REDESIGNING AMERICA'S COMMUNITY COLLEGES

Redesigning America's Community Colleges

A Clearer Path to Student Success

THOMAS R. BAILEY

SHANNA SMITH JAGGARS

DAVIS JENKINS

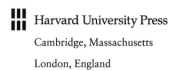 Harvard University Press

Cambridge, Massachusetts

London, England

2015

Ninth printing

Library of Congress Cataloging-in-Publication Data

Bailey, Thomas R. (Thomas Raymond)
Redesigning America's community colleges : a clearer path to student success /
Thomas R. Bailey, Shanna Smith Jaggars, Davis Jenkins.
pages   cm
Includes bibliographical references and index.
ISBN 978-0-674-36828-6 (alk. paper)
1. Community colleges—United States.   I. Smith Jaggars, Shanna.   II. Title.
LB2328.B26   2015
378.1'5430973—dc23   2014035124

Contents

Preface

The impetus for this book arose from a goal and an observation. Our goal is to conduct research to help improve student success at community colleges. Our observation was that despite an expansive reform movement built on the dedicated participation of thousands of faculty, administrators, policymakers, state education officials, researchers, and others, there is little evidence that the nation is moving toward a widespread and significant improvement in the outcomes of community college students.

Collectively, the three of us have studied and worked with community colleges for over sixty years. Throughout those years, we have been continually reminded how important community colleges are in achieving the aspirations of their students, many of whom are from disadvantaged backgrounds. A well-functioning community college system is instrumental in improving educational equity and in efficiently developing skills and talents essential for a thriving economy and society. And yet, while these colleges have helped educate millions, it is also true that many, probably a majority, of students who enter higher education through a community college do not achieve their long-term educational objectives. Thus in our recent work, we have redoubled our efforts in building a foundation of knowledge and insight to help substantially improve the outcomes of community college students.

In pursuing that goal we joined many educators, policymakers, philanthropists, and other researchers who have also worked to improve the functioning of community colleges. Indeed, since the late 1990s, a vital reform movement has germinated, flourished, and produced many exciting and interesting innovations. Through our participation in that movement, we have studied a variety of programs and policies that have yielded positive yet limited effects on student success, and have observed that while some individual institutions have improved their performance, the sector as a whole has not.

In this book, we set out to identify the barriers that have limited the effectiveness of reforms to date. We find no deficiencies in the enthusiasm, dedication, or skill of the faculty and staff of community colleges, but rather observe problems in the structure of the colleges and of the overall system of higher education—a structure that may have served this country well in the 1960s and 1970s when community colleges were a core part of the nation's effort to dramatically expand access to higher education, but which is not well suited to the needs and challenges we now confront. The reform movement has operated within that structure, rather than questioning whether the structure itself may be contributing to students' lack of progress. We thus argue that that structure needs to be fundamentally rethought, and we present proposals for what should take its place.

This book focuses on community colleges. This is our area of expertise, and our thinking and recommendations have been built on interactions with thousands of community college educators. However, research and recommendations in this book may also be quite relevant to open-access public four-year colleges, which serve similar populations of students. Indeed, across the past decade, community colleges have surpassed the open-access four-year sector in their attention to student outcomes, as well as in the energy they have focused on innovating and experimenting with new strategies to improve those outcomes. If four-year colleges and universities heed the mistakes, lessons learned, and occasional triumphs of community colleges across their decade or two of reform, we believe that the four-year sector can move forward with its own reforms more quickly and effectively. This book, then, is for all colleges that serve economically disadvantaged students and that are committed to supporting the success not only of those students but of all students from all backgrounds.

In one sense, the book has been built on the research that we have carried out at the Community College Research Center (CCRC) since it was founded nearly twenty years ago in 1996. The idea for a community college research center came from Jesse Ausubel, a program officer at the Alfred P. Sloan Foundation, who invited Teachers College, Columbia University, to develop a research center devoted to the study of these colleges. Jesse had the insight that turned out to be the foundation of the CCRC mission—while close to half of undergraduates in the United States attend community colleges, outside of the colleges themselves, within the vast universe of education research throughout the nation, only a handful of researchers focused their attention on the country's two-year public colleges.

More directly, our work on the book started in 2009 with funding from the Bill & Melinda Gates Foundation, when we initiated a set of reports designed to review research—and report the results of our own studies—on some promising but largely untested ideas for how to move beyond the incremental improvements of the reform movement thus far and substantially improve student success. We called this the Assessment of Evidence Series, and the reports were released beginning in 2011. We have drawn extensively on that work, and subsequent Gates-funded projects, for this book. We particularly want to thank Diane Troyer, our first program officer at Gates, who worked closely with us as we started the project. Her suggestions and advice are reflected in all of the reports. We also thank the many other Gates Foundation program officers—particularly Brock Grubb, Kendall Guthrie, Hilary Pennington, Ann Person, and Suzanne Walsh—whose personal and intellectual support was vital to the work of this book.

We participated in the founding and development of Achieving the Dream: Community Colleges Count (ATD), an initiative originally funded by Lumina Foundation but subsequently supported by many other foundations. Our participation in ATD has had a profound influence on our thinking for this book. We were also a partner in the development of Completion by Design (CBD), an initiative funded by the Gates Foundation. Our experience with CBD has also shaped our ideas about how colleges should be organized.

Other funders have also provided support for research that has found its way into the book's pages. These include College Spark Washington, the Ford Foundation, the James Irvine Foundation, the Kresge Foundation, the William and Flora Hewlett Foundation, Lumina Foundation, and the U.S. Department of Education through the Institute of Education Sciences. We want to thank our many program officers at these organizations, especially Leah Meyer Austin, Sam Cargile, John Colborn, Cyrus Driver, Heather Gingerich, Allen Ruby, Caroline Altman Smith, Anne Stanton, Katina Stapleton, and Dennis Udall.

Members of the CCRC advisory board also helped us shape the book and indeed all of the work of CCRC. These include Carole Berotte Joseph, Cynthia Bioteau, Gerardo de los Santos, Jim Jacobs, William Law, Jeffrey Rafn, Scott Ralls, Karen Stout, Henry Shannon, and Susan Wood. We also drew on the help of a special advisory board that we organized for the initial three-year Gates Foundation grant, which included several members of the CCRC advisory board as well as others: Anthony Bryk,

Norton Grubb, Rob Johnstone, Henry Levin, Bridget Terry Long, Kay McClenney, Donna McCusick, Daniel Solarzano, and Holly Zanville. Each of these dedicated individuals served as our "critical friends," providing advice, incisive feedback, and encouragement. Our work was immeasurably strengthened by their thoughtful reviews of the initial drafts of reports and working papers that contributed to this manuscript, as well as reviews of the manuscript itself.

We are also grateful to the many individual college faculty, administrators, staff, and students whose words and viewpoints appear throughout the book, with particular thanks to Peter Adams, Michelle Andreas, Elaine Baker, Marcia Ballinger, Joanne Bashford, Andrea Buehman, Tina Bloomer, Brad Bostian, Ed Bowling, Susan Burleson, Mary Chikwinya, Kathleen Cleary, Michele Cuomo, Tristan Denley, Kathy Drumm, Victor Fichera, Michael Heathfield, Katie Hern, Maria Hesse, John Hetts, Vicki Legion, Cynthia Liston, Russ Little, Mary Beth Love, James Mabry, Terri Manning, Susan Mayer, Byron McClenney, Mark McCullough, Sharon Morrissey, Randy Parker, David Prince, Mary Rittling, Lenore Rodicio, David Rothman, Bill Schneider, Myra Schnell, Kristi Short, Bill Storms, Kristi Wellington-Baker, Pat Windham, and Jan Yoshiwara.

During the past fifteen years, CCRC has collaborated with the social policy research organization MDRC on several projects that informed this book, including the evaluation of Achieving the Dream and the National Center for Postsecondary Research (NCPR), a center funded by the U.S. Department of Education's Institute of Education Sciences. Many researchers worked on these projects, but we particularly want to thank Thomas Brock, Oscar Cerna, Dan Cullinan, Rob Ivry, Lashawn Richburg-Hayes, Elizabeth Zachry Rutschow, Mary Visher, Michael Weiss, and Evan Weissman.

During the course of our research, we have benefited from the collaboration, friendship, insights, and enthusiasm of many individuals from a number of other research and policy organizations whose missions overlap broadly with those of CCRC. In particular, we would like to thank Elif Bor, Sue Cleary, Michael Collins, Lara Couturier, Will Friedman, Alison Kadlec, Richard Kazis, Adrianna Kezar, John Lee, Carol Lincoln, Derek Price, Isaac Rowlett, Gretchen Schmidt, Nancy Shulock, and Heather Wathington.

The research and recommendations we set forth in this book were shaped in large part by the senior research staff here at CCRC, many of whom were first authors on reports and working papers from which this manuscript draws. CCRC researchers who were authors of the Assessment of Evidence reports include Nikki Edgecombe, Michelle Hodara,

Katherine Hughes, Melinda Mechur Karp, Dolores Perin, and Judith Scott-Clayton. Other CCRC researchers who have shaped our thinking and collaborated with us on research used in the book include Elisabeth Barnett, Clive Belfield, Susan Bickerstaff, Sung-Woo Cho, Maria Scott Cormier, Peter Crosta, Kevin Dougherty, Dong Wook Jeong, Monica Reid Kerrigan, Olga Rodríguez, Madeline Joy Trimble, Michelle Van Noy, John Wachen, Di Xu, and Matthew Zeidenberg. Our CCRC colleagues also provided invaluable input and feedback on manuscript drafts. We also thank the many research associates and research assistants who contributed to those reports and working papers, and particularly Jeffrey Fletcher, who assisted us with the preparation of several case studies that appear in these pages. Special thanks are also due to Rebecca Jones, who assisted with references and citations; Gladys Perez-Mojica and Sarah Phillips, who helped with a multitude of practical matters; and Georgia West Stacey, who has worked tirelessly to make sure that our work is widely known. Nothing would happen at CCRC if it were not for Lisa Rothman, our associate director, who makes the organization function. Most of the manuscript was expertly edited by Justin Snider, and we thank him for helping us to strengthen our language and sharpen the argument. We also worked closely with Doug Slater, CCRC's managing editor, in the final stages of the writing. We know that we can rely on his judgment to help us hone the content, tone, and emphasis of our writing. Elizabeth Knoll was our editor at Harvard University Press throughout most of the work on the book. She urged us to write this book in the first place, and kept us on track with grace and enthusiasm. The project was completed under the guidance of Andrew Kinney.

Finally, much love and gratitude go to our spouses and children, who have supported us through the process: Carmenza Gallo, Erika and Daniela Bailey, Damon and Ian Jaggars, and Olive Jenkins.

REDESIGNING AMERICA'S COMMUNITY COLLEGES

Introduction

COMMUNITY COLLEGES in the United States provide access to higher education for over 10 million students each year, representing nearly half of the nation's undergraduates.[1] These open-door institutions—which are expected to serve nearly anyone who wants to attend college—are a manifestation of our society's commitment to educational opportunity, and they reflect a common understanding of postsecondary education as the foundation for economic growth and upward mobility. The role community colleges play in providing postsecondary access to underrepresented students is obvious when one examines the demographics of their enrollment: they serve a disproportionate number of low-income, immigrant, first-generation, and ethnic minority students. Indeed, a majority of low-income, Hispanic, and Native American students who are undergraduates are enrolled in community colleges.[2]

Yet most students who enter these colleges never finish: fewer than four of every ten complete any type of degree or certificate within six years.[3] The failure of students to complete college represents a loss to the overall economy, which has prompted calls from the federal government, major foundations, and public intellectuals for a significant increase in the number of people with postsecondary degrees. But just as important as the economic consequences is the fact that a large majority of new community college students aspire to some kind of degree; thus, these low completion rates reflect widespread failure, disappointment, frustration, and thwarted potential among the millions of students who do not achieve their educational goals.

The disappointing outcomes of community colleges and indeed many four-year institutions have not gone unnoticed by policymakers, who have called for more transparency in and accountability for postsecondary performance. As a result, we have seen the birth of consumer information efforts such as the U.S. Department of Education's College Navigator website, which allows students and parents to compare graduation rates at prospective colleges. In an attempt to create incentives for colleges to improve student outcomes, a growing number of states have also adopted college funding systems that financially reward colleges based on outcomes (such as the number of graduates, or the earnings of graduates) rather than exclusively on enrollments. In late 2013, the Obama administration proposed the development of a rating system for colleges based on outcomes. One possible consequence of such a system would be that students enrolled in more highly rated colleges would receive favorable treatment concerning grants and loans.

But while policymakers are applying pressure to colleges to improve their outcomes, this pressure is not likely to be accompanied by significant increases in resources. Indeed, while the discussion about higher education toward the end of the first decade of the twenty-first century focused on increasing degree completion, by 2012 the criticisms also included the problem of affordability. Colleges were expected to improve outcomes and lower tuition at the same time. In general, although state higher education budgets recovered somewhat after the extreme cuts following the 2008 Great Recession, state funding had been declining for years before the recession.[4] Typically, budgets are cut during downturns but are never completely restored; thus, there has been a long-term downward ratcheting in state support. Community colleges in most states, as with other public higher education institutions, have raised tuition in response to the cuts in state funding, but these increases have not made up for the loss of state funds. Given the outcry about the cost of college, it seems unlikely that colleges will be able to rely on tuition increases for additional revenue. Thus, colleges face a difficult situation: They are being asked to improve their performance without being able to count on additional revenue. And they are doing this in an environment of greater public scrutiny, skepticism, and criticism of college performance.

How can colleges improve their performance without a substantial infusion of new resources? In this book, we draw on a wide variety of research to propose a strategy for improving student outcomes at community colleges and other broad-access institutions. Our argument can be simply stated. Community colleges were designed to expand college enrollments, particularly among underrepresented students, and to do this at a low cost. They have been extraordinarily successful in achieving these goals. However, colleges designed to maximize *course enrollment* are not well designed to maximize *completion of high-quality programs of study*. In particular, the emphasis on low-cost enrollment has encouraged colleges to offer an array of often-disconnected courses, programs, and support services that students are expected to navigate mostly on their own. Students are confused by a plethora of poorly explained program, transfer, and career options; moreover, on closer scrutiny many programs do not clearly lead to the further education and employment outcomes they are advertised to help students achieve. We refer to this as a *cafeteria-style, self-service model*.

We argue that to improve outcomes, colleges need to move away from the prevailing cafeteria-style model. Instead, they need to engage faculty and student services professionals in creating more clearly structured, educationally coherent program pathways that lead to students' end goals, and in rethinking instruction and student support services in ways that facilitate students' learning and success as they progress along these paths. In short, to maximize both access *and* success, a fundamental redesign is necessary. We refer to the resulting strategy as the *guided pathways model*.

These ideas build on more than a decade of efforts by community colleges to improve student outcomes, and in particular to increase the rates at which students complete credentials. In this introduction, we examine some of the notable reforms that have unfolded under this "college completion agenda." We argue that these reforms have not produced the desired outcomes because they have stopped short of making the systemic changes necessary to shift colleges' organization and culture from a focus on *access* alone to a focus on *access with success*. We then lay out the basic features of the guided pathways model and end with a summary of the remaining chapters of the book, which explore the design features of the guided pathways model and propose steps that colleges can take to redesign programs and services on a large scale.

The College Completion Agenda

In 2014, higher education has a prominent place on the nation's policy agenda, as the public becomes more aware that most people need at least *some* college in order to find decent, family-supporting jobs. At the same time, there are growing concerns that the quality of a college education is suspect and that the cost of college is now beyond the means of a middle-class family.

These concerns about higher education are relatively new. As few as twenty years ago, colleges and universities were rarely mentioned in the extensive public discussion of education reform, which focused on K–12 schools. Until recently, American higher education enjoyed a stellar reputation. The public image of the sector was shaped by a relatively small number of prestigious and selective colleges: the Ivy League, the elite residential liberal-arts colleges, and the flagship public universities. These colleges and universities were well regarded and attracted students from all over the world. It is fair to say that it was never completely clear what students learned there, but a degree from these institutions was widely believed to open doors to well-paying careers and upward social mobility. Of course these institutions in reality account for only a small percentage of college students. Yet the entire postsecondary sector was bathed in their positive aura, and the quality or effectiveness of higher education more generally was rarely questioned.

If quality was not doubted, then the most important postsecondary policy issue had to do with access. Access was important from two perspectives. First was the growing economic need for more highly educated workers—the need to find employment for the millions of returning veterans after World War II and the rise of the Baby Boom generation in the 1960s gave impetus to the expansion of higher education, but there was also a general conviction that the economy needed more trained workers. Second, the access issue had to do with equity. In particular, in 1947 the Truman Commission noted the desirability of severing the strong link between socioeconomic background and educational achievement, advocated for increased education for African Americans, and recommended an expansion of community colleges.[5]

In order to facilitate access, the higher education sector expanded significantly over the next decades. Total fall enrollment increased nearly tenfold from 1947 to 2011, from 2.3 million to 21.0 million. During that time, fall enrollment in public higher education institutions grew from 1.2 million to 15.1 million.[6] In the forty years between 1970 and 2010, fall enrollment at community colleges more than tripled from 2.2 million to 7.2 million.[7] By the early part of the twenty-first century, the majority of high school graduates had some contact with higher education.[8] But racial and income inequalities continued to be important problems, and postsecondary observers became increasingly concerned about racial disparities in access. Affirmative action became the most salient and controversial issue in U.S. higher education in the 1990s. Here once again, the selective elites dominated the conversation, given that racial representation was hardly a problem at open-access institutions.

Outside of affirmative action, the broad education reform movements of the 1980s and 1990s had little to say about higher education. The influential 1983 publication *A Nation at Risk* barely mentioned college. The accountability movement of the late 1980s and reforms of the early 1990s that led to the School-to-Work Opportunity Act of 1994 were also primarily concerned with K–12 schooling.

The shift from a predominant focus on college access to a consideration of the performance of colleges and universities—the outcomes for enrolled students—was signaled by the passage of the Student Right-to-Know (SRK) and Campus Security Act of 1990. In order for students attending a particular college to be eligible for federal financial aid, the college was required to provide extensive information to the U.S. Department of Education, including graduation rates. For the first time, there was a specific outcome measure that would, at least in principle, allow comparisons among colleges in terms of performance.

Although the 1990 SRK Act did call for college outcome measures, five years would pass before the required graduation rates were defined, and it was nearly a decade before institutions were required to publish their graduation rates.[9] The definitions underlying these rates were—and continue to be—widely criticized, especially among community colleges,[10] but they represented at least some attempt to measure colleges' performance in terms of student outcomes.

Thirteen years after the first rates were published, President Obama proposed the development of a policy that would not only require colleges to publish outcomes but also create strong incentives for colleges to improve performance, possibly providing more generous financial aid to students attending higher-performing colleges. This proposed incentive system came after several years of growing efforts by state policymakers to tie state funding to outcomes rather than enrollments. In 2013, nearly two-thirds of states had enacted or were developing performance funding policies that base at least some state subsidies for colleges and universities on student outcomes.[11]

This sequence of events clearly indicates that a concrete and consistent national focus on postsecondary outcomes is a very recent phenomenon. Why did this shift occur? We can point to several factors that were likely influential.

First, the publication of graduation rates was eye-opening. For many community colleges, the percentage of first-time, full-time students who graduated from their original institution within three years (150 percent of the time in which a full-time student would be expected to graduate) was below 20 percent. Some colleges had single-digit graduation rates. Public four-year "open-admissions" institutions had a national six-year completion rate of 29 percent—compared to 82 percent among their more selective peers.[12] Although college personnel argued that these rates reflected the weak preparation and diverse goals of entering students, it was hard to argue that rates in the teens or twenties represented successful organizational performance. These rates reinforced the idea that quality varied greatly among higher education institutions. The elites continued to be seen as world-class, but other sectors of higher education were apparently not as successful.

Second, as the economy and underlying technology evolved, a consensus developed that at least some college was necessary to earn a family-sustaining wage. College was no longer an opportunity that should be open only to the ambitious, but was a basic economic necessity, much as high school was viewed a generation earlier. Thus, policymakers became more concerned about what happened to students while they were in college and whether they graduated. Although studies indicate that attending college without earning a credential provides some benefit in the labor market, they also show that earning occupational credentials, such as certificates or associate degrees, provides further labor market benefits, and that, on average, higher-level credentials provide even better returns.[13]

Third, prospective students also heard the discussion about the importance of college and increasingly set their sights on completing a degree. The vast majority of students who enroll for credit in community colleges state that they want to complete a credential or transfer to complete a degree at a four-year school.[14] Indeed, over 80 percent of entering community college students indicate that they intend to earn a bachelor's degree or higher.[15] Yet six years after initial enrollment, only 15 percent have done so.[16] This number would rise if we considered a longer time window, but it still represents a large gap between students' stated goals and their actual outcomes.

Fourth, over the last decade, the cost of college has become a much more controversial issue. College tuition has increased faster than prices overall. During an era of earnings stagnation, this means that paying for college takes a much larger share of a typical family's income than it did a generation ago. Although much of the rise in tuition (for public institutions, at least) is attributable to cuts in state subsidies rather than rising college costs, the hikes in tuition nevertheless created an environment in which students, parents, and policymakers began to ask what they were getting in return for their money. And while broad-access institutions—and community colleges in particular—remain relatively affordable to students, critics have cited their low completion rates in arguing that these institutions are making poor use of taxpayer dollars.[17]

Finally, international comparisons have suggested that the United States is no longer the most educated country in the world. Widely referred-to data published by the Organisation for Economic Co-operation and Development (OECD) indicate that in 2011, the United States ranked twelfth among OECD countries in the percentage of the population age 25 to 34 that had attained a tertiary education. But among 25-to-64-year-olds, the United States ranked fifth—suggesting that other countries are overtaking the United States.[18] This apparent threat to American international competitiveness has been a rallying cry for postsecondary reform.

For all of these reasons, the first fifteen years of this century saw a rapid growth of reform efforts focused on improving student outcomes in both two- and four-year institutions. In 2009, the Obama administration called for 10 million additional college graduates by 2020. In the same year, Lumina Foundation, one of the largest private funders of postsecondary reform, announced its "Big Goal": by 2025, 60 percent of the U.S. population would have a high-quality postsecondary credential or degree. Many states set similar goals, which were sometimes backed up by funding for reforms (although the overall funding for colleges and universities in most states was cut). Soon after he took office in 2009, President Obama proposed a $12 billion initiative to improve the performance of community colleges. Although in the end only $2 billion was funded, this amount of money was still historically unprecedented.

Private philanthropy also invested in reforms, and much of the foundation funding focused on improving outcomes in community colleges, given the disproportionate number of low-income and otherwise disadvantaged students these institutions serve. Early in the last decade, the Ford Foundation funded the Bridges to Opportunity project, which worked with six states to improve outcomes for low-income adults in community colleges. In 2004, Lumina Foundation launched Achieving the Dream: Community Colleges Count (ATD). This initiative was explicitly designed to improve institutional outcomes, including helping academically underprepared students succeed in college-level work, increasing semester-to-semester persistence, and improving rates of degree completion. Lumina and many other national and local funders eventually invested over $150 million in ATD.[19] In 2008, the Bill & Melinda Gates Foundation launched a postsecondary program designed to increase college completion among low-income young adults, and by 2013 they had invested $343 million.[20] After an initial focus on community colleges, both the Lumina and Gates foundations branched out to less selective four-year colleges as well as minority-serving institutions. Many other foundations—including the James Irvine Foundation, the William and Flora Hewlett Foundation, and the Kresge Foundation—also invested in college-completion-related reform efforts.

How did colleges respond to the increasing focus on student outcomes? Although the public push for college improvement may be relatively new, faculty, staff, and administrators at community colleges across the country have been working for decades to improve instruction and student services. For example, the League for Innovation in the Community College was founded in 1968 to host conferences and workshops, conduct research, and provide services to its many community college members, as part of its continuing effort "to make a positive difference for students and communities." Perusing the conference programs of professional associations, such as the American Association of Community Colleges and the American Association of State Colleges and Universities, reveals workshops on many types of innovations and reforms, particularly from the 1990s onward. However, developments in the last decade have provided more visibility and resources to colleges' improvement efforts, and these efforts have also been examined more systematically, which has allowed researchers and practitioners to pull together syntheses in terms of what colleges were doing and what seems to be effective. For example, in 2002, the National Center for Developmental Education published a guide to improving the outcomes of academically underprepared students, who make up a majority of incoming community college students and who are typically supported through a set of precollege courses known as "developmental education." The center's recommendations included thirty-three "best practices," such as making developmental assessment and placement mandatory, teaching critical thinking in all developmental courses, and creating a clearly defined mission, goals, and priorities for the developmental program.

The experience of the Achieving the Dream initiative during its first five to seven years provides a good picture of the state of community college reform in the first decade of the twenty-first century, just as the completion agenda took hold. As mentioned, ATD began in 2004 with funding from Lumina Foundation. The initiative was explicitly designed to increase the academic success of community college students by building a "culture of evidence" in which administrators, faculty, and others would use data to identify barriers to student success and develop reform strategies to overcome those identified barriers. The initiative assigned experienced administrators—usually retired community college presidents—as coaches for the participating colleges. These coaches helped colleges develop and implement their reform strategies. The initiative also assigned the colleges "data facilitators," who were often institutional researchers, to help assemble, analyze, and interpret their data. In addition, Lumina Foundation funded several organizations, including the Community College Research Center (CCRC), our own organization, to provide research and policy support. Overall, ATD represented an ambitious and well-supported effort, based on extensive operational experience and expertise, that drew on the best research and evidence available to develop strategies with the explicit goal of improving student outcomes, including completion of credentials.

In 2011, the research organization MDRC, in partnership with CCRC, published a report on the first five years of the Achieving the Dream experience, focusing on the twenty-six colleges in five states that were the first to join the initiative.[21] The report grouped the various colleges' reform-oriented "interventions" into three broad categories: student support services, instructional support, and changes in classroom instruction. Student support services interventions—including advising, student success courses, early alert programs, and the like—accounted for nearly half (48 percent) of all ATD-related interventions. The other half focused on instruction, but half of those involved "instructional support," such as tutoring or summer "bridge" programs for new students. Only about a quarter of interventions involved new instructional techniques, reforms of college-level curricula, or changes in classroom instruction. Across all types of interventions, about half—and at least one in each of the twenty-six colleges—were devoted to improving outcomes for developmental students. Between these reforms of developmental education and changes to new student orientation and advising, the majority of ATD reforms focused on helping students during the early stages of their college experience. When these types of reforms have been rigorously evaluated, the studies have found mixed results for the reform participants, often consisting of modest positive effects that fade over time.[22]

The ATD report also investigated the *penetration* of reforms—the percent of potential target students reached by the practice. About half of the ATD interventions enrolled fewer than 10 percent of the college's potential target students, and only 31 percent reached at least one quarter of the target students. The few interventions that were large-scale tended to be low-intensity, such as an orientation program that engaged students for fewer than five hours in total.

To promote the scale-up of promising practices, the Bill & Melinda Gates Foundation funded the Developmental Education Initiative in 2009. Fifteen ATD colleges were chosen to participate, and each received $743,000 to assist it in these efforts. The chosen colleges were engaging in practices that had evidence of initial positive results and therefore seemed worthy of scaling up. However, the typical college was still only able to extend a given practice to about one-third of the target population.[23] Thus, even with supportive leadership, encouragement, and technical assistance from national organizations, as well as grant support, colleges have had difficulty scaling up programs that they perceive to be successful.

In general, the experience during the early years of ATD illustrates the dominant characteristics of reform in community colleges during the "completion agenda" era—more or less since the early 2000s. Colleges have been willing, and often enthusiastic, to experiment with new practices and strategies. These innovative practices are frequently directed at one segment of the student experience—usually at the beginning—and they generally reach a relatively small number of students, although very "light touch" efforts are more likely to reach a larger group of students.

Across the past decade, this approach to reform gave the impression of widespread innovation, experimentation, and commitment to improving student outcomes. Yet further results from the ATD study suggest that these reforms have not changed colleges' overall outcomes in any substantial way.[24] At its inception, the ATD initiative established five categories of performance metrics against which to judge participating colleges: developmental education program completion rates; "gatekeeper" course completion rates (particularly for the first college-level courses in math and English); completion of attempted courses with a grade of C or better; term-to-term and year-to-year persistence; and attainment of credentials. Despite the ATD colleges' many interventions—including some with at least modest positive effects on participating students—four categories of performance metrics remained essentially flat for the colleges included in the study.[25] In the remaining category, there was a modest positive effect on completion of gatekeeper English. A follow-up study with two more years of data found the same results.[26]

To be sure, the authors of the ATD report emphasized that this was not a rigorous study with an appropriately chosen control group; thus, we cannot definitively say that the ATD reforms did not cause overall improvements. Nevertheless, these data would suggest strong positive effects only if we expected that *without* ATD, performance would have dropped significantly during the years of the study. In any case, if one is looking for significant improvements in outcomes—the types of changes that would give the country a chance to achieve the ambitious goals set by the federal government, many states, and foundations—the reform model represented by early years of ATD cannot achieve this change on its own.

There are several reasons why ATD and similar reforms had a limited effect on student outcomes. As we have mentioned, most of the reforms either benefited a small number of students (and were not scaled beyond this select group), or they affected larger numbers but provided only low-intensity, or "light touch," support. In addition, most of the reforms implemented under ATD and similar initiatives focused on only one segment of the student experience: usually the intake process, developmental education, or in some cases the first year of a student's experience.

It is not surprising that colleges have focused on getting new students well established in college, but concentrating on this segment of the experience alone is insufficient. Indeed, we have conducted a simulation using data from one community college to estimate the change in graduation rates that would be generated by improvements in various first-semester or first-year outcomes. For example, we calculated that a 20 percent increase in the share of students who complete a college-level math course in the first year (a very large increase) would lead to only a 2.5 percent increase in the graduation rate.[27] This research suggests that to substantially improve rates of student progression and completion requires changes in practice throughout the students' experience with the college, and not just at the front end. Indeed, while students deemed "college ready" upon entering community colleges are more successful than those referred to remedial instruction, the majority of such students do not end up earning a college credential, suggesting that there are barriers to success in college-level coursework even for those considered academically prepared for college.[28]

Moreover, most instructional reforms have focused on tutoring and other supplemental support services rather than on classroom instruction. When instruction has been the target of reform, it has tended to be developmental education rather than college-level coursework. As a result, most faculty in the college—and particularly those teaching in college-level programs—have been largely uninvolved in, and unaffected by, reform efforts.[29]

To achieve significant institutional-level improvements in student success, reforms need to involve more thoroughgoing organizational change. In fairness, ATD sought to change colleges' wider organizational practice and culture through its emphasis on five organizational improvement practices: leadership commitment; use of data to prioritize actions; stakeholder engagement; implementation, evaluation, and improvement of strategies; and establishment of an infrastructure for continuous improvement.[30] These practices—together referred to by the ATD organizers as a "culture of evidence"—are similar to those that research suggests are characteristic of high-performing organizations in higher education, K–12 schools, and the private sector.[31] And the twenty-six colleges included in the ATD evaluation report did indeed make some progress toward a culture of evidence. The evaluators categorized the colleges into three groups: strong or very strong culture of evidence, some culture of evidence, or weak or very weak culture of evidence. In the spring of 2006, only 23 percent had been in the strong group; three years later, 42 percent were in that group.[32]

But this degree of organizational change seemed insufficient to change institution-level performance. While performance measures rose for some colleges and dropped for others, the researchers were not able to identify any relationship between improvement in the culture of evidence and improvement in institutional performance.

Achieving the Dream and other related reforms have made important contributions to the community college reform movement in the country. By emphasizing the crucial role of data analysis and calling for broader institutional change, they have changed the reform conversation. Many of the ideas that we propose in this book were influenced by our own participation in ATD and our reflections on its successes and limitations.

Yet why didn't a movement toward the type of thorough organizational change represented by the culture-of-evidence model help improve student outcomes? We suspect that principles such as "stakeholder engagement," "leadership commitment," and "continuous improvement" are too abstract to promote deep change. Colleges interpreted these goals in many different ways, and no outlines of a common strategy emerged. Thus, calling for fundamental change based on abstract principles is apparently an inadequate strategy. Current organizational structures, hierarchies, and cultures are too powerful and well entrenched to be threatened by abstractions, no matter how ambitious. Deeper organizational change likely needs to be supported by a more concrete set of reform plans, accompanied by an explicit strategy to win over and engage faculty, staff, and administrators. One purpose of this book is to further the reform movement by proposing a comprehensive, concrete, and evidence-based approach to reform, while including suggestions for engaging the cooperation and enthusiastic participation of college personnel. Just as important, recent reforms did not question the fundamental design of community college programs and services, but rather sought to improve performance within the same design framework that had been in place since the 1960s and 1970s, when most of these institutions were established. In this book, we argue that to improve their outcomes on a substantial scale in an environment very different from the past, colleges must undertake a more fundamental rethinking of their organization and culture.

The Cafeteria College

Community colleges and other broad-access institutions are well designed to serve the mission of providing low-cost access to college. However, the same features that have enabled these institutions to provide broad access to college make them poorly designed to facilitate completion of high-quality college programs—that is, programs that support deep student learning and that prepare students for success in further education and employment. We refer to the prevailing model as the *cafeteria* or *self-service* college because students are left to navigate often complex and ill-defined pathways mostly on their own.

The next four chapters of this book discuss different components of a typical community college: program structure, intake and student support services, instruction, and developmental education. Within each chapter, we draw on research first to describe how the cafeteria college operates in terms of the given component and then to suggest how the component can be redesigned following the guided pathways model to promote student completion of high-quality credentials that better enable students to achieve their goals for employment and further education. Below, we summarize our description of each component as it appears within the typical community college—which is currently organized as a cafeteria college. Later in this chapter, we will summarize our recommendations for redesign under the guided pathways approach.

Program Structure

Because they are designed to provide access to a wide variety of students with a wide variety of goals, community colleges give students many choices. Students have broad flexibility to decide when to enroll, which courses to take, how many to take per term, and what programs to pursue. Most colleges offer an extensive array of courses and programs, which allows students to explore different areas and discover their interests. Yet students are expected to explore these options more or less on their own, with minimal guidance. Moreover, the courses available within a given program are often not closely connected or coherently sequenced in ways that build to a clear set of meaningful learning outcomes. As a result, students end up taking courses merely to meet program requirements—"checking off boxes" rather than mastering skills and knowledge relevant to their goals. Too often, program learning goals are also not well defined or are poorly aligned with requirements for further education and employment.

Intake and Student Supports

The intake process for new students often consists of a placement test, a brief face-to-face or online orientation, and an abbreviated (and not always mandatory) advising session, typically focused on registering for the first semester's courses rather than on exploring the student's longer-term goals. After their initial registration, most students remain confused about their potential goals, and how these might align with the college's program offerings. Even if the student chooses a specific program or transfer goal, most colleges do not closely monitor students' progress toward their goals over time; both the college and the students themselves are thus unclear about how far students have progressed and how far they still need to go. Advisors and faculty have no way to know when a student is going "off track," and it is therefore up to students to recognize when they need help and seek it out on their own. Unfortunately, it is students most in need of such help who are the least likely to seek it.

Instruction

Just as students must rely on themselves in the cafeteria model, instructors are often isolated and unsupported in their teaching, a situation reinforced by the extensive use of adjunct instructors. There is little opportunity for cooperative work to improve teaching and learning. And while many professors in community colleges are excellent instructors, their innovations tend to result from individual initiative rather than institutional policy or culture. Consistent with a culture of faculty isolation, curricular content is developed course by course, with less emphasis on programs as a whole. Rather than recognizing and explicitly working to improve students' weaknesses in self-direction, time management, academic motivation, and other factors critical to students' success in college, faculty often regard these weaknesses as outside the scope of course instruction. Moreover, course content and instruction often seem irrelevant to students' interests and career and personal aspirations, thus contributing to a demotivating learning environment. To provide students with more flexible learning options, community colleges are increasingly turning to fully online instruction, which tends to reinforce the cafeteria model of disconnection and isolation, while undermining many students' academic success.

Developmental Education

The typical community college devotes considerable resources to helping academically underprepared students—who represent the broad majority of incoming students—reach the college's standards of academic readiness. However, the current system of developmental education is hampered by inadequate placement information, lengthy prerequisite sequences, and, in many cases, uninspiring instruction. As a result, most students who enter developmental education never successfully emerge from it to embark on a college-level program of study.

Overall, across the four components of structure, intake and supports, instruction, and developmental education, the various parts of the college are consistently characterized by a lack of interaction and alignment toward students' end goals. Students must rely mostly on themselves; professors and advisors generally work in isolation; and there is little coordination between instructors and student services personnel. Meanwhile, options abound: students can chose from a large menu of courses, which ultimately confuses and frustrates them, while faculty can choose to engage in instructional improvement or not. Of course, even in a cafeteria college, there will be areas of excellence and collaboration; however, the fragmented or "siloed" structure of the college does not encourage this in a systematic way. Community college faculty and administrators seeking to shift away from the cafeteria model must overcome an entrenched organizational structure and culture. The weaknesses that we have observed emerge from the logic of the college structure, not from the failings of individual institutions or certainly not of individual faculty and staff.

When considering the path to reform, it becomes clear that the typical approach to reform in community colleges is also consistent with their underlying cafeteria structure. As we have argued, reforms have been sporadic, focused on one element of the college in isolation from other elements and reforms, and based primarily on the initiative of individuals or small groups of individuals. Thus, reforms have sought to strengthen elements of the prevailing model without challenging that model. But if the problems originate in the model itself, then it is not surprising that the results of these reforms have been disappointing. In the next section, we outline how these elements would change under a more ambitious and comprehensive guided pathways model.

Designing Guided Pathways to Student Success

Research on organizational effectiveness in and outside of higher education indicates that, in contrast to the disconnection and isolation that characterize the cafeteria college structure, high-performing organizations implement their "core functions" in a coordinated, complementary fashion that is aligned with organizational goals.[33] The offerings and support services provided by community colleges under the prevailing model are well designed to achieve the organizational goal of access to college *courses*. They are not well designed to help students enter and complete college *programs* that prepare them for further education and employment. From this perspective, it would appear that Achieving the Dream and other similar reforms have been too limited in their goals. To support student success, it is not enough to try to find ways to improve student completion in courses as they are currently designed; rather, courses need to be incorporated into larger program redesigns. The guided pathways approach to redesign starts with students' end goals in mind, and then rethinks and redesigns programs and support services to enable students to achieve these goals. A growing number of colleges and universities are doing just this. Instead of letting students find their own paths through college, they are creating "guided pathways" to completion of credentials, further education, and advancement in the labor market. In the process, they are redesigning the conventional college in fundamental ways.

Within the next four chapters of the book, after describing the prevailing cafeteria design of key college functions, we review research that supports a shift to a guided pathways model and describe the work of some colleges that are implementing redesigns consistent with this approach. Below we summarize the guided pathways approach that is unfolding across these and other innovative colleges.

Program Structure

In guided pathways colleges, faculty clearly map out academic programs to create educationally coherent pathways, each with clearly defined learning outcomes that build across the curriculum and are aligned with requirements for further education and career advancement in the given field. Students who enter without clear program or career goals are assisted in choosing a broad initial field of interest (such as business; allied health; education and social services; social and behavioral science; science, technology, engineering, and math; or English, arts, and humanities), each of which features a default curriculum that gives students a taste of the given field and helps them either narrow down their choice to a specific program or switch to another area of interest. While each broad field and the programs nested within it are built upon a default sequence of courses, students can opt out of the default if they wish. Rather than restrict students' options, the guided pathways structure is intended to help students make better decisions without limiting their options.

Intake and Student Supports

In guided pathways colleges, intake processes are focused on helping new students develop or clarify goals for college and careers, and advising and other necessary supports are integrated into the student's everyday experience. Mandatory student success courses, well-designed web-based information, and explicit career counseling help students explore their options and choose a college-level program of study as quickly as possible. Advising is redesigned to ensure that students are making progress, based on academic milestones that faculty have incorporated into each program pathway. Students' progress on their academic plans is tracked using "e-advising" systems, which provide frequent feedback to students and their advisors and instructors. "Early alert" systems signal when students are struggling, and set in motion appropriate support mechanisms. Close cooperation between professional advisors and academic departments ensures a smooth transition from initial general advising to advising within the student's program or major.

Instruction

In the guided pathways model, faculty define the skills, concepts, and habits of mind that students need to achieve by the end of their program, and map out how students will build those learning outcomes across courses. The college emphasizes a "learning facilitation" approach to instruction, which focuses on building students' academic motivation and metacognition; and the college systematically supports faculty in developing and improving this approach using a "collaborative inquiry" framework. Instructors work closely with librarians, technologists, and student service professionals to design courses that incorporate innovative approaches to teaching and learning. Technology is recognized as a valuable tool for learning, but it is leveraged as part of a larger pedagogical tool kit and approach.

Developmental Education

In the guided pathways model, developmental education is redesigned as a critical part of the "on-ramp" to a college-level program of study, with the goal of helping students successfully complete the critical introductory college-level courses in their initial field of interest. For many if not most students, developmental education consists of co-requisite coursework designed to scaffold students' success in critical college-level courses.

For students who need an extended prerequisite approach, developmental instruction maintains high college-level expectations while providing more intensive support, and is contextualized to students' program of interest. Colleges also partner with high schools, adult basic skills programs, and workforce development agencies to better prepare and motivate students to enter college-level programs of study.

After presenting evidence and examples about the four functional components of program structure, intake and support, instruction, and developmental education, we turn to larger implementation issues. In Chapter 5, we examine how college leaders can engage faculty and professional staff in the process of designing and implementing a guided pathways approach. In particular, leaders can rethink their approach to governance, professional development, and hiring and promotion processes in ways that build rather than undermine faculty engagement, collaboration, and enthusiasm for positive change. As part of this discussion, we address colleges' heavy reliance on part-time faculty, and how colleges might best engage these key members of the community in the college's redesign.

In Chapter 6, we discuss the cost implications of the guided pathways model. We point out that improvements in student outcomes—no matter how they are achieved—will necessarily increase the costs of college operations. Taking into account this reality, as well as transition and ongoing costs associated with shifting to a guided pathways approach, we argue that colleges need more committed support from their funding entities in order to substantially improve student completion of high-quality credentials. However, the extent of this increased support is not large; moreover, it should dramatically improve the already-strong return on student and taxpayer dollars invested in community college education. We discuss how performance funding approaches, as well as other state-level policy initiatives, could help support colleges in this effort while keeping postsecondary education affordable for both students and taxpayers.

Guided Pathways and "Unbundled" Reform Strategies Compared

The second decade of this century has seen a great deal of enthusiasm and interest in "unbundled" models of education, which are based on online delivery coupled with competency-based approaches to conferring credentials. Under most such models, students, perhaps with the help of a coach or mentor, construct their own education by using low-cost online instructional materials and demonstrating their achievement through competency-based assessments.[34] Proponents argue that this unbundled approach will result in a more efficient, customized, and low-cost college education.[35]

In broad terms, the unbundled approach, which emphasizes greater flexibility and choice for students, seems to conflict with the guided pathways model, which calls for more structure and a more coherent set of options for students. In the chapters that follow, we will explore this comparison. Some features of unbundled models—such as an emphasis on using technology more effectively to track and advise students, and a focus on defining program-level learning outcomes—we find compatible with the guided pathways approach. Yet we also find that unbundled models frequently fail to consider the particular barriers facing disadvantaged and struggling students. In Chapter 3, we argue that the unbundled approach to instruction does not help address the learning challenges of many students who enroll in community colleges. In Chapter 6, we directly address the question of cost-effectiveness. In comparison to the guided pathways model, the unbundled model may cost less per student enrollment at any given point in time, but that cost advantage may be coupled with worse student outcomes. Thus the guided pathways model, we argue, is likely to result in lower cost per successful completion.

The Evidence for Guided Pathways

Overall across this book, the evidence we present to support the various design features and implementation approaches of the guided pathways model is drawn from research in numerous domains. For example, we cite research from behavioral economics, organizational effectiveness, and learning theory to support the idea that students will benefit from more structured programs of study. We have direct rigorous evidence on the effectiveness of some elements of the guided pathways model; however, the evidence in support of other elements is descriptive or preliminary, in part because institutions have only recently begun to implement them. Moreover, it is difficult to evaluate the effectiveness of whole-institution reforms in a rigorous way; our only option is to wait several years to observe whether guided pathways improve institutions' outcomes at much higher rates (and at a lower cost per successful completion) than do other reform strategies. Indeed, this difficulty in measuring the effects of whole-institutional reform may be one of the reasons why colleges have been reluctant to rethink the basic design of their programs and support services and have instead focused on small, discrete, more easily measured reforms.

The colleges and universities profiled in this book have seen encouraging preliminary results from the early phases of their guided pathways redesigns. Still, many of the practices we examine reflect evidence-based *hypotheses* about how colleges can become more effective, rather than proven solutions. Thus, we encourage the reader to approach our recommendations critically and thoughtfully, and to recognize that each college will implement guided pathways reforms in a different way, depending on its unique strengths and priorities. Given the importance of faculty and staff engagement in a college's guided pathways redesign, it would be counterproductive for us to dictate exactly how a college should be changed. Rather, we present general principles and design elements, along with examples of how real colleges have implemented them. Colleges can then combine these principles with their own unique values and perspectives to create the most effective guided pathways design for their students and community. As more and more colleges redesign their practices based on the model, we will accrue a growing body of evidence regarding specific implementation approaches, which will help future college leaders in their own efforts to redesign the community college to improve student success.

1

Redesigning College Programs

Nowhere are the features—and disadvantages—of the cafeteria model more apparent than in the design of community college degree and certificate programs. To achieve their goal of serving a diverse array of students, community colleges offer a wide variety of courses and programs, including both for-credit and noncredit options. In this book, we narrow our focus to for-credit programs leading to postsecondary credentials: "associate of arts" and "associate of science" programs, which are generally designed to prepare students for transfer to bachelor's degree programs; and occupational certificates and "applied associate" programs, which prepare students for direct entry into jobs as diverse as respiratory therapy, protective services, and early childhood education. If a college serves large numbers of both occupational and transfer-oriented students, then it may offer hundreds of such degree programs. And when this number is multiplied by the dozens of programs offered by four-year transfer destinations, transfer-oriented students may have thousands of options—too many for even the most experienced advisors, let alone students themselves, to understand and evaluate.

In addition to the multiplicity of program choices, the course-taking path within each program is often unclear—many programs have a plethora of electives and course alternatives. This problem is particularly acute in transfer-oriented programs, which give students broad flexibility in the introductory liberal arts and science courses they must complete to meet requirements for "general education" curricula. Faced with a wide range of choices, students seeking to transfer to four-year institutions often express confusion about which courses to take. Moreover, in both transfer and occupational programs, *course* learning outcomes are not always tied to *program* learning outcomes, making it difficult for students to build a coherent set of skills as they progress across the curriculum.

In this chapter, we describe the cafeteria model's focus on courses rather than programs, and examine the effects of this focus on students. We find that the typical student is overwhelmed by the many choices available, resulting in poor program or course selection decisions, which in turn cost time and money, and likely lead many students to drop out in frustration. In particular, the lack of coherence in transfer-oriented programs, and the poor alignment of such programs with requirements for transfer with junior standing in a specific major at a four-year college, create barriers to advancement for students.

What is a solution to the chaotic and confusing environment that confronts students when they arrive on campus? We argue that the guided pathways model can provide a route through college that is relatively easy to understand and follow, and that helps structure student choices. In this model, students who have chosen a major or program are provided with a program map that defines a default sequence of courses, each with clear learning outcomes that build across the curriculum into a coherent set of skills, which in turn are aligned with requirements for successful transfer or career advancement. New students who are undecided about a major must choose one of a limited number of exploratory or "meta-majors" that expose them to educational and career options within broad fields. The meta-majors also include program maps of default sequences of courses.

While this approach provides a more structured pathway through college, it does not eliminate student choice. Students can choose among programs or meta-majors; they can change programs; and they can customize their initial program map. But once they have chosen a program, if they do not explicitly decide to alter the default map, they will be in a coherent program that leads to a defined educational credential and explicit objectives for further education or career advancement. The maps are designed to enable students to complete credentials as quickly as possible, and make it possible for students and their advisors and faculty to track progress and intervene if students are not making headway or stray "off-map."

The chapter is divided into four sections. First, we describe the confusing and inefficient pathways inherent in the cafeteria model that lead to low completion rates and weak student outcomes. In the following section, we present the guided pathways model and explain how and why it can overcome many of these problems. Then we describe some examples of the model in practice. In the final section, we argue that the redesigned program pathways described in this chapter provide a structure around which colleges can engage faculty and staff to rethink and improve the effectiveness of student support, instruction, and intake—examples of which are examined in subsequent chapters.

Complexity and Confusion in the Cafeteria College

As they enter community colleges, students are confronted with a series of complicated decisions they must make, often with little assistance. In this section, we review research from behavioral economics that analyzes the problems individuals face when confronted with a complex environment like a college, and we show that students often make poor decisions as they try to navigate through college programs. Next, we focus on transfer. Transfer is fundamental to the community college mission, since the large majority of students in credit programs state a desire to transfer and earn a bachelor's degree. We show that the transfer process is particularly inefficient and confusing to students. Then we argue that the course-based structure of community colleges makes it difficult to create coherent pathways based on defined program-level learning outcomes.

Choice Architecture and Student Behavior

In a review of research from psychology, marketing, and behavioral economics, CCRC researcher Judith Scott-Clayton argues that the complex choices facing community college students may lead to poor decisions.[1] She cites three overarching findings that have implications for community college students. First, individuals are not necessarily aware of their own needs and preferences, and their choices may be affected by a variety of seemingly irrelevant contextual factors. In the community college context, this finding suggests that student decisions about programs and courses could depend in part on how various options are presented, or on other factors such as convenience of schedule or which courses their friends are taking—in other words, considerations that may be unrelated to the merits of particular options.

Second, even when individuals are aware of their own needs and preferences, they do not have unlimited time to research available options for a given decision, nor do they have an unlimited capacity to process vast amounts of information. Particularly when one is unfamiliar with a specific type of product or service, it is time-consuming and intellectually challenging to identify relevant information, understand it, apply it appropriately, and judge how well each option matches one's needs and preferences. The process is even more difficult when choices involve trade-offs. For example, a short occupational certificate program may be relatively easy to complete and may reduce a student's earnings only briefly (while the student takes courses); but, on the other hand, it may increase the student's long-term employment prospects only modestly. In contrast,

a longer-term program will be more academically demanding and may reduce earnings for the longer period required to complete the program, but
it may also lead to higher earnings and better advancement opportunities
in the long run. Attempting to compare multiple dimensions of costs and
benefits across a variety of options is a formidable exercise. Indeed, while
people enjoy having choices in general, they dislike these types of complex
balancing acts, and they tend to avoid situations that require such decisions.
Perhaps as a result, when faced with complex decisions, people commonly
choose the easiest or most obvious option, even when the benefits of doing
otherwise are substantial.

Third, sometimes the easiest decision is *not deciding*—or at least delaying the decision. Researchers have found that people defer decisions
when they are faced with multidimensional tradeoffs, when they are uncertain how to weigh different types of costs and benefits, and when they
are unsure about the long-term consequences of each option. This notion
of "decision deferral" is particularly troubling when we consider the choices
that college students must make. If a student is confused about various
course options for the upcoming semester, the easiest path may be to defer
the decision. However, "later" may be too late if the student misses the
financial aid deadline, or if required courses have filled up, or if life circumstances have conspired to make it easier to put off enrollment until
the next term.

Scott-Clayton argues that the decision-making context confronting students at community colleges may be even more complex than that of their
peers at elite four-year institutions, and the consequences of suboptimal
decision making may be more negative.[2] In contrast to community colleges, which give students a broad choice of courses and programs and
limited guidance, elite four-year institutions often offer many fewer program options, and much more individual guidance in selecting from a
smaller set of majors; some also provide a more structured curriculum of
first- and second-year courses. Scott-Clayton points out that Harvard University, for example, offers limited choices to its undergraduates: they can
attend only full-time, they must complete a required core curriculum in a
face-to-face setting, and they must choose one of forty-three majors leading
to a bachelor's degree.[3] In contrast, nearby Bunker Hill Community College offers over seventy associate degree or certificate programs in more
than sixty academic and applied fields, with no required core curriculum.
Advisors are available, but there are too few to offer individualized support. Many students are left to decide on their own whether to enroll full-
time or part-time, or whether online or face-to-face courses are optimal
in each subject area. At Harvard, most freshmen follow a limited set of

curricular paths, and they can consult with one another on their relatively limited options in terms of courses, professors, and programs. At Bunker Hill, a given student may not know another student who is following a similar path, and thus may garner only limited advice from his or her peers.

If community college students confront a more complicated set of choices than do students in elite four-year institutions, they also have fewer resources for managing complex decision making. James Rosenbaum and his colleagues have argued that the lack of structure in community college programs increases the importance of "social know-how" or "college knowledge," which in turn tends to place already disadvantaged groups commonly served by these institutions—including low-income, minority, and first-generation college students—at a further disadvantage.[4] Since they are often unable to ask a parent or sibling who has already been through college, these students are especially in need of effective guidance. Rosenbaum also finds that lack of clear guidance can lead students to make costly mistakes, such as taking credits that are not accepted for transfer credit in the specific major a student wants to pursue at a university and pursuing credentials that have limited labor market payoffs.[5]

It is also worth noting that, on average, compared to undergraduates at elite institutions, community college students are more often employed, are more likely to have young children, and have fewer family financial resources.[6] Outside obligations and pressures further complicate their lives and may tax their mental and emotional capacities to make good decisions.[7] Compared to their peers at elite four-year colleges, community college students may also be more easily derailed by bad decisions. In a 2006 article in the *Journal of Public Policy and Marketing,* economist Marianne Bertrand points out that low-income people make the same types of mistakes as high-income people, but the consequences of their mistakes are more devastating:

> People who live in poverty are susceptible to many of the same idiosyncrasies as those who live in comfort, but whereas better-off people typically find themselves, either by default or through minimal effort, in the midst of a system composed of attractive "no-fee" options, automatic deposits, reminders, and so forth, that is built to shelter them from grave or repeated error, less-well-off people often find themselves without such "aids" and instead are confronted by obstacles—institutional, social, and psychological— that render their economic conduct all the more overwhelming and fallible.[8]

Along the same lines, a student from a high-income family who discovers that he or she has taken a course that does not count toward graduation or transfer can shrug off the time and money spent as a minor hassle. In contrast, for a low-income student, the time spent on a semester-long course translates to at least a full week of time away from wage earning. The forgone wages, together with any tuition not covered by financial aid, may require cuts in basic household expenses for items such as groceries, health insurance, or children's clothing. To realize that such painful sacrifices were wasted on an unnecessary course is no minor hassle. The outsize consequences of these types of small mistakes mean that the poor can afford fewer mistakes, and they may feel the need to avoid or exit contexts that tend to cause them.

Students Lost in a Maze

The research described above suggests that confusing pathways can make it difficult for students to make good decisions, and some empirical evidence reinforces this idea. Quantitative analyses of student transcript data show that many students pursue suboptimal enrollment patterns. For example, several studies have found that students who eventually earn an associate degree tend to earn a significant number of "excess credits."[9] A CCRC study of community college students in one state found that associate degree holders earned 12 percent more credits than required by their program.[10] Some excess credits may result from course taking that is not problematic, such as early experimentation in order to discover interests, or study in subjects that are not required for a credential but do broaden knowledge, such as supplemental career-oriented courses. Other excess credits are more troublesome, insofar as they result from poor course selection by students or unavailability of courses needed to graduate.

Students are often confused about their options, or lack the information they need to make wise choices. In a 2006 survey of students in a large urban community college district, Rosenbaum and his colleagues found that many students felt they did not receive enough information about program requirements and options.[11] Other research has found that community college students "develop information by taking courses almost at random."[12] Many students are surprised to find out that the courses they completed when they were exploring options do not count toward the major they eventually select.[13]

Similarly, in a 2013 survey of California community college students regarding the supports they thought would be helpful to succeed in college, 79 percent said that being "directed"—making a connection between their success in college and their life goals—was very important to their progress in college.[14] In focus groups associated with the study, most participants reported that they found direction by selecting a major and mapping out related academic requirements in an educational plan. Some reported struggling to find the information they needed to establish a plan, and suggested that colleges should be more proactive in helping students, particularly those who are undecided about a major or those who are the first in their family to attend college.

No Clear Path to a Bachelor's Degree

Community college students who want to transfer to a four-year institution face a particularly daunting set of choices. Over 80 percent of first-time community college students indicate that they intend to earn a bachelor's degree or higher.[15] Yet only about a quarter of students transfer within five years, and fewer than two-thirds of them (62 percent) earn a bachelor's degree within six years of transferring.[16] Why do so few achieve these goals?

To begin with, although students may wish to complete a bachelor's degree, many entering students have not chosen a four-year college from which they hope to graduate, nor have they settled on a major. In a national survey of beginning college students, nearly 40 percent were undecided about their major—and the real number may be much higher, as students must declare a program of study (even a vague program such as "general education") to qualify for financial aid.[17] Besides the major of "undecided," the largest single major field for new community college students is business, which students may choose because it sounds practical and remunerative. Many students, particularly those who are recently out of high school or who come from disadvantaged backgrounds, do not have a clear idea of the opportunities available to them in business (or in any other field, for that matter).[18]

CREDITS DON'T TRANSFER

Students who do not have a clear idea of their major but who want a bachelor's degree are typically advised to take introductory liberal arts and sciences courses in a "general education" or "general studies" program.[19] The advantage of a general studies track is that it allows students the opportunity to take a variety of courses and explore different subject areas without limiting future options.[20] Unless aspiring transfer students have selected a destination institution and major, they cannot know precisely which courses will transfer and which will not. To minimize the risk, colleges often advise students to take courses such as Psychology 101, History 101, English 101, and Biology 101, which are a relatively safe bet to be accepted for credit after transfer to a four-year institution.

Given the need for undecided students to explore, together with the conflicting demands of transfer destinations and their specific majors, community colleges build flexibility into their general studies program requirements. Students in this track are generally asked to pick from a long list of courses that meet "distribution requirements" in a variety of subject areas, such as science, social and behavioral sciences, arts and humanities, English, and math. In addition to fulfilling distribution requirements, students can select from almost any course in the college to fulfill the leftover electives required to reach a sixty-credit associate degree.

The general studies track is designed to be flexible enough to allow students to transfer anywhere; unfortunately, however, universities (or departments within them) will often pick and choose among the courses on a transfer student's transcript, accepting a few for credit in the major, accepting some only for general education credits, and rejecting others entirely. Some universities will not even apply "safe bet" courses in the way a student might expect, because of the institution's or individual program's unique core curriculum courses. For example, a student's destination major may offer a signature course in ethics that also fulfills the humanities requirement for graduation. If a transfer student arrives with a humanities course already completed, that course may fulfill the destination college's humanities requirement, but not the major's ethics requirement. Thus, the student must take a second humanities course, having already spent time and money on the first course at a community college.

POOR ALIGNMENT BETWEEN TWO- AND FOUR-YEAR PROGRAMS

To avoid requiring transfer students to retake the same or similar courses at destination colleges, over thirty states have developed "common core" agreements that require public four-year colleges to accept an agreed-upon set of general education courses from community colleges.[21] These agreements stipulate that credits earned in the core will transfer to any public four-year institution in the state. Other states have agreements that require public universities to grant junior standing to students who earn an associate degree (with the state-sanctioned general education core) from one of the state's community colleges.

However, not all states have such agreements. Moreover, even when they do, most do not guarantee that community college credits will be accepted for credit toward junior standing in a particular major. This is because major requirements are often stipulated by departments within universities. Programs such as business, engineering, and nursing typically have specific general education prerequisites that are not part of the core. As Matthew Reed, the author of *Confessions of a Community College Administator*, explains:

Typically, students who transfer have to declare an intended major at the destination college. When they do that, the destination college usually allows the department of the intended major to decide which credits to accept and which not to. In most cases, the destination department has no issue with the courses outside the major, but will frequently become unreasonably picky about courses within the major.[22]

A few states have tried to smooth the process of transfer into specific majors by creating policies that not only guarantee transfer of all associate degree credits but also stipulate which community college courses will be accepted toward specific majors at any public university. Arizona was among the first to adopt such a policy, but more recently California, Connecticut, and Tennessee (among others) have adopted "associate degree with major pathways" transfer policies. These policies are promising, but simply having a state policy in place does not mean it will be effective in improving the transfer process. For example, although North Carolina had a statewide transfer agreement in place since 1997 that included major pathways, in practice many courses were only accepted as electives by some of the state's public four-year institutions.[23] Perhaps because of the frequent disconnect between policy and practice, researchers have not found a statistically significant relationship between statewide articulation agreements and transfer rates.[24]

In numerous instances, colleges and universities have worked together in pairs to create their own transfer agreements, independent of state policy. However, many of these local agreements apply to a limited number of specific programs. Moreover, having multiple agreements—some of them with specific departments within a university rather than one that encompasses all programs—is inefficient and contributes to confusion among students, advisors, and faculty, as we will discuss in more detail later.

Losing credits in the process of transfer can derail students' progress toward a bachelor's degree. For example, a 2014 study using a nationally representative sample found that students who were able to transfer almost all their earned community college credits to a four-year institution were two and a half times more likely to earn a bachelor's degree, compared to students who were able to transfer fewer than half of their earned credits. Unfortunately, less than 60 percent were able to transfer most of their community college credits, and about 15 percent could transfer very few credits and essentially had to start over.[25] The study examined ideas often posited for why many community college transfers fail to earn a bachelor's degree—including lowered expectations, the vocational focus of many community college programs, or the sometimes presumed inadequate academic rigor of community college instruction—and found that none of these had a substantial negative effect. Instead, the biggest barrier to bachelor's degree completion for community college students who transferred was the credits lost in the transfer process.[26]

In addition to the problem of lost credits, the higher education model based on using general education courses to explore options and choose majors faces particular obstacles in the community college. The need to ultimately choose a major is often not communicated to new students entering a community college.[27] Moreover, many community colleges do not offer disciplinary majors such as biology or economics. Thus, unlike students at four-year institutions, community college students are not typically exposed to a particular major by interacting with faculty from a department that offers both introductory and more advanced courses in the field, which puts them at a disadvantage after transferring. Take the example of psychology, a highly popular field for transfer-oriented students. At most community colleges, there is neither a psychology "program" in which to enroll, nor are there psychology-specific advisors to help students navigate course requirements. Rather, students interested in psychology usually must investigate the requirements of prospective transfer schools' psychology programs on their own, and match their community college's offerings to those requirements as closely as possible.

Furthermore, community college students often do not understand the value or utility of their general education courses, which tend to be broad surveys of a field in which many students have no preexisting interest. While the courses are intended in part to provoke students' interest in new and unfamiliar topics, students do not always perceive them this way. In general, students tend to be interested and excited to enroll in courses they think might help them in their future goals. In contrast, when they think courses are irrelevant to their goals, they label them as "stupid," "useless," or "boring."[28] And students in career-technical programs, who are focused on preparing for specific jobs, are sometimes reluctant to take general education courses that are required for degrees but seem irrelevant to their interests.[29]

THE PERPLEXING TRANSFER PROCESS

Student interviews expose the confusion and inefficiency of the transfer process. In fifty focus groups that discussed the transfer experience with students from two- and four-year colleges in one state, researchers at Public Agenda found that many students had lost time and money because of courses that did not transfer.[30] Some students had been advised to take courses that were not accepted by the university to which they transferred.

In other cases, community college credits were accepted as electives but not as credit toward a major. Interestingly, another paper that drew from some of the same focus groups found that students faulted themselves, rather than their institutions, for these missteps: "Instead of outrage and recrimination, most students sounded deflated and defeated—and blamed themselves even for those problems that, from the outside, appear to result from the clear failures of institutions to collaborate effectively."[31]

CCRC researchers found similar confusion and frustration among transfer students in an in-depth study of advising at a Detroit-area community college.[32] Several students suggested that the college should create clearer sequences of default courses for particular programs of study. As one said,

> I feel like they should put one way to do it, and then if you want another option, if you want to take a different class . . . then there's like different classes that will go with it. But they should just kind of lay out one way to do it.

This sentiment was echoed by student participants in another focus group study by Public Agenda on community college students' experiences along educational pathways and their ideas about ways colleges could support student progress.[33] A common theme among students in the study was that they were confused trying to navigate through college, and that being in programs with well-defined pathways would improve their chances of completion.

Given the complexity and confusion students encounter when seeking to transfer, it is perhaps not surprising that, while the majority of community college students intend to get a bachelor's degree, only about one-fourth actually transfer to a four-year institution within five years of starting college.[34] Among community college students who transfer to a four-year college, about three in every five earn a bachelor's degree within six years of transferring.[35] About 80 percent of students who transfer do so without first earning an associate degree.[36] In the end, the majority of students who enter a community college seeking to transfer end up with no credential—neither an associate nor a bachelor's degree.

Curricular Incoherence Limits Learning

Allowing students to cobble together their own programs from a wide menu of courses not only creates barriers to program completion, it may also limit students' learning. A large body of research on learning shows that new knowledge is gained by connecting it to previous knowledge.[37]

Based on a synthesis of current research on student learning, researchers at Carnegie Mellon University's Eberley Center for Teaching Excellence found that "how students organize knowledge influences how they learn and apply what they know."[38]

> Students naturally make connections between pieces of knowledge. When those connections form knowledge structures that are accurately and meaningfully organized, students are better able to retrieve and apply their knowledge effectively and efficiently. In contrast, when knowledge is connected in inaccurate or random ways, students can fail to retrieve or apply it appropriately.

The implication is that if students are to achieve meaningful learning outcomes and associated skills in a program, then they need to develop knowledge and skills systematically and cumulatively over time, not in a haphazard fashion. It is difficult to see how a college program could help students learn effectively without establishing clear learning goals that are interconnected across courses in a program. Yet community college faculty have been slow to make use of information about student learning outcomes—information that could facilitate discussions and reforms to create more coherent curricula. According to a 2013 survey by the National Institute for Learning Outcomes Assessment (NILOA), while 84 percent of colleges and universities have developed learning outcomes for students, most colleges did not systematically use information about learning outcomes to improve teaching and student progression.[39] Another study of a sample of community colleges in Washington State found that, among faculty respondents, only 30 percent reported making frequent use of data on measures of learning other than grades (such as student learning outcomes, licensure exams, achievement tests, or other competency assessments).[40] If faculty are unlikely to use assessments of learning other than grades, then they are unlikely to be able to assess, discuss, and improve the achievement of learning outcomes by students—not only within courses but across courses in a program.

The organization of the cafeteria college makes coordination to create coherent programs of study particularly difficult. For example, many community college students who want to transfer are in liberal arts or general education programs,[41] but liberal arts and sciences faculty in community colleges are often organized into academic departments by disciplines such as math, economics, and psychology. Faculty in these departments owe their primary allegiance to their discipline, not to the general studies curriculum. As a result, we have observed, they are unlikely to meet with faculty in other departments to discuss program goals and to design a coherent curriculum for students taking general education courses. Thus, it is unclear how under this model faculty can effectively align teaching and learning outcomes across the curriculum.

The cafeteria model affords flexibility in the selection of distinct courses and provides opportunities for students to explore their interests and options. But, in the end, it offers little guidance in establishing career goals, choosing a program, or crafting a strategy for efficient transfer. Moreover, the course-based curricular design thwarts coherent program-level planning and may weaken student learning. Thus, the cafeteria model is not well designed to help uncertain students recognize the options available to them, understand what they need to do to achieve their goals, and offer a framework for building knowledge and skills across the curriculum.

The Guided Pathways Model

How can colleges minimize student confusion over the many choices available to them and thus reduce the mistakes that students make while navigating college? And how can colleges create curricula that enable students to develop competencies that they will need to succeed? In this section, we describe the guided pathways approach that provides students with more simplified programs based on maps developed by faculty and defined according to coherent sequences of courses and competencies aligned with the requirements for success in further education and employment. Such maps help to structure students' decisions while preserving their ability to choose among options. We also draw on learning science to discuss the benefits of using learning outcomes to define programs.

One way to minimize student confusion is to offer a much narrower set of program options, together with highly prescribed courses and course sequences that allow little to no room for students to go off track. James Rosenbaum and his colleagues argue that since the types of students served by community colleges often lack knowledge about college procedures and options, they would be better served by highly structured programs, which are often found at private career colleges. Advising at these private two-year colleges is also more structured and intrusive. Rosenbaum and colleagues refer to the complementary combination of highly structured programs and mandatory, well-integrated support services afforded to students by career colleges as a "package deal."[42]

The highly structured programs at the Tennessee Colleges of Applied Technology (which are public institutions) have attracted a good deal of positive attention for similar reasons. Like the private career colleges that Rosenbaum and his colleagues have studied,[43] the programs offered by the "Tennessee Techs" are much more structured than those at a typical community college: students enroll in block-scheduled programs with prescribed curricula for six hours a day, five days a week. Attendance is mandatory.[44]

While it is true that private career colleges and the Tennessee Techs have higher graduation rates than public community colleges, these institutions attract types of students different from those at public community colleges.[45] Research has not shown that these programs would be more effective for the same types of students served by community colleges. Moreover, while such programs may work well for students who have made a clear decision about their career goals—especially older students—they have been criticized for being too rigid and for limiting student choice. This can hinder students—especially younger students—from exploring their options and from benefiting from the choice process itself.

Scott-Clayton argues that providing students with highly structured pathways to completion is not without tradeoffs, particularly if more structure is taken to imply less choice and flexibility.[46] Creating a model that is too restrictive could threaten students' autonomy, which research suggests is critical to their intrinsic motivation.[47] Community college educators also sometimes object to mandatory structures because they seem overly paternalistic—such structures, it is argued, ignore the fact that students are adults and have the right to make their own decisions.[48] Some college faculty also believe that making one's own choices and finding one's own path are important parts of the college experience. Indeed, as we have mentioned, general studies curricula are often explicitly designed to allow students latitude to choose courses so they can explore different fields without limiting future options.[49] And yet, as we have argued, such curricula do not provide the level of guidance that many students want and need.

Guiding Student Choices without Restricting Options

As we have discussed, behavioral economics research provides insight into why complexity might be a barrier to students' completing college programs. At the same time, behavioral economics also suggests ways that colleges can help students make decisions to increase their likelihood of completion without restricting their options. One key conclusion from this research is that it helps to have a map or plan. Studies show that prompting individuals to state a plan for how they will undertake something they want to do increases the likelihood they will do it. For example, in a field experiment during the 2008 presidential primary, voters who were asked to identify when and where they would vote (thus creating a mental plan of how to do the activity) were 10 percent more likely to vote than those who were not prompted. In contrast, a standard "get out the vote" intervention had no effect on turnout.[50] Referring to such studies, Cass Sunstein, a Harvard Law School professor whose writing has helped popularize behavioral economics concepts, argues that

> when people are informed of the benefits or risks of engaging in certain actions, they are far more likely to respond to that information if they are simultaneously provided with clear, explicit information about how to do so.... In many domains, the identification of a specific, clear, unambiguous path or plan has an important effect on our decisions. Vagueness can produce inaction, even when people are informed about risks and potential benefits.[51]

Of course, the decisions involved in choosing a program of study and then getting through it are vastly more complex than those involved in figuring out how to get to a polling place. How can colleges create maps that help guide students through this complicated process without unduly restricting their options? Behavioral research offers a number of tools to help colleges do this. These tools can be described generally as *nudges,* or actions that guide decision making while preserving freedom of choice.[52]

One such nudge is the use of *defaults.* Research suggests that defaults help people make decisions that they want to make and believe they will benefit from, but which they might not make on their own because the options are too complicated or technical.[53] For example, studies of employer retirement plans have shown dramatic increases in participation when people are enrolled by default but allowed to opt out.[54] Similar results have been found in studies of European organ donation programs tied to driver license applications.[55]

As applied to community colleges, defaults avoid the problem of forcing students to cobble together their own programs. Instead, colleges can enroll students in a default sequence of courses in their chosen program of study. Particularly when it comes to students with poor academic preparation and limited exposure to higher education, having to plan an academic program can be daunting. Faculty members are best qualified to design a meaningful course of study. A default curriculum, designed by faculty, with input from advisors, can give students a map of the path they need to take to reach their academic and career goals.

Studies also show that offering a default with the possibility of opting out can have a strong influence on behavior because people assume that the defaults have been selected by experts for a good reason.[56] In focus groups with California community college students about the supports they think they need to succeed in college, students underscored the value of faculty involvement in helping them establish goals and plans for achieving those goals.[57] This finding suggests that students trust faculty and advisors (until given reason not to) and will for the most part be happy to follow a suggested default pathway.

A particular default pathway may not be appropriate for all students in a program, however. It is important to point out that a default program map is not the same as a mandated one, as students can opt out of the default and customize it to their needs and goals. For example, if a student has a very specific goal in mind for her studies, she can work with an advisor or faculty member to create a custom map. A default map is also not the same as the lockstep programs of the sort students typically experience in high school or in the private career colleges described by Rosenbaum and his colleagues.

On the other hand, some studies suggest that defaults have disadvantages because individuals are not as motivated to implement a decision they did not actively make. As one team of researchers noted, "because opt-out policies yield decisions through the inaction of the decision maker, they are less likely to engender the kind of committed follow-up that is often useful when it comes to implementing the decision."[58] For example, while default enrollment can greatly increase participation in employer retirement plans, workers who are automatically enrolled in retirement accounts seem less motivated to pay attention to their plans. They may not, for example, check to ensure they are saving enough, or confirm that their investments align with their goals for saving.[59]

While research of this kind has not been conducted on program course defaults at colleges, it does raise a reasonable concern. To address it, we need to look to another kind of "nudge" that can guide decision making while still bolstering commitment. This sort of nudge is called *active choice*. With active choice, individuals are required to choose from among a relatively small set of clearly defined options; however, individuals are not defaulted into any one option. Sunstein maintains that active choice works best when the choice set is diverse, when experts are unsure which choice is best, and when choosers prefer to choose.[60]

As an example of active choice, colleges might require entering students to choose from a limited set of broad program areas with which to begin their studies. Requiring choice from a limited set of options has two strong benefits. First, it is much easier to choose from a limited set of well-defined options than to choose from a large set of ill-defined ones. When options are clearly delineated, students may more readily recognize the option that best matches their own nascent interests and preferences. While it is true that many incoming students do not have a clear idea of what they want to study, most probably have at least a vague sense of an area of study that might interest them. In a survey we conducted of incoming students at one large comprehensive community college, only 17 percent had no idea what they might like to study. The majority of students had some idea about the area they wished to pursue—for example, business, health, or liberal arts—but had not developed their preferences beyond that point.[61] For these students, choosing among a limited set of clearly defined options should be a relatively simple and straightforward process, freeing up advising time and resources for the smaller set of students who need more intensive help exploring their interests and preferences.

A second benefit of active choice is that it is more motivating than defaults that offer no choice. In two field experiments, participants not only made better health-related decisions but were also more committed to their decision when they were made through active choice.[62] Some members of a prescription benefit plan were given the choice to opt into an automatic refill program that would help them maintain compliance with their doctor's recommended dosage. Other patients in an "enhanced active choice" group were required to choose whether or not to enroll in the refill program, and were given information about the costs and benefits of each option. Patients in the latter group were much more likely to enroll than patients who were given the choice to opt in. Moreover, the enhanced active choice group patients were more likely to stay committed to the program. Applied to the case of entering college students, this research suggests that requiring students to choose from among a set of broad program streams rather than allowing them to be "undecided" about their college goals could be beneficial, especially if each option is accompanied by information about the particular program stream, its core requirements, and its relationship to further education and careers.

It is possible to combine active choice with defaults such that students are required to choose among several broad program streams from the start, and within a given stream are then provided with a default curriculum created by faculty. Default curricula within broad streams can be designed to give new students exposure to their initial field of interest while also exposing them to other subject areas, providing a foundation in fundamental cross-cutting skills such as critical thinking, quantitative reasoning, and reading in different disciplines. Over the course of their first semester, this can help students choose a major or concentration in the broad field, or switch fields if they do not find the initial field a good fit.

This approach also has the advantage of enabling students to explore a field, but without being locked into a specific major. Active exploration is likely a better way to enable students to decide on a particular course of study rather than just presenting students with information on program options, even within a particular broad field. In this case, some experience is probably the best guide.

In focus groups with two- and four-year college students who were asked about the idea of requiring them to pick a "broad major" upon entry, along with default curricula and guaranteed availability of required courses, researchers from Public Agenda found some resistance to the idea among students who valued the opportunity to explore and who believed that once in college, students can and should take responsibility for their course selection. Other students, as well as advisors who believed that students need to select a major and complete a degree as quickly as possible, liked the idea.[63] According to the Public Agenda report, "Several students said that nowadays it's 'just too expensive to explore,' and they were attracted to the idea of accelerating the exploration process."[64] Those who supported the idea said that students often choose majors without being fully informed about the courses required and the further education and careers to which a given major might lead. Students generally liked the idea of grouping majors into areas of interest to help organize their thinking about potential paths. For this idea to have the greatest impact, students indicated that institutions would have to provide adequate advising to help them choose a specific major within a broad program stream that is a good fit for them.

Aligning Program Learning Outcomes with Student Goals

Having a map is important for navigating college, but it is also important that the paths to students' end goals are clearly delineated with signposts along the way. As we have discussed, part of the reason that college programs are confusing is that their learning outcomes are too often poorly defined and not aligned with the requirements for further education and successful employment in the given field. Research from several domains suggests that colleges can improve student learning by mapping out programs using learning outcomes that are aligned with student goals beyond just program completion.

First, studies on the psychology of learning show the importance of setting clear learning goals and providing students with a concrete sense of how they are progressing toward those goals.[65] For example, some studies indicate that the amount of time one spends in deliberate practice toward a specific goal is more predictive of learning in a given field than time spent in more generic practice.[66] If a learning outcome is clearly specified, students have a concrete goal toward which to "practice." Research on the elements of effective teaching in higher education also suggests that providing students with a "big picture" of the key topics within a specific course, and how they fit together, helps improve learning.[67]

Second, studies in K–12 education find that schools that are able to achieve greater gains in student learning, particularly with students from disadvantaged backgrounds, are characterized by higher levels of "instructional program coherence."[68] This is defined as "a set of interrelated programs for students and staff that are guided by a common framework for curriculum, instruction, assessment, and learning climate, and that are pursued over a sustained period of time."[69]

Third, studies of organizational effectiveness in higher education and other sectors suggest that innovative organizational practices have the greatest effect on performance when they are implemented in concert with one another and are well aligned to achieve organizational goals.[70] If organizational goals—for example, enabling students to complete programs of study that prepare them for success in further education and employment—are not clearly defined, disparate units of the organization are less likely to work together to achieve those goals, and may instead turn inward toward their own unit's more clearly understood goals. This fragmentation of resources and energy hampers institutional performance. In community colleges, clearly defining programs with a coherent set of learning outcomes aligned with the requirements for further education and career advancement helps to ensure that efforts by faculty to improve instruction in their courses pay off through improved learning across the curriculum. In colleges organized according to the cafeteria model, faculty typically lack reliable information about student learning outcomes beyond grades. Without other measures of student learning, it is difficult to see how faculty can systematically improve instruction not only within courses but also across courses within programs.

The notion of aligning and sequencing learning outcomes along a program pathway may bring to mind the notion of competency-based education, which we discussed briefly in the introduction. At their best, competency-based models define the specific set of skills and competencies needed for students to complete a degree or program, with program completion based on authentic demonstrations of those competencies, rather than on the accumulation of course-based credits. Such models are highly consistent with the guided pathways emphasis on defining, mapping, and tracking learning outcomes. Yet competency-based assessments are often used in conjunction with an "unbundled" approach to teaching and learning that we argue will be less effective for the typical community college student. We will return to this issue in Chapter 6.

Guided Pathways in Practice

The implementation of the guided pathways model requires a significant change in the design of college programs, the professional interaction among faculty and between faculty and advisors, and more extensive relationships among two- and four-year colleges and among colleges and employers. The overall approach is relatively new and still being developed. In this section, we describe how some colleges have put the notion of default curricula and active choice into practice in redesigning their academic programs. We begin by providing illustrations of how individual colleges and universities have mapped guided pathways. We then describe how maps and guided pathways have been used to help students transfer from community colleges to four-year institutions.

Mapping Clearer Paths

ARIZONA STATE UNIVERSITY

To help students choose from among the 300-plus majors it offers, Arizona State University (ASU) faculty have mapped out the path to a degree in each program.[71] These maps identify the courses that are most important to the major and indicate which one of a group of "critical courses" should be taken early in a student's program (critical courses are ones that most strongly predict later success in the major). ASU's maps provide a default curriculum for students to follow each semester, and also list milestones that students are expected to achieve, such as completing college math by a particular semester, if they are to stay on track. ASU officials say that the program maps are continually updated and reflect the interdisciplinary work that the university has emphasized in recent years.

New ASU students who are undecided on a major are required to enter an "exploratory track" in one of the university's seven most popular program areas: business; education; health and life sciences; humanities, fine arts and design; math, physical sciences and technology, social and behavioral sciences; and pre-engineering. Administrators and faculty believe that requiring students to choose exploratory status, instead of allowing them to be "undecided," helps to overcome inertia and procrastination. At the same time, exploratory status does not limit students' choices. Students who declare an exploratory status can immediately begin meeting the general education requirements that all ASU graduates must fulfill, while taking some time to engage in structured exploration of a variety of academic courses that may spark interest in a potential major. Exploratory students in the School of Letters and Sciences can take up to three terms or forty-five credits before they must choose a specific major, while exploratory students in business have two terms to make a decision.

Like students in specific ASU majors, students in exploratory majors are required to follow a "major map" that shows the prescribed sequence of courses by term, including "critical courses."[72] Students in exploratory majors are also required to enroll in a sequence of one-credit major and career exploration courses, which are designed to lead students through the process of choosing a specific major. According to ASU vice provost Maria Hesse, these courses were developed by counseling psychologists to provide "a clear plan for what students need to do each semester to move closer to deciding who they are and what they want to become." From a behavioral economics standpoint, exploratory status helps guide students' decision making about a major, using *active choice* to require students to choose an initial broad program area and a *default* curriculum within each area. Scaffolding students' decisions in this way makes it easier for students to choose from among the more than 300 majors ASU offers, but without limiting their options. Hesse reports that identifying students as "exploratory" also allows advisors to target information and other supports that help them choose a major.

QUEENSBOROUGH COMMUNITY COLLEGE

Outside of their occupational programs, community colleges that do not offer bachelor's degrees typically do not have majors; instead, most transfer-bound students enroll in vaguely defined general studies or liberal arts programs. But it is nonetheless possible to engage new students in structures resembling ASU's exploratory majors in a community college setting. In 2009, Queensborough Community College, an institution in the City University of New York (CUNY) system, began requiring all first-time, full-time students to enroll in one of five "freshmen academies" based on their interests and goals. The five Queensborough academies are clustered around related occupational programs and bachelor's degree majors: business, visual and performing arts, STEM, health-related science, and liberal arts. Students are required to choose an academy before they enroll. Those who enter undecided are usually recommended to enroll in the liberal arts academy.

Each academy is designed collaboratively, with at least one faculty coordinator responsible for working with faculty and student affairs staff to improve practice and build an academic community of students and faculty with similar interests and aspirations. A dean and faculty member explained: "The idea is that students begin to see themselves as students in a particular field, pretty much from the start."[73] According to a college researcher who oversees evaluation of the academies,

> Students say that being in an academy gives them a sense of identity as a student. . . . Within an academy, student interactions with Academy Advisers (before fall 2013, Freshman Coordinators), faculty, and their peers result in increased opportunities for reflection on what it will take to move ahead in their field of interest.[74]

Faculty and administrators say that the academy structure works particularly well for students in fields such as health care, education, and business; these students tend to have career goals in mind, which makes it easier for them to identify with a community. In the past, for example, nursing students would initially go into liberal arts, as they took the required prerequisites to be accepted into the nursing program. Within that context, it might be difficult for them to meet and connect with other students applying to the nursing program. Now they are part of the health-related science academy from the start, working through the prerequisites alongside other students with similar goals.

At Queensborough, students are not locked into a particular academy. The experience within an academy leads some students to change their minds about what they want to study and do. Indeed, approximately 15 percent of students switch academies in the first year.[75] Thus, the process of deciding what course of study to pursue continues for many students after they enroll.

The academies also provide a useful structure within which faculty work together to define and assess learning outcomes and improve teaching practices. Queensborough has initiated a formal process to assess student mastery of learning goals, using the VALUE rubrics (Valid Assessment of Learning in Undergraduate Education) developed by the American Association of Colleges and Universities.[76] For example, David Rothman, a coordinator in the liberal arts academy, pointed out that they used the VALUE rubrics "to see if we could find evidence about whether students were learning and what they were learning." According to Rothman, this process generated discussion across the liberal arts departments and

> made us ask questions like: "Do my course objectives make sense?" "How do I know a B is a B?" . . . A lot came out of the discussions among faculty in [the liberal arts academy] about how they teach writing. . . . Some changed their curricula as a result to better teach writing in their subject areas.

Thus, Queensborough designed academies and worked to align the content and courses based on program-level learning goals. Moreover, although the academies were initially developed to smooth the transition of new students into the college and get them on a path in a program of study right away, in 2013 the college took steps to build transfer connections, starting with Queens College, the closest four-year CUNY institution. We will discuss the extension of pathways to transfer institutions later in the chapter.

MIAMI DADE COLLEGE

In searching for reasons why so few students completed programs and degrees, faculty at Miami Dade College, a community college in Florida, realized that the curriculum was not coherent to students. Students had too many course choices and too little guidance in selecting a path. Academic support was often misaligned with academic programs, and the information students received to help them navigate academic programs and support services was often unclear and inconsistent. These realizations provided the impetus for a comprehensive college-wide effort to redesign programs and supports in ways that help students more easily navigate college and achieve their goals.[77]

As part of this effort, in 2012 the college convened a task force of twenty-seven faculty members, who, in consultation with their departments and college-wide instructional committees, mapped out program pathways in the five largest program areas, which account for over 80 percent of degree-seeking students at the college. The charge to the pathways mapping team was to create maps that specify a default sequence of courses for students pursuing degrees in those fields.

Some task force faculty members were skeptical that default program maps were necessary or valuable. Thus, to demonstrate the problems facing students, team leaders provided faculty participants with a sample transcript for a Miami Dade student seeking to transfer to a local university to pursue a bachelor's degree in biology. Faculty were asked to help determine the most appropriate courses for the student to complete in the second year of his studies so that he would be able to transfer with junior status in his field. Based on the existing program information sheets, task force members could decipher neither which prerequisites were required by the transfer institution nor which specific courses would transfer. The assignment was further complicated by the addition of information about state prerequisite requirements. One faculty member said half-jokingly, "I think I'll recommend that the student major in English, because I can figure that out." This experience helped galvanize support among task force members for more clearly structured program pathways.

Members of the task force began by agreeing on four guidelines for each program-area map. First, each program curriculum would integrate opportunities for students to master all of the ten learning outcomes that Miami Dade faculty had previously defined for all programs.[78] Second, each pathway would need to satisfy the statewide general education core requirements, although faculty were encouraged to indicate specific general education courses relevant to the given major field (for example, which social science course is recommended for criminal justice majors). Third, all courses in each pathway should transfer seamlessly to enable students to achieve junior standing in target bachelor's programs offered by Miami Dade and its university partners. And fourth, each program area would include curricular pathways for both full-time and part-time students, as well as curricular "on-ramps" for students who started in developmental and English-as-a-second-language programs.

At the same time, Miami Dade redesigned its intake process, so that all entering students are now required to see an advisor and develop an academic plan based on the faculty-created pathway maps. The college is also creating "communities of interest," which introduce students to a specific field and help them evaluate whether to pursue more specialized study in it or switch to another field. These changes are affecting all of Miami Dade's students. Thus the college is innovating at scale—redesigning programs and support services in ways that affect thousands of students.

FLORIDA STATE UNIVERSITY

Building coherent and well-mapped pathways will not by itself significantly improve student outcomes. They will have little effect if students do not make use of them. Florida State University (FSU) was a pioneer in the guided pathways approach, and its experience is instructive. In the late 1990s, FSU tried several strategies for reducing the large number of students who graduated with excess credits (that is, more than the 120 typically needed to graduate with a bachelor's degree in most programs). Realizing that students lacked clear paths to degrees, the university introduced program maps. The maps resulted in a slight improvement in graduation rates and retention rates (second-semester enrollment rates for first-time students), but not in a reduction in excess credits. The reason, the university discovered, was that many students were not following the maps. FSU only saw significant improvements in student outcomes when the university made maps the *default* program of study, designated critical courses as milestones to gauge student progress, and required new students who were undecided about a major to enter an exploratory major. After these changes were implemented around 2002–2003, FSU experienced a 6 percentage point increase in retention in 2009 compared to 2000, a 17-percentage-point increase in the four-year graduation rate, and a decrease from 30 percent to 5 percent in the share of students graduating with more than 120 credits.[79]

Bridging the Transfer Divide

The examples we have discussed so far have involved colleges and universities that developed program maps and pathways for students in their own institutions. For four-year institutions, such as Arizona State and Florida State, intra-institution pathways can get many students all the way to a bachelor's degree, and for two-year colleges such pathways can get them to an associate degree or certificate. But the ultimate goal for most community college students involves transfer to a four-year college; thus community college program maps need to be aligned with transfer goals. In this section, we describe an example of a university—Arizona State University—that extended its program maps backward to community colleges, and two community college entities—Guttman Community College and its parent, the City University of New York (CUNY) system—that extended their pathways forward to transfer-receiving institutions and the labor market.

ARIZONA STATE UNIVERSITY MAPPS

In 2009, Arizona State University formed a partnership with the Maricopa County Community College District to launch the "Maricopa to ASU Pathways Program" (MAPP) to help students transfer seamlessly from Maricopa colleges to ASU and earn an associate degree along the way. Building on the program maps ASU faculty developed for all ASU majors, ASU and Maricopa worked together to create "MAPPs" that specify all the courses students must take to complete the requirements for the Arizona General Education Curriculum (AGEC) and an associate degree, while also completing the lower-division prerequisites for their intended major at ASU. The mantra, according to an ASU brochure on transfer partnerships with community colleges, is "No surprises." In addition to specifying all the required courses, MAPPs clearly indicate any other important requirements, such as minimum grade point averages. Maricopa students who complete a MAPP enter the university as a true junior with a maximum of sixty credits remaining to complete a bachelor's degree. MAPPed students are not only guaranteed admission into their desired major, but also receive a tuition reduction through ASU's Tuition Commitment Program.

Historically, ASU and the Maricopa colleges had a strong relationship but did not have strong, clearly identified transfer pathways. Before MAPP, Maricopa colleges relied on a course equivalency guide to advise students on which courses to take. The guide focused on which courses transferred from a community college to ASU, but did not provide information about how those courses applied to a program or major. In 2008, ASU and the Maricopa colleges convened a work group to examine data on transfer student success. The group found that, in contrast to the relatively poor outcomes of students who transferred to ASU with only a few credits, almost 90 percent of community college students who completed the AGEC and a transfer-oriented associate degree were successful in completing a bachelor's degree. Those who completed associate degrees that included preparatory courses specific to their intended majors were the most successful.

To spearhead the process of designing clearer transfer pathways, ASU in 2009 hired Maria Hesse, who had been president of the Maricopa system's Chandler-Gilbert College. Hesse explained to us what changes were needed:

> Just because a course transfers does not mean it addresses a requirement for a particular ASU major. Students were frustrated when they would transfer to ASU and find that what they had been told would transfer did not "count" towards their degree. There was growing realization in the [Maricopa] system that the approach we were using was engrained in the culture but it was not working to prepare students to transfer with junior standing in a major. One goal of this work is focused on having students take more credits [at the community college], which decreases the student's distance to a degree. At the same time we want to help students become more aware of the right courses to take that are applicable to their degrees so that they can come in as true juniors. This has been a cultural shift as students traditionally just took any course that transferred.[80]

Andrea Buehman, who oversees transfer relations for the Maricopa colleges, also explained: "We wanted to be more intentional about how students go through the process, and get them thinking about applicability [of courses to majors], not just transferability."[81]

In 2009, ASU and the Maricopa colleges began collaboratively developing MAPPs, starting with thirty-two majors. After the initial success with MAPPs at Maricopa, ASU expanded to develop similar Transfer Admission Guarantees (TAGs) with every community college in Arizona and more in California. To develop the TAGs, ASU sent teams to each community college to meet with administrators and faculty to examine program offerings and negotiate alignment of requirements. Like MAPPs, TAGs include all lower-division requirements for an ASU major, ensure students are on a path to complete the AGEC and an associate degree, and guarantee TAG completers admission to ASU as juniors in their selected major.

As of spring 2014, there were TAGS in over 160 majors, and over 9,000 Maricopa students were enrolled in MAPPs. A brochure from ASU, citing *U.S. News & World Report,* claims that ASU now has more transfer students than any other public university in the country.

Both ASU and the Maricopa colleges acknowledge that MAPPs are most appropriate for students with clear goals—that is, those who know they want transfer to ASU in a specific major.[82] As we have discussed, many community college students do not have a clear sense of what they want to do—and even those who do may not understand the differences among specific majors in a particular field. To address this, ASU and the Maricopa colleges launched "exploratory pathways" in the summer of 2013 for community college students who are interested in transferring but are undecided about a major. In a process similar to ASU's exploratory status, such students can enroll in an exploratory pathway in one of four broad fields: health and life sciences; humanities and arts; social and behavioral sciences; and math, physical sciences, engineering and technology. Students in these pathways take introductory courses in the given field as well as courses that satisfy the Arizona general education core. While they are enrolled in an exploratory pathway, students receive targeted communications and counseling from ASU about their career interests and are provided opportunities to explore education and careers in the given field. By the time students earn thirty credits, they are required to choose a MAPP in a specific field. According to ASU's Maria Hesse, "Just identifying one of these broad fields can help you move closer to what you want in life; and then in year two, you go on to select an appropriate major."[83]

GUTTMAN COMMUNITY COLLEGE

Students who are new to the City University of New York's Guttman Community College, which opened in 2012, are required to take a common first-year curriculum. In their second year, however, students are asked to choose a program of study in a particular field. The college's designers selected the fields for these programs of study after conducting extensive research on New York City's labor market projections and after consultation with experts. According to a 2013 case study undertaken to document the work involved in starting the college,

The goals of the research were to identify fields of study that would be attractive to students, would be relevant to the College's mission of sustaining a thriving New York City, and would provide the greatest possible range of academic transfer and career development opportunities.[84]

The college has been phasing in its selected programs of study over time, beginning with five: associate of arts (AA) in business administration; AA in human services; associate of applied science (AAS) in information technology; AA in liberal arts and sciences; and AA in urban studies. An additional program in health information technology (AAS) was started in the fall of 2013, and other AAS programs in energy services management and environmental science will be phased in later.

One purpose of the common first-year curriculum is to guide students through the process of choosing an appropriate program of study. This includes exposure to workplaces in related fields, and visits to bachelor's programs at four-year CUNY colleges.[85] Each associate degree program is also designed to transfer seamlessly to any of CUNY's many nearby four-year colleges—a goal that is supported in part by the larger university's new "Pathways" transfer initiative.

THE CITY UNIVERSITY OF NEW YORK

In the fall of 2013, CUNY (a system that includes eleven "senior" colleges and seven community colleges) implemented the Pathways initiative, which was designed to ease transfer among CUNY undergraduate institutions. Pathways established a new system of general education requirements and new transfer guidelines across the university, including a thirty-credit general education common core.[86] After bachelor's degree students transfer, each CUNY four-year college can require them to take another six to twelve credits of general education through the "college option." Once fulfilled at one CUNY four-year college, these general education credits carry over seamlessly to other CUNY colleges. Faculty committees representing several popular transfer majors at CUNY have designated a minimum of three common and transferable "gateway" courses that are required of all students in those majors. Students anticipating majors in these fields can begin their coursework at any CUNY college with the assurance that if they transfer to another CUNY college, their prior coursework will count toward their continued pursuit of that major.

The CUNY Pathways initiative has been controversial in part because it was perceived by some as a top-down initiative led by administrators rather than faculty.[87] Despite the controversy, both Guttman and Queensborough Community College have used the Pathways initiative as an opportunity to create "concentrations" for liberal arts students that include the gateway courses identified by CUNY faculty committees for popular major fields. Queensborough identified concentrations in ten fields—including English, psychology, and gender studies—in which its students frequently transfer. According to a former dean at the college who oversaw the CUNY Pathways work, faculty had long wanted to create concentrations for liberal arts majors as a way to create "a more intentional curriculum" and to give students "a focus for their studies [in liberal arts and sciences], which often to them seem too disconnected."

If the guided pathways model is to be meaningful for community college students, then pathways must extend into the receiving colleges. This requires coordination among the faculty from different types of colleges. This works well when a large four-year institution such as ASU is the primary target transfer institution for one or more community colleges. In the ASU case, it was important that the four-year institution took the lead. It is more difficult for community colleges to try to coordinate with reluctant receiving institutions. But where there are many possible "receiving" institutions, then state-level coordination might facilitate the process. In Chapter 6 we describe efforts by states to encourage colleges and universities to create clearer pathways for students to further education and career advancement.

A Framework for Rethinking Other College Practices

All of the institutions we discuss in this chapter have redesigned (or are in the process of redesigning) their programs according to the guided pathways approach on a large scale, in that the changed practices affect most or all of their undergraduate students. Although most of the colleges are in the early stages of implementation, and most have not yet incorporated all of the design elements of the guided pathways model that we discuss in this book, they have nevertheless seen some evidence of improved student outcomes.

ASU officials report that the university's fall-to-spring retention rates for first-time freshmen increased from 77 percent in 2006 to 84 percent in 2010.[88] ASU and the Maricopa colleges have formed a task force to collect data on whether Maricopa MAPP students are progressing faster toward transfer and degree completion than are other students intending to transfer into similar majors.[89] However, finding an appropriate comparison group for MAPP students is a challenge, as MAPP students have clearly indicated an intent to pursue a particular degree at ASU. It is much more difficult to identify students with similar intent from the general population of Maricopa students.

Queensborough Community College reports that after implementing the freshman academies in the fall of 2009 for all first-time, full-time students (over 5,000 students per year), first-year retention rates have increased.[90] In the baseline year of 2006, the rate was 65 percent. The rate was 72 percent in 2009 and 2010, and 69 percent in 2011. Queensborough research staff reports that the college's three-year graduation rate for the 2006 first-time, full-time cohort was 12 percent; the rate for the 2009 cohort was 16 percent.[91] While it is impossible to determine the extent to which its freshman academies are responsible for this upward trend, because of these positive results with the college's full-time students, in fall 2013 Queensborough started to require all new students, including part-timers, to select an academy upon entry.

At Guttman, implementation of guided pathways is too recent to track students' long-term degree completion outcomes. However, Guttman's goal for its inaugural cohort was to achieve a three-year graduation rate of 35 percent. According to data reported to the Integrated Postsecondary Education Data System, the median three-year graduation rate for the latest available entering cohort (2009) for degree-granting two-year public institutions located in large cities was 12.9 percent.[92] In August 2014, the college announced that 28 percent of its inaugural class completed an associate degree within two years and reported that it was on track to meet or exceed its three-year goal.[93] Although these results do not constitute definitive evidence, these preliminary descriptive data are encouraging.

While program maps, including well-aligned learning outcomes, may be a necessary foundation for substantial improvements in student outcomes, they alone will likely prove insufficient. Simplifying and clarifying program pathways requires complementary changes to other college practices, particularly in how colleges approach student support services, instruction, and the intake process. These complementary changes can also help students progress.

For example, in addition to helping students choose majors, program maps that identify critical courses and other key milestones can help students and their advisors monitor progress and identify when students are struggling, which we will discuss in more detail in Chapter 2. Program maps can also help rationalize and simplify the scheduling of classes, which in many colleges is a chaotic process in which deans and department heads attempt to guess how many sections of a given course they should offer. If students are progressing along well-defined program pathways—and assuming, of course, that colleges are able to track their progress—college departments will be better able to anticipate how many students will need a particular course in a given semester. Program maps that include learning outcomes (aligned with requirements for further education and career advancement) can help faculty identify the skills and concepts most important to teach in each course, and guide faculty efforts to improve teaching—issues we will address in Chapter 3.

As we will discuss in Chapter 4, the intake system of the cafeteria college, which typically includes extensive developmental education offerings, in practice serves more to divert students into a remedial track rather than to build their skills to succeed in college-level coursework. In contrast, in colleges organized according to the guided pathways model, rather than an "off-ramp" that diverts students from their college goals, the intake system is redesigned as an "on-ramp" with the aim of helping students choose and successfully enter a program of study as quickly as possible.

Bringing about these complementary changes requires broad-based engagement of faculty and staff as well as a rethinking of hiring and professional development, which we will describe in Chapter 5.

In summary, the program pathway maps described in this chapter can provide a framework for redesigning other key college functions to support student learning and success. How colleges are changing each of these other functions, and engaging faculty and staff in the process, is described in more depth in the chapters that follow.

2

Guiding Students

BECAUSE of their commitment to provide open-access education to all members of their community, two-year public colleges enroll a disproportionate number of students who face academic, social, and economic challenges. Moreover, while some of these students apply months in advance and learn about the colleges before they arrive, others apply only a few days or weeks before the start of classes. Students and the colleges are ill prepared for each other, yet they have very little time or resources to sort out the process. Furthermore, as we have just discussed, incoming students face a complex and often bewildering choice of courses and programs. Given these circumstances, it is not surprising that far too many students fail to become comfortably and productively settled into programs and courses that match their interests and skills. Indeed, a fifth of all entering community college students exit school before they manage to earn even ten credits.[1]

In this chapter we review the college intake process—the practices and policies designed to launch students on a successful path to meet their goals—as well as the ongoing advising and support processes designed to keep students on track. We point out that many students arrive at college with unclear goals and are often unaware of available services. Even when students have goals, they often have trouble selecting the most appropriate courses, resulting in wasted time and money and the accumulation of credits that do not count toward their degrees. We then discuss how the potential of advising-related services typically available to students—in-person advising, technology-based advising systems, and student success courses—is hampered by the structure of the cafeteria college. Next we describe how these services could be redesigned to complement the guided pathways approach to create a more integrated, systematic, and helpful infrastructure for student advising. The central idea is that advising services need to build upon and reinforce the guided pathways program design features, by helping students select and enter a program of study, tracking students' progress through program milestones, providing frequent feedback to students on their progress, and intervening with individual students who stray off track.

New Student Intake in the Cafeteria College

Like much about postsecondary education, the public's view of the college intake process is dominated by an image of four-year colleges, especially selective colleges. For students who aim to attend selective colleges, the application process involves months or years of planning and preparation, including studying for standardized tests. Applicants weigh their alternatives far in advance, and colleges receive extensive amounts of information about each applicant. A network of contacts and interactions connects selective colleges and the high schools that typically send their students to those colleges, including relationships between high school counselors and college admissions staff. At such high schools, the curriculum is also designed to prepare students for selective colleges through advanced placement courses and other rigorous coursework. The transition between high school and college is further smoothed by parents, siblings, other relatives, and friends who have been to college and can help high school students prepare. Finally, entering students typically benefit from several days of orientation.

The process is fundamentally different for community college students, as well as students in many broad-access four-year colleges. Many community college entrants apply only to the nearest college, often only a few weeks in advance, with little sense of the options available at the college. They often arrive at college with no clear goals or firm ideas about their prospective majors or programs. In particular, younger students may move from high school to college simply because it is expected of them, or because they have a general sense that they need college to get a good job.

In turn, community colleges generally have little information about incoming students. While they may, for example, know whether a given student graduated from high school, is a veteran, or has applied for financial aid, they have relatively few other pieces of basic information, aside from the student's scores on a developmental education placement test. In this section, we examine two key issues that weaken the intake process at the typical community college: poor linkage between the college and its local feeder institutions, and a very light-touch orientation, advising, and registration process.

Linkages with Feeders

Relationships between community colleges and their feeder institutions are generally weak, including the colleges' links to both high schools and local adult basic education programs. The disconnect between high schools and colleges was described in the report *Betraying the College Dream: How Disconnected K–12 and Postsecondary Education Systems Undermine Student Aspirations*. The report's authors conclude that

> the current fractured systems send students, their parents, and K–12 educators conflicting and vague messages about what students need to know and be able to do to enter and succeed in college. . . . Current data systems are not equipped to address students' needs across systems, and no one is held accountable for issues related to student transitions from high school to college.[2]

A survey of local high schools by the *Los Angeles Times* revealed a telling distinction. In the fall of 2013, the Webb Schools in Claremont, California—a private high school with 106 seniors—hosted 113 visits from recruiters from selective colleges from all over the country. Public high schools from affluent neighborhoods had similarly packed recruiter scheduling. In contrast, only eight recruiters from local institutions visited Jefferson High School, a low-income public school in South Los Angeles with 280 seniors.[3]

An extremely limited data interchange is another indication of the disconnect between high schools and community colleges. Other than self-reported information from enrollees, many colleges do not have timely access to the transcripts or records of entering students. While some colleges maintain relationships with local high schools that might provide information, this is not helpful for students who show up close to the beginning of the semester. And even these relationships, when they exist, cannot provide information on students who did not attend local high schools or on older students who have been out of school for several years.

As a result, when students arrive, community colleges have scant information regarding their academic strengths and interests—and thus little basis on which to help students identify potential fields of study to explore. There are some encouraging signs and potentially promising efforts working to strengthen the connections between high schools and community colleges, which we will discuss in Chapter 4. Nevertheless, forward-looking reforms continue to be on the margins of the high school–college interaction, especially for low-income students from public high schools.

Orientation and Registration

Most community colleges have a very limited orientation process. Students may be required or merely encouraged to review online information regarding the college's program offerings, developmental education placement process, and other rules and regulations.[4] For many students, the most time-consuming portion of the orientation and registration process is taking the college's developmental education placement tests, which assess students' academic readiness in math and English. After taking their tests, students typically proceed to a short registration-oriented advising session, although a survey of students contacted within the first three weeks of enrollment suggests that as many as 40 percent of students do not take advantage of even these limited services.[5] To field the large number of personnel potentially required to help new students with registration, colleges may hire part-time advisors or recruit academic faculty to help out. Part-time advisors tend to be unfamiliar with the college's larger programs and course offerings, and academic faculty tend to be familiar only with their own. Moreover, these initial advising visits often last only ten to fifteen minutes, given the long line of other students waiting for assistance.[6] Within this short time frame, advisors review the student's developmental education placement test scores and create a suggested course schedule for the first semester.[7] Typically there is no time for an in-depth discussion of the student's interests and strengths, potential transfer schools, career plan, or how the student might embark on an exploration of those issues. The Community College Survey of Student Engagement found that only 38 percent of students reported that an advisor helped them to set academic goals and create a plan for achieving those goals.[8]

In a CCRC study of advising at a Detroit-area community college, students who had already decided on a program of study were relatively content with this type of advising, calling it "straightforward" and "efficient."[9] In contrast, undecided students reported feeling rushed. As one student complained, "It's like they want to get you in and out as fast as possible. Like they kind of threw some papers at you, and then [it's] like, 'have a good one.'" Another explained:

I feel like it's very impersonal, and they're kind of like: "Okay, get in, say a few words, okay you're out. Next!" I don't know if they don't have enough advisors or they just don't care enough. . . . I felt like they were just rushing me, and I couldn't really get out what I wanted to get out in time, and I was out of the door before I got my help.

One result of the limited availability of advising services is that undecided students are encouraged to enroll in a general studies track, because of its flexibility. Yet the general studies curriculum is perhaps the most confusing and complex program for students to navigate. Accordingly, undecided students who enter this track tend to be particularly perplexed by the process of course selection. As one student at the Detroit college recounted:

[The advisors] basically printed out a list of classes that I could take, but they didn't say which one would be the best one. They just highlighted every single one and said "pick from these," and I really didn't know which would be the best one to take. . . . It was more confusing [to me] for them to give me those classes than it was to just choose what I think would be right.

In general, undecided students were either actively frustrated by, or passively resigned to, the fact that they could not be sure which courses were appropriate to take, given that they had not yet chosen a program of study. As one explained:

I still don't know what I'm doing. Honestly, I'm taking classes all on my own. I have no idea what basic courses you have to take, your prerequisites. [The advisor] couldn't tell me that, because apparently they are all different for whatever you want to go into. I don't know what I want to go into yet.

Overall, during the orientation and registration process, colleges learn little about entering students, besides the basic information included in their application form and the standardized English and math scores gathered by the placement test. Meanwhile, students learn little about their college's available program offerings and related opportunities for transfer or a career; instead, they embark on a slate of courses whose relevance to their own nascent goals and interests may not be entirely clear.

Services to Get and Keep Students on Track

As new students begin their first semester of courses, they often remain confused about their goals and how they will select programs and courses in the future. In a study of community college teaching, instructors reported that younger students in particular are often unsure what they want to do with their lives. As one instructor remarked, "They want to do something, they want to succeed, but maybe they haven't tapped into what it is yet."[10] Without a specific goal to work toward, it can be difficult for students to maintain their motivation to persist in school. For example, current and former community college students in a recent Public Agenda study agreed that having a goal—whether oriented toward a career or transfer—helps students stay on track in college. As one student explained, "I think it's really hard for people when there's no end in sight and there's no goal in mind to even continue to go, because you're probably just going to get really frustrated and want to drop out."[11]

To help students choose majors and courses and chart progress toward their goals, the cafeteria college provides an array of support services, which can seem as complicated and confusing as the program structure itself. These may include financial aid assistance, academic advising, career services, tutoring, academic workshops, student activities, special services for at-risk groups, and psychological counseling.[12] Often, services are located in separate offices, which may be physically and organizationally distant from one another, with few lines of communication among them. The result is frustrated students who—unsure which office is the most appropriate for a given issue or problem—often do not make use of available services.

Campus services are typically advertised through flyers, posters, and occasional visits by representatives to selected classrooms. Many students, however, remain unaware of these services. In a CCRC study of students' experiences in their first year at two community colleges, we found that both colleges offered additional counseling and assistance to first-generation, low-income, and minority students. Almost all of the forty-four students interviewed would have qualified for these special services, yet only five had taken advantage of them. Most had learned about the services from friends. As one student explained:

> Actually, they don't tell you about it. I just heard about it from somebody who's in my class. I don't know if it's a secret, but it's not really out in the open. People hear about it from word of mouth, and they just happen to tell me, and I was like, oh wow, I really need that, so I went.[13]

Among the most important support services that can help community college students choose a program of study and stay on track are academic advising, technology-based advising resources, and student success courses, which we describe in detail in the following sections, noting how they interact with the cafeteria college structure.

In-Person Academic Advising

At community colleges, the academic advisor is the most important resource to help new students clarify their goals and select courses that lead
toward those goals. Theories of advising suggest that these goal exploration sessions ought to unfold as a sustained, multiphase process: Advisors
should begin by guiding students through an exploration of their own skills
and interests, followed by a structured investigation into various occupational and professional career areas, and then help students draw connections between their new self-understanding and their developing knowledge of various careers.[14] After students have carefully explored and
tentatively settled on a set of life or career goals, an advisor can work with
each student to create a coherent plan for academic and career progress,
which should integrate continuing and structured exploration of the student's preliminary selection of college major or career area.

Some theorists conceive of this goal-setting process as a problem-solving
exercise, which draws on (and develops) a variety of critical student skills.
For example, the process of deciding on a long-term career goal may require students to process large amounts of information and select a smaller
subset of relevant information, evaluate costs and benefits of various goal
options, prioritize alternatives, and, more generally, identify emotional reactions that may be blocking effective decision making and learn how to
defuse them.[15] According to this view, if advisors can help students master
career-related problem-solving steps, including the larger emotional and
cognitive considerations required to execute each step successfully, students will be able to resolve career-related issues throughout their lives—
an important proficiency, given that the typical worker switches employers
several times.[16]

Similarly, the leading professional association for advisors regards effective advising as a form of teaching.[17] That is, advisors should not only
provide students with information but also help students build the skills
needed to reach a defined set of learning outcomes. Learning outcomes
vary across schools, of course, but one example might be using "complex
information from various sources to set goals, reach decisions, and achieve
those goals."[18] This complex and long-term process of teaching students
how to self-advise is thought to require sustained one-on-one interaction
between the student and an advisor, not merely during the student's first
semester but throughout his or her college career.[19]

The intensive and personalized approaches to advising described above
are often termed "developmental advising." While it may represent the ideal
approach to advising, it is nevertheless unusual. Most community colleges

are able to fund only one advisor for every 800 to 1,200 students, and advisor duties include not only academic advising but also a variety of other time-consuming tasks, such as helping students request disability accommodations or deal with unexpected financial or life crises.[20] As a result, after the student's first (and often quite rushed) registration session with an advisor, follow-up visits are generally left to the student's discretion. Moreover, those most in need of follow-up advising visits are also those least likely to take advantage of them.[21]

If a student does attend some type of follow-up session to explore his or her goals, the session will typically begin with a process of student self-examination to identify goals, interests, and strengths, which advisors assess through online or on-paper career inventories.[22] Research suggests that such inventories increase "career decidedness" and "career maturity," but there is no evidence that they improve longer-term outcomes, such as progress toward a credential.[23] Drawing on developmental advising theories, CCRC researcher Melinda Karp argues that while inventories can help students build self-knowledge, students are not likely to incorporate this knowledge into their academic and career planning unless they receive further assistance.[24] Thus, inventories may be most useful to initiate a longer-term process of self-reflection guided by advisors, which very few students experience.

What is more, in general, when students do make time to go see an advisor, it is unlikely to be the same advisor they saw in the past.[25] Different advisors frequently offer conflicting advice, because of differing philosophies, a different awareness of program-specific rules, or a change in the student's situation.[26] For example, advice that is sensible when a student is undecided on a program or transfer school (for example, "Go ahead and finish the standard math sequence, because most transfer schools will accept it") may no longer be appropriate once the student has made a decision ("For this program, you need to take the business math sequence"). If the same advisor meets with the same student over time, the advisor can help the student understand how and why relevant information and advice change as one's context changes, thereby helping the student develop an ability to identify and apply the appropriate information across shifts in context. If the student meets with a different advisor each time—particularly if each new advisor is unaware of the student's academic arc and previously received advice—the advisor's new and conflicting advice may reinforce a notion that the college's requirements are arbitrary, or that its advisors are incompetent.

In CCRC's study of the Detroit college, students were deeply frustrated when different advisors provided different guidance. For example, students complained that "I will go to one advisor [and] they will tell me one thing; then I go to another advisor and it's different," and "Every advisor I talked to kind of sent me in a different direction, like no straight answer from any of them."

In addition to receiving guidance from different advisors, students may also receive advice and assistance from specific professors. But cultural and professional differences between student services professionals and academic faculty, exacerbated by breakdowns in communication between the two groups, often mean that the two sources provide conflicting advice to students. Academic departments and their faculty, who are responsible for updating their own programs' requirements, often fail to communicate these changes to advisors in a timely way; as a result, advisors often find out about such changes from the students they are attempting to advise.[27] In one study, while advisors complained that faculty did not communicate with them, professors in turn complained that advisors were "unprofessional" and did not understand the curriculum.[28] These problems seemed to result from a structural separation between faculty and advisors at the departmental level; when advisors were embedded in departments, the relationship between the two groups was more collegial and productive.

Typically, colleges lack shared case-management systems that would allow them to coordinate assistance across the disparate offices, personnel, and services that a given student may visit. Only the student may be aware of which services he or she has accessed, and the different advice he or she may have received from each provider. And only the student is aware of how these disparate services relate—or fail to relate—to the academic challenges, tasks, assignments, and habits of thinking required in his or her classes.

While the portrait we have drawn of the advising process is accurate for the bulk of community college students, a small proportion of students may also receive "enhanced" advising services, which attempt to bring the reality of advising into closer alignment with the aspirations of developmental advising. Enhanced services often include mandatory meetings, an assigned advisor for each student, and longer advising sessions. Because of the increased costs associated with enhanced advising, however, these programs are often limited to specific, small populations deemed to be particularly at risk of failing or dropping out.

Rigorous studies of enhanced advising have tended to focus on activities that are less intensive than those implied by the ideal model. Perhaps as a result, these studies have shown modest effects of limited duration. In two separate studies, a two-semester intervention in which randomly assigned students were required to meet with a specific advisor twice per term (and encouraged to meet more frequently) increased registration rates in the following semester, but had no wider or longer-term effects.[29] Another study randomly assigned developmental math students to courses that included a mentoring component. Across one semester, the course mentor visited the classroom at least three times, providing information about advising and counseling, financial aid, and other services. Mentors also encouraged students to meet with them outside of class if they had questions or concerns about any issues, whether academic or nonacademic. Although only about half the students took advantage of this opportunity, students in mentored courses were more likely to report that they knew where to go for help if they needed it, and they were more likely to visit the campus learning center. Despite these benefits, the program had only modest positive impacts on students' academic performance in the mentored course, and it did not affect their wider performance that semester or their likelihood of persisting to the following term.[30]

This fade-out effect suggests that first-semester activities, at least in their current incarnation, do not represent a strong enough "dose" to inoculate students when future challenges arise. At some point, nearly all students will encounter an anxiety-provoking situation that poses a barrier to their progression through college: loss of anticipated financial aid to a student's chosen destination university may lead to a reassessment of her academic future; poor performance in a required course may lead a student to wonder if his chosen major is a good match; divorce may lead a student to question whether she can remain in school; or a student who is still undecided on a major after two years may feel lost and depressed about his future prospects.[31] Accordingly, a truly "enhanced" advising system may need to more explicitly teach students how to self-advise in the face of new decisions and challenges; in order to achieve such a system, colleges may need to either provide a much stronger dose of advising assistance during a student's first year or integrate advising activities across the student's entire college career.

Online Advising and Tracking Resources

In the absence of ongoing personalized assistance, many students turn to the college website to understand the programs available, to see whether a potential program is a good fit for them, and to learn the steps necessary to complete a credential.[32] Ideally, the website should provide detailed information about each program, allowing students to answer questions such as: How long does the program typically take? Can students attend either full-time or part-time? Is there a certificate that can be earned on the way to earning an associate degree? Program web pages should also offer information on opportunities for employment and further education, including the kinds of occupations that program graduates work in, typical entry-level wages, the extent of labor market demand, and whether there are articulation agreements with nearby colleges where students can transfer to earn a bachelor's degree in a related field. Finally, websites should provide contact information for a person who can answer any additional questions.

Unfortunately, most colleges' websites do not feature such detailed and clear information. In a CCRC study of eight career-technical programs across several community colleges, we rated the quality of information provided by each of the programs' web pages, using a rating scale ranging from 1 to 5. Program websites tended to have at least one significant problem that kept them from earning our top rating of 5, with the typical program earning a 3.25. In another recent study of three community colleges' websites, researchers found that students were usually able to locate basic information about a program of interest, such as its course requirements.[33] However, the presentation of the information was frequently unclear, such that students had difficulty understanding and correctly applying it. Moreover, most students were unable to find useful information regarding the program's job prospects and typical starting salaries.

In CCRC's study of the Detroit community college, the college's website provided a page listing all areas of study and promised that each page would include a detailed set of information: "an overview of the area of study, career and transfer options, and faculty as well as links to program and course descriptions and external resources."[34] However, a student exploring different program pages would find that most—particularly those in transfer-oriented areas—did *not* include all of this promised information. Many areas' web pages merely provided a link to their department's course descriptions, with no overview or information about transfer or eventual career options; others provided an overview of the program area, with no information about specific courses. The website also did not allow students to sort through or compare their program options. To compare more than one hundred areas of study (connected to nearly twice as many degrees and certificate programs), students would have to scroll down the list alphabetically and visit each web page separately.

To understand how the typical community college student might use the website to make decisions about a program of study, CCRC provided a sample of students at the Detroit college with a particular career goal, and asked them to select a program of study that would help them achieve that goal using the resources available on the college's website (including the college catalog).[35] Overall, students correctly identified a relevant program of study three-quarters of the time. Yet one student summarized the frustration inherent in trying to explore different program options:

> I mean, there's tons of programs online, but figuring out what each one actually does is kind of daunting sometimes. So you go to the advisor for help, but if they don't know the programs themselves, they can't really be much help to you. So [they might say], "You like computers? Well, try this." I mean, that's not really the best way to go. So I don't know. I guess [I would like] more information online or better-educated advisors—one of the two.

CCRC also asked students to identify appropriate courses for a particular degree or transfer program. For example, one item asked students to choose four introductory college-level courses they should take at the community college if they wished to transfer to an elementary education program at a specific nearby university. Overall, students performed very poorly on these tasks—they scored an average of 40 percent correct when selecting courses for the college's own programs of study, and 50 percent correct in understanding transfer requirements. While all of the information necessary to answer each question was available on the college's website, students had a difficult time locating, interpreting, and applying it to the specific question at hand. Several students confessed that they were not confident in their ability to extract relevant information for their own advising questions. For example, one said: "I'm not really good with that kind of stuff. . . . It's easier to go to an advisor and talk . . . so you don't mess up." Another reflected,

> I would like the advisor option better rather than the Internet. I don't know; I just feel more confident when a real person tells me it. Because on the Internet, they don't know exactly what your needs are. . . . And you might think you're searching for something, and it might be something different that you're looking for, but I don't know. I just think explaining it to an advisor is easier.

The first and most basic step toward tracking student progress is identifying the program of study each student is pursuing, including (for transfer-oriented students) the student's intended transfer destination and major. Yet many colleges do not maintain up-to-date information about students' programs of study, in part because incoming students often declare a program almost at random for financial aid purposes and then pursue a different program without informing anyone. Even fewer colleges keep systematic track of students' transfer objectives.

Most colleges have "degree audit" systems that track the courses a student has completed and, if the student has declared a program, the courses the student still needs to complete. Yet advisors check on an individual student's progress only if the student comes in for an advising appointment, which many continuing students never do.[36] To further complicate matters, while some colleges incorporate bilateral transfer agreements into their audit systems, many do not. At the latter colleges, the audit system may show a student making good progress toward an associate degree in general studies, even though the student is making little progress toward meeting the requirements for the desired transfer destination and major.

Often the first warning sign that a student is "off track" comes when he or she fails to meet "satisfactory academic progress" (SAP) requirements and is in danger of losing federal financial aid.[37] Despite the label, SAP requirements do not track student progress through a program but rather indicate students' basic academic achievement—for example, students might be required to maintain a cumulative grade point average of at least 2.0 and complete at least two-thirds of the courses they attempt. By the time it is clear a student is failing to meet such basic standards, it is often too late for an advisor to help the student get back on track.

Based in part on growing frustration with the use of technology both for advising and student tracking and the results of studies like ours, college administrators and vendors have started to recognize the limitations of online advising and information systems, and many innovations are emerging. We will discuss these innovations, and how they might be used to support the guided pathways model, later in this chapter.

Student Success Courses

Student success courses (also sometimes called "College 101" or "Introduction to College" courses) are one way to provide students with more intensive advising assistance. Most student success courses are also designed to build students' time-management and study skills, as well as to provide information about other college resources and support services.[38] Success courses have become popular in the last few decades; they are now offered by an estimated 83 percent of community colleges, with almost one in four community college students participating at some point in their college careers.[39]

In some older studies, participation in student success courses is positively related to a range of academic and nonacademic outcomes, such as academic motivation, critical thinking, academic course performance, and persistence in college.[40] Students in these courses also tend to view them positively; for example, many have told us that their success course helped them build a sense of confidence and belonging.[41] Similarly, in surveys of community college students, success course participants report that these courses helped them improve their study skills, understand their strengths and weaknesses, and learn about useful services.[42] Studies attempting to control for the background characteristics of students who choose to enroll in such courses also suggest mild long-term positive effects in terms of academic performance, persistence, and completion and transfer rates.[43] However, a set of random-assignment studies that strictly controlled for students' preexisting characteristics found only short-term positive effects that dissipated over time, resulting in no long-term increases in persistence, graduation, or transfer rates.[44]

A 2012 CCRC study of student success courses at three community colleges in Virginia revealed some reasons why their positive short-term effects may not last.[45] Across all Virginia community colleges, a student success course is required for graduation, and students are strongly encouraged to take it in their first semester. To offer the course on such a large scale, Virginia colleges typically rely on a one-credit course taught by adjunct faculty, advisors, or administrative staff. The Virginia system requires courses to cover six content areas: career exploration, information literacy (including exposure to library resources), college policies, college services, study skills, and "life management" (for example, time management and financial literacy). Many colleges also add other topics, such as diversity, ethics, or personal relationships. For example, one college has added content around health issues (including nutrition, stress management, healthy relationships, and drugs and alcohol), and expanded the financial literacy topic to include subtopics on budgeting, financial aid, balancing a checkbook, and retirement planning. Including the required and supplemental topics, each college covers between sixteen and twenty-one topics in its course.

Covering so many topics in a meaningful way within the scope of a one-credit course seems unrealistic, however. As one instructor told us, "There's not enough time to deliver the content we're expected to deliver—not in any meaningful way. Students don't have time to really engage either with the professor or the content—or at least, we haven't found a way that might be an option to."

As instructors scrambled to cover all of the course's required content, they often assigned activities that were superficial in the development of knowledge. For example, when learning about student services in their success course, most students merely received a list of available resources, with little discussion of when, how, or why to use each service. Thus, in most courses, there was little *teaching for application,* although there were some exceptions.

As is typical in community colleges, Virginia's student success courses were taught by a variety of staff, including administrators, adjuncts, and advisors. Full-time faculty neither taught these courses nor were aware of the content covered in them. Accordingly, they did not reinforce the student success topics in their own courses, even though students were often unsure how to apply the academic skills they learned in the student success course to their other classes. Some were also confused about how to apply their new knowledge about campus resources and other, more abstract skills. As one student said: "I really don't understand. . . . There's a place that I can go for job placement or something like that. I know that these things are out there, but I really don't know how to utilize them."

The success courses provided students with important information and seemed to improve some concrete academic skills; students reported that practice with skills such as note taking was helpful in the other introductory courses they were taking. But it was unclear whether students would be able to build on their application of those skills as they moved on to more-advanced courses. The student success curricula did not include guidance to help students understand when different types of study strategies might be appropriate for different courses. As a result, students did not recognize that the effectiveness of given strategies will vary by course. For example, one student remarked that the study strategies taught in the success course were not necessary for her: "I just kind of do it my way, just stare at it until it sticks. It works. I got an 85 on my first test." Without an awareness of the academic challenges ahead of her, this student is unlikely to adopt the very useful strategies taught in her success course and apply them when they become more necessary in the future.

Similarly, in many success courses, students created "program plans" that mapped out the courses they would take to meet their academic or career goals, but they did not learn how to reevaluate and modify plans if their goals or circumstances were to change. Given the broad syllabus, career exploration was also typically covered in a perfunctory way. Students were exposed to planning tools and inventories but were not given much guidance in how to use such tools thoughtfully. Accordingly, students did not seem able to integrate their interests, academic plans, and career goals effectively.

To apply skills and information about careers, course sequences, and study strategies effectively in the long run, students need to develop the metacognitive skills that allow them to recognize change as it occurs, reflect on how change affects their own situation, and create plans to manage the change. Building such skills requires practice, which could be accomplished through in-class reflection and discussion as well as out-of-class applied assignments.[46]

Our study of student success courses suggests that the initial positive effects of such courses may tend to fade out over time because the courses are only partially integrated into students' academic experience. Packaging a holistic set of supports into a for-credit academic course that students regularly attended was no doubt helpful. In a truly integrated experience, however, the success course would incorporate hands-on activities that help students directly meet the challenges they encounter in other courses, and instructors of other courses would reinforce the lessons learned in success courses. Without this integration and reinforcement, student success courses may have only modest long-term effects.

To sum up, in this section we argue that the typical suite of support services provided by the cafeteria college is not effective in helping students choose a program of study, select appropriate courses, avoid excess credits, and stay on track. Well-meaning support strategies such as advising and student success courses often merely provide information, without teaching students how to correctly and effectively apply that information in different contexts across time. Support services also often exist in isolation and are disconnected from students' academic programs of study.

The limitations of traditional support services are inherent in the fact that they rarely challenge the underlying academic and cultural structure of the cafeteria college. Innovations in support services, such as enhanced advising or student success courses that integrate teaching-for-application, fit in around the edges of usual practice. They engage the most interested and enthusiastic faculty and staff, while allowing the rest of the college to continue with business as usual. In order to provide more coherent, integrated, intensive, and sustained supports for students, colleges should redesign their support services to serve three goals: to help students choose an appropriate program of study and (if applicable) transfer destination and career goal; to teach students how to use available resources to effectively self-advise; and to track student progress, intervening at the first sign that students are going off track. In the next section, we discuss what such a redesigned support system might look like.

Redesigning Student Supports

As we have discussed, many students arrive at a complicated and confusing institution with unformed goals. If they do have clear goals, they often have only a vague sense of exactly what they must do to achieve those goals and are often unsure about the progress they are making to achieve those goals. How would a restructured college address these problems?

First, colleges can leverage in-person advising services and student success courses to help students make an initial decision about enrolling in a "meta-major" or exploratory major in their general area of interest, help them clarify their goals over their first semester or two of enrollment, and in general teach them how to self-advise when faced with new decisions and challenges. For example, for students who initially make a poor program choice, advisors need to help them recognize the mismatch and find their way into a better-match program as quickly as possible, minimizing any loss of credits. Second, the guided pathways model provides students (and advisors) with a simpler set of clearly mapped-out majors and program pathways, which makes it easier for students to plan their pathway through college using online resources, in turn making it feasible for colleges to require students to create and update their academic plan every semester. Third, with students' current academic plans on file, colleges can effectively track students' progress through their specific program and put automated feedback mechanisms in place, which can encourage a student who is making progress and alert both the student and an advisor if the student begins to go off track.

The basic outlines of a redesigned system would involve an initial mandatory meeting with an advisor, accompanied by online career and program exploration, which would help the student choose a broad meta-major. Within each meta-major, students would receive developmental advising—and learn how to better self-advise—through enhanced student success courses that are reinforced by academic faculty in English, math, social science, and other subject areas.

Advisors clearly play a crucial role in this vision, but they cannot work in isolation from faculty. They need faculty to create more coherent and easily understood programs through more coherent program mapping, which would help ease the weight and complexity of the advising burden.

In addition, effective student success courses and online advising systems are important tools to maximize the effectiveness of scarce advising resources. These tools could free up advisors to work one-on-one with the students who need them most: those who change programs, fall off track, or encounter unique challenges. In the rest of this chapter, we will discuss how colleges can strengthen student success courses and electronic advising to help students on their guided pathways.

Strengthening Student Success Courses

Student success courses are an important element of the guided pathways model, as they represent a cost-effective method of providing students assistance in goal formation and program planning. Based on a 2013 study of such courses, CCRC researchers have three recommendations for strengthening them: narrow the course content, focus on teaching-for-application, and engage the academic side of the college.[47]

First, student success courses usually try to cram too many topics into the semester, and as a result they tend to cover each topic superficially. Instead, colleges need to identify the essential advising needs of new students and focus the success course on those needs. For example, if students will be expected to use the college's online advising system to create and update their academic plan each semester, then they need hands-on training in how to use the system, and practice in how to create and update an appropriate academic plan. As another example, in our study of Virginia's student success courses, we observed several that were specific to certain types of students—for instance, students interested in nursing. As colleges develop exploratory or meta-majors, it may be sensible to create success course sections for each meta-field, which can focus on the specific program paths, transfer options, and the career exploration needs of students in that area of study. Similarly, students who are entirely undecided about their area of study might benefit from a success course that explores a variety of program and career areas.

Second, for student success courses to be effective, instructors need to teach students how to apply the information they learn to their own lives and goals. Thus instructors must be skilled teachers who are comfortable with interactive, reflective, and guided practice pedagogies. However, success course instructors often teach part-time: some are adjunct faculty, and others are full-time advisors or administrators who teach the course as part of their larger job duties. Typically, these instructors do not receive professional development designed to improve their pedagogy. Accordingly, colleges should provide opportunities for these instructors to reflect on and improve their own teaching (an issue we will discuss in more detail in Chapter 3).

Third, student success courses are usually the responsibility of student support professionals and are thus disconnected from academic coursework and faculty. This separation encourages a negative view of the courses among faculty and undermines their status as "real" college courses. Instead, academic courses should reinforce the skills taught in student success courses, which suggests that academic faculty should be involved in the development of success courses and be informed of the courses' goals, content, and outcomes. It might also make sense to house the courses in academic departments where they are overseen by an academic dean, as many four-year colleges do.[48] This model would foster stronger and more intentional linkages between academics and student support services.

Of course, given the extensive course requirements of many existing academic programs, colleges are often reluctant to require more than a single one-credit success course, and such a limited intervention may have little impact. Guttman Community College has addressed this problem by more explicitly incorporating success course material into academic coursework. At Guttman, all students take a common core curriculum embedded in a set of linked courses that include a student success course, a "City Seminar," and an "Ethnographies of Work" course, which allow students to grapple with issues that affect their urban community and explore their own career interests. According to the course catalog:

> Ethnographies of Work I introduces students to sociological and anthropological perspectives on work as they investigate a range of careers. The course approaches work as a cultural system invested with meanings, norms, values, customs, behavioral expectations, and social hierarchies. Students pose key questions through the lens of ethnography in order to investigate workplaces, occupations, and career pathways in an urban context. . . . The centerpiece of the course is for students to compose and present ethnographic accounts of workplace relations and vocational pathways as they contemplate their own career journeys.[49]

The required Ethnographies of Work course, which helps reinforce and build on the skills that students learn in their student success course, is also fully transferable as a social science course to Guttman's four-year sister institutions in the City University of New York.

Leveraging E-Advising Systems

In the early years of the current decade, a number of vendors began to market new tools designed to support more efficient, effective, and integrated advising systems while maintaining the human interaction that is often vital to student success. In this section, we discuss two key ways in which e-advising tools can help: by integrating services in order to support students through their program pathways, and by providing "just-in-time" progress information to students and their advisors. We then caution that e-advising systems will likely prove ineffective unless they are incorporated in a college culture that takes advantage of their potential strengths. In particular, colleges must set in place some foundational program structures, encourage end-users to use the tools in their daily lives, and integrate human points of contact into the system.

INTEGRATING SUPPORTS ALONG THE PATH

As we have discussed in previous sections, the cafeteria college offers a fragmented array of self-service student supports, often scattered across a campus. Typically, information is not shared among these offices. Thus, for example, a math faculty member may notice that a student rarely comes to class and seems disengaged when she does; a counselor may know that the student is worried about losing her apartment; and an advisor may know that the student qualifies for housing assistance; but no single person puts these pieces of information together to help the student. E-advising systems can create some degree of integration among multiple support services by allowing access to the same case-management interface. Such integrated systems may also reduce the frequency with which students receive conflicting advice from different sources of support.

While integrating multiple sources of student information into a case management system will certainly help improve efficiency and reduce confusion, colleges will reap stronger benefits from such systems if the underlying student support services are also more intentionally aligned toward a common goal: helping students choose and make progress through a program of study. Rather than working separately in a disjointed and ad hoc way, services should be designed to work together to provide support at each point along the student's program pathway. For example, during the new-student intake process, the college's placement and assessment services should work more closely with advising services in order to help students choose a meta-major. During the assessment process, students might fill out a short metacognitive assessment, indicate their top two or three interests in terms of a program of study (and transfer school, if applicable), and answer further questions that probe how "decided" or "undecided" they are on these options. Case management systems allow advisors to pull up survey results when students arrive for their appointments, which could help guide the discussion of choosing a program stream.

As students begin to progress through their meta-major, case management software could automatically track individual students' progress through the milestones on their program map and prompt staff to intervene with targeted supports when necessary. For example, "early warning" tools allow faculty to note when students fail to come to class or turn in a first-week assignment, triggering a professional advisor or student peer advisor to reach out immediately. Similarly, when students perform poorly in a critical course within a specific program, advisors can reach out to help them reevaluate their options, and help them decide whether they wish to switch programs or get the help they need to proceed with their current one.

PROVIDING "JUST IN TIME" FEEDBACK

Early-warning tools are one form of "just in time" feedback, which research from behavioral economics suggests can help improve students' persistence in school. For example, Cass Sunstein's research on late fees demonstrates that timely reminders about upcoming loan payment deadlines significantly decrease late payments.[50] Other research has shown that simple reminders can help reduce the "summer melt" that occurs after high school graduation, when an estimated 15 percent of students fail to matriculate in the fall even after they have gained admission to college.[51] Similarly, short reminders for first-year college students to fill out financial aid forms have been shown to improve persistence.[52]

Thus e-advising systems that provide students with direct and automatic feedback on their progress (such as a progress "dashboard" with green, yellow, and red lights) may also help students stay on track through their program of study, particularly if yellow and red lights are accompanied with suggestions as to specific actions students can take to improve their standing. From research on teaching and learning, we know that feedback significantly improves student learning—but to be effective, feedback should be appropriate (the student needs it), timely (the student receives it in time to use it), and actionable (the student is willing and able to use it).[53]

Keeping track of students' progress also provides an important source of information to the institution. Research on organizational effectiveness in higher education and other sectors suggests that high-performing organizations use measurement to improve processes and better align them with organizational goals.[54] If colleges are unable to monitor students' progress through the institution and have little idea of outcomes after students depart, then colleges do not have the information they need to improve programs and services in ways that promote student success. Tracking students' progress over time in relation to their program map can enable colleges to gauge how well students are doing in general, pinpoint where students tend to struggle, and thereby identify which programs and support services need to be refined.

THE ROLE OF COLLEGE ORGANIZATION AND CULTURE

Since 2013, CCRC has been engaged in a study of how colleges adopt and implement e-advising tools.[55] Our preliminary observations—together with our ongoing on-the-ground work with the colleges profiled in this book— suggest that in order to be maximally effective, e-advising systems must build upon clear program structures, and they must be incorporated into users' daily lives while allowing for human points of contact when needed. We discuss these points in more detail below.

Simplifying information on programs and services.   No matter how flawlessly it is programmed, software cannot produce useful results if the user provides no inputs or if the provided inputs are mismatched to the software's processes. And in a college with an incoherent curriculum, the necessary inputs for an e-advising system may be nonexistent or, at best, inconsistent.

The development or implementation of an electronic system may expose problems that new technologies will not solve. For example, most colleges today rely on electronic degree audits, which one might consider the parent of the new generation of e-advising tools. When colleges first piloted electronic degree audits, the tools made apparent a variety of previously unnoticed inconsistencies in degree policies. According to one study, colleges discovered "extensive course substitutions not included in the published degree requirements," and inconsistent enforcement of requirements, such as academic residency and the maintenance of a certain minimum grade point average.[56] For the tool to work properly, these inconsistencies had to be resolved. This process required explicit conversations, negotiations, and changes in the way people did their jobs.[57]

Similarly, in CCRC's study of a Detroit-area college, an effort to simplify online information showed that descriptions of majors were inconsistent and confusing. To address this problem, the college created a team composed of academic administrators, operational administrators, and student support service representatives to create a "program template," which listed all the information that should be provided in a standardized format by each program to its potential students. Simply having complete information for each program, as well as consistent elements of information across programs, paved the way for a much more useful set of online self-advising resources.[58]

Indeed, program maps can provide a strong foundation for an e-advising system. When colleges have well-structured, clearly mapped-out pathways that include key milestones, such as critical courses that experience shows students need to pass to succeed in the program more broadly, it is relatively straightforward to determine when a student is straying from the path or not on track to meet the next milestone. Later in this chapter, we give some examples from Arizona State University, Austin Peay State University, and Florida State University to illustrate the centrality of well-mapped pathways to the development of useful e-advising systems.

Incorporating the human role.   A key challenge in implementing any new technological system is integrating it into users' everyday lives.[59] A sophisticated technology will remain ineffective if students are unaware of its capabilities, do not explore its potential usefulness, or do not understand how to leverage the information provided. For example, in 2009 Virginia's community colleges deployed a very useful e-advising tool known as "the Wizard." In their student success courses, students were informed about the Wizard and encouraged to explore the tool on their own. However, the Wizard was not a primary focus of the course. Thus, after its initial introduction, the tool was never revisited in a subsequent session or assignment in most class sections. Accordingly, most students had visited it once but not fully explored its capabilities.[60]

Some students may also be skeptical about the value of a technology tool, in comparison to that of a human advisor. In our discussions with students about their advising needs, some felt that talking with a "real person" was important regardless of the quality of online information.[61] Although these students had some difficulty articulating the reasons for their preference for face-to-face advising, many believed that a person would have a more nuanced understanding of their problems and would therefore answer their questions more effectively and efficiently. For example, in a CCRC focus group, one student recounted her recent visit to an advisor, and the moderator asked why she went in person as opposed to handling the process on the website. She answered,

> Because I feel like they can give you more information than a website, because they know what direction I'm going through, and the computer doesn't really know that. . . . Like, they don't know what school I want to go to. I don't know. I guess I prefer a counselor.

Another student explained:

I'm a person that likes that personal one-on-one. I like that face time with somebody. It allowed me to ask questions that may not have been answered on the website. I did look at the website a few times, but I thought, it's just easier for me to go in and talk to the registration [office] and say, "What do I do? Talk to me like I'm stupid; say this is what you have to do." . . . It was much easier and I'm better with talking with people and getting information from them than online.

While the new and more user-friendly generation of e-advising tools may effectively provide students with the information necessary to make informed decisions on their own, colleges still need to consider how they will teach students the process of how to identify the most relevant information, interpret it in light of their own individual situations, and apply it appropriately. If students are not explicitly taught these skills—in a student success course or elsewhere—then they will continue to need advisors to lead the process for them.

Regardless of their own sophistication or comfort in self-advising, however, students will continue to need advisors when complex or unusual problems arise. Accordingly, an effective e-advising system needs to integrate human points of contact. This could be facilitated by a screen button that allows students to chat online with an advisor or make an in-person appointment, or through an algorithm that determines when a student seems lost navigating the online system and flags the case for advisor follow-up. If we can recognize when students need more personalized help, and advisors can provide that help in a way that builds student self-sufficiency, then we will better enable students to tackle similar problems on their own in the future.

Overall, e-advising tools, when coupled with clear program maps that include progress milestones, should free advising staff from low-level and routine tasks to focus on more complex and interesting cases. Rather than spending most of their time helping confused students register for courses, advisors may be able to help a poorly performing student understand how to balance academic, family, and financial issues more effectively; talk with a student about why she is exiting a certain course or program stream and provide feedback to the stream coordinator; or work with faculty in the sociology and economics departments to design an assignment that helps first-semester students understand the short- and long-term financial tradeoffs of different types of programs and degrees. That is, e-advising tools could help address the issues of integration, implementation, and scale that we discussed earlier in the chapter. This fundamental change in the advisor's role, however, will not occur without first altering the culture of the college and, in particular, how various stakeholders on campus—including advisors themselves—view the advisor's role. We will return to these issues in Chapters 3 and 5.

Examples in Practice

In this section, we provide some examples of institutions that have reorganized their student services to do a better job of helping students choose programs and guiding them through those programs to graduation. In some cases, these colleges use new e-advising and tracking systems, but in all of the cases the services were designed to support students throughout their college experience. The examples we discuss include the City University of New York, Miami Dade College, Arizona State University and its partnership with Maricopa's community colleges, Austin Peay State University, and Florida State University.

The City University of New York offers the Accelerated Study in Associate Programs (ASAP) to financially needy students who commit to attending community college full-time. ASAP is a comprehensive reform program, integrating a variety of components designed to ensure that at least 50 percent of entering students earn associate degrees within three years.[62] Consistent with the guided pathways model, the program uses a block scheduling structure in which students in the same program take the same prescribed set of courses, combined with intensive and sustained counseling. Students are required to meet with their advisors at least twice a month, and with career specialists at least once a semester, throughout their college career. Across students' first two semesters, advising is supplemented by a student success course that helps students reflect on their experiences and plan for the future, through activities such as discussion, group research, and reflective writing. According to ASAP's website, the purpose of the course is to empower students to "make informed decisions and develop academic and life skills to become confident, proactive, and accountable participants in their educational and professional lives."

A random-assignment study found in 2013 that after two years, ASAP students in need of remediation were more likely to enroll in college, remain enrolled, accrue more college credits, and graduate at higher rates than similar, non-ASAP students.[63] The program is expensive, costing approximately $16,600 per student annually, compared with $9,800 for a "regular" CUNY student. Much of the program's cost is due to its low student-to-advisor ratio: ASAP counselors work with fewer than one hundred students each. However, given that many more ASAP students graduate, the cost *per graduate* for ASAP is actually lower than it is for regular students.[64] Due to the higher cost per student in ASAP, CUNY is working to lower its up-front costs so that the program—which thus far has served fairly small cohorts of students—can be scaled to serve more students. ASAP has made little use of technology and e-advising thus far, both of which could offer additional savings.

In Chapter 1, we introduced Miami Dade College, a community college that is restructuring its programs by developing meta-majors and default program plans. To support implementation of these changes, the college recently hired twenty-five new advisors—thereby lowering the ratio of students to advisors, but only to 600 to 1. The college came to realize that it needed to rely on a combination of human advisors and technology—along with the more clearly structured program pathways—to keep students on track.

In Miami Dade's redesigned intake system, each entering student works with an assigned advisor to develop an individual education plan (IEP) based on the faculty-designed program pathway maps. Students' course taking is tracked by the college's degree audit system, and students check in regularly with their advisor to compare the courses checked off in the degree audit to ensure they match up with their IEP. The college hopes to automate this process and make the information directly available to students, but has held off doing so until plans to replace the college's existing student information system can be implemented.

Students stay with their assigned advisor until they have completed 25 percent of their program requirements, at which point they are transitioned to advisors in their program area (that is, program-specific advisors, departmental staff, or faculty mentors). To prepare program faculty and staff for this new role, the college provided six hours of required training, including role-playing in situations they would likely encounter with students. Prospective mentors also spent two to four hours shadowing student services staff who serve as liaisons to their programs. Even after the transition of students to a specific program area, student services staff are responsible for handling certain issues such as academic probation or financial aid. The college has also designated "reassignment coordinators" for students who wish to change pathways.

In Arizona State University's development of program maps, the university relied heavily on electronic advising, using a sophisticated homegrown system called eAdvisor.[65] The system automatically provides feedback to students on their progress, and refers them to an advisor if they are not making progress or have gone "off-plan." If students fail a "critical course" on their map, the system prevents them from registering for classes until they have seen an advisor or taken appropriate action. The system also provides advisors with tools to monitor students' progress. For each student, advisors can see a "retention dashboard," which provides summary information on the student's status in terms of financial aid, academic progress, probation, transfer requirements, and other metrics. These tools allow advisors to make the best use of the limited time they have with students. Deans and department chairs use eAdvisor to see how students in their programs are progressing. If large numbers of students are going off-plan, faculty can pinpoint the problem areas. The information provided by the system also helps with enrollment management— for example, to ensure that enough seats are available for students in critical courses when they are needed.

As part of their Maricopa to ASU Pathways Program (MAPP), ASU and the Maricopa community colleges have developed software tools that allow Maricopa students and their advisors to see which courses on the MAPP plans they have already taken and which ones they still need to take to earn junior standing in their target major at ASU. The university uses the system for enrollment management, to help anticipate when students will arrive at ASU and in which programs. According to Maria Hesse, vice provost for academic partnerships at ASU, in the past all transfer students "looked the same" when they arrived at the university. Hesse noted that ASU is using this information on students while they are still in community colleges to better understand their needs, and is working with them and their Maricopa faculty and advisors to ensure that they are well prepared when they arrive at ASU.[66]

Like Arizona State, Austin Peay uses its homegrown electronic advising system, called Degree Compass, to track student progress and provide timely information to students and advisors.[67] Austin Peay also uses data from the system to run predictive analytics for use in advising students before they take a course or enter a program. For example, one set of analytics uses information on each student's academic background and performance, together with data on how similar students have performed in a course, to predict the grade a given student will receive in the course. If students are not expected to do well in a course, they might want to choose another course; or if they do decide to take their original choice, they and the college can take steps to ensure that supports are in place to help them beat the odds. Like ASU, Austin Peay also uses the system information for enrollment management. According to former provost Tristan Denley, "We want students to take the courses they need, not the courses that are left over." The university analyzes information in the system about where students are in their programs to identify courses that will be in high demand and plan accordingly to avoid scheduling bottlenecks.

The experience at Florida State University, on the other hand, provides an example of how e-advising systems may not be effective in the absence of changes in program structure and other services. FSU has been using program maps to guide students since the early 2000s. It has also had an electronic student tracking system that provides information on academic progress to students and their faculty and advisors.[68] However, FSU has found that even with the guidance provided by default program maps, exploratory majors, and a tracking system, a robust system of advising and other supports remains necessary. In-person advising is especially needed to help undecided students select majors as well as to assist transfer students, veterans and other special populations, and students who go off track or are not making progress. As a result, since the time that FSU first implemented program maps, the university has restructured its approach to advising to help students complete the pathways laid out by the maps. According to Karen Laughlin, FSU's dean of undergraduate studies, the university's approach to advising is "centralized decentralization." Advisors are hired by the undergraduate studies division, but many are "embedded" in specific academic departments. Advisors also participate in an enrollment management group that meets regularly to identify bottlenecks in student progression and success, and to assist with program planning and course scheduling.

To be clear, both ASU and Austin Peay also recognize the importance of face-to-face advisors, and both have developed approaches to advising and guiding students that integrate technology with individual advising: technology provides information that assists students with more routine decisions, freeing advisors and faculty to help students when face-to-face contact is more essential. Like Florida State, ASU and Austin Peay have built into their pathway maps key "touch points": when a student reaches each point, the system cues advisors that specific supports may be needed. Acknowledging the importance of human advisors in guiding students, ASU also hired transfer specialists to work with students participating in MAPP and in the Transfer Admission Guarantee (TAG) program in Maricopa and other community colleges across Arizona. According to Hesse, the job of these transfer specialists is to get to know "intimately" a small number of community colleges and help their students transfer to—and be prepared to succeed at—ASU.[69] These specialists hold regular office hours at the community colleges and meet with community college advisors.

Under the guided pathways model, a key role for student support services is to help students choose and successfully complete their programs. In the course of this process, colleges must help students set goals for college and careers, develop a plan to achieve those goals, track their progress on the plan, and provide help when students get off track. Colleges have several tools at their disposal—advisors, student success courses, and e-advising systems—that can be combined to provide this support cost-effectively.

Program design reforms based on the guided pathways model represent a good first step toward strengthening student support services. More coherent program maps can simplify course selection and scheduling processes, freeing up more advisor time to help students with goal setting and planning. When combined with a robust case management system, program maps also facilitate student progress tracking, allowing advisors to identify and reach out to students who experience unexpected challenges as they progress through their programs. With the combination of more clearly defined default program pathways, more effective use of group counseling via student success courses, and e-advising technology for monitoring and providing feedback on students' progress, advisors and counselors can focus their in-person efforts on helping the students who need them most, before it is too late to get them back on track.

Student support services are also crucial to two other college processes: academic instruction in general, and "developmental education," or the programs designed to address the needs of students who enter college underprepared for college-level work. In Chapter 3, we will examine instruction in the guided pathways college and discuss how student services professionals can collaborate with faculty to better support students in both academic and nonacademic arenas. In Chapter 4, we examine the services provided to students who enter college with weak academic skills and discuss how colleges can use the guided pathways approach to integrate developmental skill-building with the process of helping students enter and succeed in a college-level program of study.

3

Rethinking Student Instruction

T HE VOLUME of scholarship on teaching and learning is immense.[1] Our goal in this chapter is not to comprehensively review or analyze research related to teaching and learning in the community college, but rather to contrast the instructional structures and philosophies of the self-service cafeteria-style college with the instructional approaches suggested by the guided pathways model.

As we have already pointed out, the goal of the cafeteria college is to provide students with low-cost access to courses. Such courses often do not connect with one another to create a clear and coherent learning pathway; instead, course selection is fraught with complexity and risk. Similarly, complex and disconnected processes characterize the cafeteria college's approach to faculty hiring, professional development, and curriculum design. In contrast, a more coordinated, collaborative, and strategic approach to instruction is necessary to achieve the potential benefits of the guided pathways approach.

In this chapter, we first delineate the academic challenges common among students who matriculate at open-access colleges, describe how the cafeteria-style college only partially addresses those challenges, and discuss how a guided pathways approach to instruction could respond to them more effectively. Next, we provide recommendations and examples for how colleges can implement this approach to instruction.

As part of this discussion, we devote a section of the chapter to online and technology-mediated instruction. We argue that technology alone cannot improve student outcomes; rather, technology must be thoughtfully implemented as part of a larger curricular and pedagogical redesign. In Chapter 6, we will return to the issue of online education and consider how it factors into the relationship between institutional quality and costs.

Academic Challenges Facing Students

The typical community college student embarks on postsecondary education with a weak foundation of academic skills. Indeed, a significant majority of entering community college students are referred to developmental education, or precollege preparatory work in math or English. Although we are skeptical about the assessments and processes that lead to such referrals (as we will discuss in more detail in Chapter 4), it is nevertheless clear that many entering students struggle to succeed in college-level courses. The academic barriers they face include not only poor preparation in math and English, but also a poor foundation of *metacognitive skills* (or the ability to perceive their own weaknesses and apply strategies to overcome those weaknesses).

Given the demographic characteristics of typical community college students, it is not surprising that many are poorly prepared for college. About a quarter are low-income and thus more likely to have received poor instruction and academic support in their previous schooling than their more affluent peers.[2] In addition, over a third departed high school more than a decade ago; thus, even if they received a quality high-school education, they have likely forgotten a good deal of what they learned. Taking these factors together, approximately two-thirds of community college students are deemed by their college to be "academically underprepared."[3] Even if they are judged "college ready," however, incoming students may not be prepared for the level of conceptual and critical thinking expected in college-level courses because they were not exposed to that type of thinking in their previous educational experiences. As we will discuss in more detail below, instruction in primary and secondary schools in the United States tends to focus heavily on procedural rather than conceptual learning.

Moreover, these academic problems are exacerbated and their solutions thwarted by the complicated lives that most community college students lead. Approximately four-fifths are employed, working an average of thirty-two hours per week.[4] Many are continually concerned about their finances, with perhaps half being vulnerable to drop out because of financial concerns.[5] Over one-third care for dependents, including 15 percent who are single parents.[6] Such students have less time than others to spend on campus and to devote to studying, and they have more difficulty balancing academic responsibilities with external demands. As a result, many attend part-time (which, at best, significantly delays their progress) or rely on online courses. In part because of the complicated nature of their nonacademic lives, some students also seem detached from and unmotivated by their academic work.[7] To shed light on the origin and development of many students' academic difficulties, we first discuss the distinction between procedural and conceptual learning, as well as the concept of metacognition.

Procedural and Conceptual Learning

Throughout their educational experience, entering community college students have been exposed to pedagogical techniques that emphasize rote learning activities and assessments, including multiple-choice and fill-in-the-blank activities, wherein the appropriate approach and correct answer are always clear-cut, leaving little room for creative or critical thinking.

In math, middle- and high-school teachers focus on teaching mathematical *procedures* rather than mathematical *concepts and connections*. For example, according to a large-scale observational study of eighth-grade classrooms in the United States, 69 percent of math problems simply require students to apply a particular memorized procedure (for example, "Solve for x in the equation $2x + 5 = 6 - x$").[8] Only 13 percent ask students to demonstrate understanding of a concept (for example, "Draw an isosceles right triangle"), while 17 percent require mathematical reasoning to construct relationships among different ideas, facts, or procedures (for example, "Graph the following linear equations, and then examine the role played by the numbers in determining the position and slope of the lines"). And regardless of the type of problem, when teachers discuss how to solve it, they typically provide students an answer without explaining why it is correct or demonstrate the step-by-step problem-solving process without explicating the underlying concepts. Thus, students can pass their math courses by memorizing procedures and applying them when told to do so, with little accompanying understanding.

In English, the situation is not much brighter. The level of reading complexity in eleventh- and twelfth-grade textbooks is substantially lower than that of introductory college textbooks. Moreover, most textbook assignments only require students to follow a simple procedure: scan and extract specific facts from the text.[9] Similarly, the vast majority of high school writing-related assignments consist of fill-in-the-blank, short-answer exercises.[10] In both reading and writing, students are not required to absorb, evaluate, or analyze information. Accordingly, while the vast majority of incoming college students have no difficulty understanding a passage's literal meaning, they have much more difficulty processing it at a deeper level, including understanding its implications and evaluating its trustworthiness.[11] As one student told us, reflecting on his first semester of college, "I didn't know that there was so much in-depth [work] that comes with reading; [you cannot] just read the material and listen and go about your business. But it's so much more—you have to understand what you're reading, you've got to know what you're reading about."[12]

Metacognitive Skills

Some students' weak academic skills may also reflect a poor understanding of how they might go about improving those skills. Metacognitive processes can help a student understand his or her own academic weakness and develop strategies to strengthen them. Yet in many high schools, students do not need strong metacognitive skills in order to perform relatively well, because teachers tend to actively manage their students' work. For example, teachers require class attendance; assign discrete homework tasks that are due within a short span of time, making it less likely students will forget to complete each task; nag students who do not complete assignments; talk to students (or students' parents) when they perform poorly; and test students' knowledge frequently.[13] High school students can also earn reasonable grades by using fairly straightforward and unsophisticated study strategies, such as reading a textbook chapter the night before the exam.[14]

In contrast, in most college courses, attendance is encouraged but not required, and homework tasks may be complex and unfold over a longer span of time. Rather than explicitly keeping students on task by reminding them of specific reading due dates or testing them regularly on the content of the reading, college instructors may expect students to use the syllabus (an unfamiliar concept to many students) to manage their own work flow. To take control of their learning, students need to practice skills such as self-regulation, task planning, time management, note taking, and organizing study time effectively. All of these rely on the student's metacognitive abilities to reflect on, organize, and improve his or her own thinking and learning.

A student with strong metacognitive skills is able to realize when she is not performing successfully, identify some potential reasons why not, and take steps to fix the problem and improve her own learning. For example, when high-achieving students run into academic challenges, they try strategies such as reorganizing the material into a more personal frame of reference, or seeking help from the library, teachers, or parents. In contrast, when motivated but low-achieving students encounter problems, they often simply "try harder," with little clear conception of how to make their time and effort more fruitful.[15] Qualitative studies of community college students suggest that many of them fall into this latter category: they are willing to try hard to succeed, but they are not quite sure how to do so.

Over time, if they do not learn strategies for success, they are likely to earn poor grades, withdraw from courses, or otherwise become discouraged about school.[16]

How the Cafeteria College Addresses These Challenges

In this section, we first describe the typical style of instruction in college classrooms—which does little to overcome the academic problems we discussed above—and how the cafeteria college encourages and reinforces this style. Next, we discuss the formal in-class and out-of-class support strategies the cafeteria college pursues to help students with academic challenges. We end the section with a discussion of the growing use of online instruction and how this interacts with student learning, academic motivation, and the organization of the cafeteria college.

Knowledge Transmission: The Dominant Model

Researchers have identified two distinct approaches to college teaching, known as *knowledge transmission* and *learning facilitation*.[17] Faculty who adhere to the knowledge transmission model tend to focus on facts rather than concepts, cover a large amount of content in class, and emphasize lectures, readings, and other use of media to impart information.[18] Implicit in the model is the assumption that when instructors transmit information, students will understand the information as sent. Instructors do not necessarily realize that this assumption is a poor one, because they themselves were able to succeed as students within the transmission model: they were intrinsically motivated to learn, confident in their intellectual abilities, easily picked up information from lectures and books, and could connect facts into a broader conceptual superstructure without much assistance. Given these instructors' own experiences of success, it seems reasonable to them that their students should learn effectively under the same model.

Faculty using the knowledge transmission model believe that deeper learning—such as conceptual understanding and critical thinking—is vitally important; but they tend to assume that such learning will be "kind of an unforeseen, unintended byproduct of what you're doing," as one community college instructor put it.[19] For example, a study of California college professors found that 89 percent saw critical thinking as a key instructional goal, yet only 9 percent were able to explicate how they taught to encourage critical thinking in a typical day.[20] College instructors also rarely require active thinking within the classroom: observational studies suggest that most professors spend the bulk of classroom time lecturing, and when they ask the class a question, it tends to be a low-level question that requires repeating facts, rather than translating, associating, synthesizing, or judging facts or ideas.[21] Moreover, national survey data suggest that 36 percent of courses at nonselective postsecondary institutions focus on basic or general material contained in standard textbooks, and 70 percent rely on multiple-choice tests supplied by the textbook publisher.[22] Of course, the facts that are transmitted by lectures and standard textbooks, and assessed through multiple-choice methods, may be a necessary foundation for deeper learning; but unless students are already highly motivated to engage with the topic, they tend to retain only a scattering of surface-level facts without the hoped-for deeper learning.[23] And by itself, surface learning is insufficient to spur students' thinking, motivate them, or get them excited about persisting in college.[24]

Under the knowledge transmission model, instructors also spend little time encouraging discussion among their students, as peer-based activities are viewed as an inefficient method of transmitting factual information (despite a wide range of studies suggesting that having students collaborate can improve their performance).[25] Community college faculty estimate that they spend 15 percent of class time on collaborative techniques, discussion, or group activities.[26] However, in a qualitative CCRC study of students' first-year experiences at two community colleges, several students who happened to participate in student success courses told us these were the *only* courses that emphasized class discussion. As one explained, new students do not necessarily realize that "it's okay to talk" in their courses, unless they are encouraged to do so via a student success course.[27]

In general, the transmission approach does not acknowledge the underlying challenges that make it difficult for some students to absorb and apply the facts they hear or read. Accordingly, students' low academic motivation or weak metacognitive skills are often dismissed as "nonacademic" problems that are best addressed outside the classroom. For example, a college might include metacognitive skills—such as study strategies and time management—in its student success course syllabus, or offer workshops on these topics through the tutoring or advising center; but it is unlikely to encourage English, biology, psychology, or engineering faculty to integrate metacognitive instruction into their courses.[28]

Because they do not see themselves as responsible for metacognitive instruction, professors using a knowledge transmission model tend to hold students responsible for their lack of metacognitive skills. For example, one community college instructor lamented to us that "we have students who are coming in [for help in] the last few weeks [of the semester], and they say they don't understand anything. Well, there's no way we can bring them up to speed."[29] Yet students may not have learned the metacognitive strategies necessary to realize that they need help until they have already failed their first exam, which sometimes occurs halfway through the term.

In contrast to knowledge transmission is the model of *learning facilitation,* which more explicitly addresses conceptual understanding, metacognition, and student motivation. The learning facilitation model is based on research suggesting that, in order for students to integrate and apply factual content, they must build and organize their conceptual understanding with the active support and guidance of the instructor.[30] Faculty who adhere to the learning facilitation model are explicitly focused on how to motivate students and help them "learn how to learn." They tend to use more collaborative, discussion-based, and activity-based teaching methods, and assess student performance through discussions, writing assignments, and projects that emphasize critical thinking.[31] College instructors who adopt the learning facilitation model find the approach rewarding. As Maryellen Weimer recounts in her book *Learner-Centered Teaching,* under the facilitation approach "you no longer struggle with passive, uninterested, disconnected students. Their energy motivates and drives you to prepare more, risk more, and be rewarded more by the sheer pleasure of teaching."[32] Why, then, does the approach remain relatively uncommon?

College instructors cite a variety of reasons for avoiding the learning facilitation approach. Some endorse the idea in theory, but are skeptical that such strategies will be effective with their own poorly prepared students. For example, some developmental education faculty believe that their students need the foundation of lecturing, or that their students are incapable of learning complex skills or concepts without first drilling on subskills.[33] Many instructors worry that class discussions and activities will take too much time away from knowledge transmission, resulting in too little time to cover the required course content.[34] Others anticipate student resistance—students who are not used to active class participation, problem solving, or interrogating their own reasoning may not initially feel competent to do so, and thus will resist their instructor's attempts to make them do anything other than passively listen.[35] The deployment of learning facilitation strategies also requires time-consuming preparation and involves a certain amount of risk, because the appropriate strategy in any given class depends on the unique needs of the students in that particular class.[36] Accordingly, instructors must prepare and plan for a wide variety of "what-if" scenarios, and practice improvisational flexibility in the classroom.

How the Cafeteria College Supports the Knowledge Transmission Model

While each of these concerns about learning facilitation could discourage faculty from using it, we suspect the largest barrier to the learning facilitation approach is the cafeteria-style structure of most colleges, which implicitly supports a knowledge transmission approach. The cafeteria college's focus on courses rather than programs implies that each course represents a discrete, disconnected unit. Each course dispenses factual information that students need to remember for the final exam, but next semester's coursework may or may not build on that knowledge. Thus, instructors need not ensure that students retain and transfer important concepts after the final exam.

Because the cafeteria-style college has not defined the critical conceptual understanding and skills that each program's graduates must demonstrate, it tends to ensure rigor by packing each course full of content, without asking "how much content is enough?" to support students in learning necessary concepts and skills.[37] As a result, most instructors feel they do not have enough class time to cover the required content through lecture, much less indulge in discussion and activities that do not forward the goal of content coverage.

Having no particular incentive to promote learning facilitation, the cafeteria college tends to default toward the less-challenging knowledge transmission model, a preference that is apparent in its faculty hiring, professional development, and promotion practices.

HIRING AND PROMOTION

There are, of course, excellent teachers in community college classrooms, many of whom gravitate toward a stronger learning facilitation style, but instructors tend to develop toward this style on their own initiative rather than as a result of institutional support and emphasis on this approach to teaching.[38] The typical college's hiring and promotion processes provide little encouragement to do so. For instructors to win tenure, their course evaluations must remain acceptable, with few explicit student complaints, and such criteria encourage the maintenance of a reliable teaching approach rather than the adoption of a new and risky one.[39] For example, in a 1998 case study of barriers to integrating critical-thinking skills into economics coursework at a regional four-year university, the authors note that faculty who are good at dispensing information and capable of entertaining students typically receive good evaluations as well as direct praise from their students. They are also considered to be effective teachers by their colleagues. Retooling a course to include aspects of critical thinking introduces new risks that may have a negative impact on one's evaluations, which, as we know, often influence merit, promotion, and tenure decisions.[40]

If learning facilitation is not emphasized in the hiring and promotion of full-time faculty, it is completely ignored in the case of part-time adjunct faculty. Often hired a few days before the start of the semester, part-time faculty have little time to prepare for their new course, and they typically receive no orientation, mentoring, evaluation, or direction.[41] Some are required to teach according to rigid syllabi that leave no room for pedagogical experimentation or their own professional expertise; others are provided with no guidance at all, not even a sample syllabus or set of learning goals.[42] Because they are often excluded from larger departmental discussions, part-time faculty also have little sense of how their courses fit into a larger curriculum (if indeed they do).

PROFESSIONAL DEVELOPMENT

In the cafeteria college, models of instructional development are very similar to models of student support services. Just as new students may be required to meet with an advisor for fifteen minutes and have the option to return for more intensive sessions (which few have the time or inclination to do), faculty are typically required to attend episodic professional development sessions on instructional strategies, and have the option to receive more sustained and intensive support (which few have the time or inclination to do).[43]

Required professional development tends to take the form of workshops or lectures, where instructors learn about a particular pedagogical tool or approach that could be applied in their classroom. Faculty professional development workshops are often top-down, designed and offered by the college's administration with little input or feedback from the faculty themselves. Workshops are also isolated from the classroom: they provide participants with an opportunity to learn more about a topic or technique, but when or how the technique can be effectively applied in each participant's own class remains unclear.[44] Furthermore, workshops are typically unaccompanied by additional structures to help faculty sustain and build on their learning across time. Taken together, the top-down, decontextualized, and short-term nature of many faculty development workshops conspire to create an experience that instructors characterize as "painful," "boring," and "insulting."[45]

In order to promote more bottom-up, intensive, and sustained professional development, some colleges have created teaching and learning centers. Such centers provide an array of useful services, such as observing classrooms and providing feedback to instructors, working with faculty to incorporate technology into their courses, designing more-useful course evaluation forms, or hosting faculty discussions about teaching and learning.[46] Given their limited staff, however, most centers provide one-on-one assistance only for the small minority of faculty who request it. Unfortunately, just as with students, it is the faculty most in need of support who are also the least inclined to seek it.[47]

Compounding the problems of the cafeteria college's typical professional development model is its culture of isolation. In most colleges and universities, instructors rarely talk with one another about teaching and learning.[48] While some instructors do connect deeply with a teaching colleague, such collaborations typically occur in scattered pockets across the college—for example, among faculty who team-teach within a learning community. Workshops and other pedagogical development activities are frequently conducted with groups of individual instructors, in isolation from their departmental colleagues. Yet if an individual instructor attends a workshop and is converted to a new approach, he or she is likely to return to colleagues who have no information about the approach, are uninterested in it, and may even actively resist it. In such an environment, it is difficult to develop and sustain a challenging new approach over time.[49]

Overall, while colleges do devote significant resources to faculty professional development each year, the cafeteria college's model of professional development is unlikely to shift the culture and practice of pedagogy toward a learning facilitation model. Just as with their student services, many colleges' development programs merely consist of "a series of loosely related activities that administrators *hope* will improve teaching and learning."[50]

Other Attempts to Address Academic Challenges

Outside of instruction in the English, math, or science classroom, colleges offer a variety of services designed to strengthen students' academic skills, study approaches, time-management strategies, commitment to school, and ability to balance academics with employment and other personal demands. Such services include student success courses, tutoring, supplemental instruction, learning communities, and flexible online course options. Consistent with the underlying structure of the cafeteria college, these services are available on an individual and voluntary basis. Below, we first discuss academic support services such as supplemental instruction and learning communities, and next turn to the option of online learning, which many colleges view as a key strategy for helping students balance multiple demands.

ACADEMIC SUPPORT SERVICES

As we have already discussed student success courses in detail, here we will focus on other forms of academic support offered by most community colleges: tutoring, supplemental instruction, and learning communities.

Tutoring and supplemental instruction share the goal of helping students more deeply understand the procedures and concepts to which they are exposed in class. Tutoring may focus on the skills and assignments required by specific courses (for example, Biology 101), or may focus on more generalized skills, such as reading or writing. Well-trained tutors do not merely correct errors, but help students diagnose where and why they commonly make mistakes. They also help students build the conceptual understanding and specific skills necessary to avoid those mistakes in the future, and apply those skills in a variety of contexts.[51] In addition to tutoring, an estimated 87 percent of community colleges offer "supplemental instruction," or peer-led discussion sessions scheduled in conjunction with one or more "high-risk" courses (often defined as courses in which 30 percent or more of enrollees withdraw mid-semester, fail, or earn Ds).[52] Supplemental instruction peer leaders are trained not to repeat course content, but rather to help students process, discuss, reflect on, and apply what they are learning.[53] Theoretically, supplemental instruction not only provides more time on task, but also allows students to connect more deeply with the content.

Qualitative and correlational studies make a strong case for the usefulness of tutoring and supplemental instruction when they are well designed,[54] yet few colleges require struggling students to use such services. In a survey of community college faculty who taught courses offering supplemental instruction sessions, 81 percent of faculty reported that they did not require any students to participate in such sessions.[55] In a companion survey, 82 percent of community college students said they had not used supplemental instruction in the current academic year, and 76 percent had not used tutoring.[56] Even students who obviously need tutoring may not avail themselves of it. In one study of students on academic probation, an intervention program strongly encouraged these students to visit the college's learning center, but still only 57 percent did so.[57] Many students, particularly those who struggle academically, may not recognize that they need help—or may be embarrassed to expose their weaknesses—and thus avoid tutoring unless they are required to use it.[58]

While tutoring and supplemental instruction services try to help students create deeper connections among concepts within a given discipline, learning communities are designed to help students make connections among disciplinary areas.[59] In a learning community, a particular group of students enroll together in a set of linked cross-disciplinary courses (typically two courses, but sometimes three or more). In addition to the benefits of interdisciplinary thinking, learning communities provide students with extended blocks of time together, which is thought to encourage stronger social bonds and provide students with a network of information and support. The learning community philosophy also encourages instructors to integrate collaborative activities, such as small-group work, into each course. And to the extent that learning community instructors communicate with one another about students, "sit in" on one another's classes, or even team-teach, students may spend more time with the instructors and build closer bonds with them.

Students and faculty who participate in learning communities give them positive reviews. Students report feeling more connected to their peers and, in some cases, to their instructors as well; faculty feel that the experience improves their own pedagogy, particularly when their course is linked with that of a more experienced faculty member.[60] Nonexperimental studies have attributed a variety of positive student outcomes to learning communities, including stronger relationships with peers and faculty, more satisfaction with the course and with the college experience as a whole, improved cognitive development and academic performance, and increased persistence.[61] However, a set of six random-assignment studies of learning communities found only modest and short-term effects on students' academic outcomes. One potential reason for these disappointing findings is that in the typical college, faculty find it difficult to adjust their course planning and pedagogy to the learning community model's emphasis on interdisciplinary collaboration and learning facilitation. For example, in those six learning communities, only a minority of instructors regularly collaborated on syllabi or assignments, communicated about shared students, or discussed course content with other instructors.[62]

One lesson from this research is that learning communities may not have a substantial effect if they exist in isolation. Even the best one-semester course or program is unlikely to improve a student's overall experience significantly if the rest of the college's courses and programs remain unchanged. And despite the good reputation of learning communities—half of all community colleges offer them—most colleges only offer a few sections. Thus, learning communities remain at the margins of college instruction, and only 13 percent of students report that they have enrolled in one.

The isolation of learning communities is consistent with the overall organization of the cafeteria college—a learning community represents an option for some students who happen to know about it and might be interested in it. Indeed, it is not at all surprising that the learning community model has trouble thriving in the cafeteria college, where an interdisciplinary and collaborative curricular model faces an uphill battle against norms of disconnected courses and a culture of instructional isolation.

In general, although research suggests that high-quality and well-implemented academic support services can help promote student success, many students in a cafeteria college remain unaware that these services exist, most do not use them, and those most in need tend to be the least likely to take advantage of them.[63]

FLEXIBLE ONLINE LEARNING OPTIONS

The availability of fully online coursework is perhaps the most important strategy colleges use to help busy students stay committed to academic work in the face of work and family demands. Approximately half of community college students take at least one fully online course at some point in their college careers, although most take the majority of their courses face to face, sprinkling in online courses here and there to create a more flexible schedule.[64] There is no doubt that the flexibility and convenience of online learning is a boon to nontraditional students, allowing them to create a better balance between school and other responsibilities. As one student explained to us:

> I think one thing that influences a full-time working adult to do distance learning is: how much time are you willing to sacrifice away from your family? . . . I just left Algebra II last semester, which was two days a week for two hours at night. That was tough. I missed a lot in my son's school and his sports, so it was more of a personal choice when I came back to register for the spring classes. I said, "You know, I think I'm only willing to sacrifice one night a week for school, for my family."[65]

The typical community college student, however, performs worse in online courses than in face-to-face courses. We conducted two large-scale studies in Virginia and Washington State (including fifty-seven community colleges, tens of thousands of students, and hundreds of thousands of course enrollments) and found that a given student is less likely to complete an online course than a face-to-face course, and students who manage to complete an online section tend to earn lower grades in the course than they would in face-to-face sections.[66] Subsequent large-scale studies replicating our methods in North Carolina and California have found similar results.[67] The negative effects for online learning among community college students remain—and, indeed, grow even stronger— when researchers control for a variety of potentially confounding effects through ever more rigorous statistical models.[68]

Although all types of community college students have a degree of difficulty in adapting to online learning, some face more challenges than others. In particular, males, younger students, black and Hispanic students, and students with lower levels of academic preparation have much more difficulty in online courses than they do in face-to-face courses.[69] These demographic groups are doubly disadvantaged: they already struggle to match their peers' performance in face-to-face classrooms, and that performance gap widens in online courses.

Given the advantages of online coursework for busy community college students, why do so many students seem to struggle in these courses? To understand student perspectives on this question, we interviewed students at two community colleges.[70] We asked students to reflect on why they took some courses online and others face to face, and how they felt about the online courses they had taken. The results of our investigation suggest that students struggle in online coursework because the typical online course does an even poorer job than the typical face-to-face course in supporting student motivation.

Community college students often have a low level of academic motivation. For example, in his 2013 study of developmental education students in community colleges, Norton Grubb observed, "Many students don't come to class on time, many students don't come to class prepared, and many don't do their homework. Many students are distracted during class by phone calls, texting, the Web, and off-topic discussions about family issues." The knowledge transmission model of instruction considers this "nonacademic" issue of student motivation to be beyond the purview of instructors, and thus these students receive little motivational support in the typical classroom. Our research suggests, however, that they receive even less support in online courses.

In general, research on motivation finds that instructors can cultivate three classroom conditions that help build students' motivation to persist and perform well at academic tasks: (1) building strong *interpersonal connections* among learners and between the learners and teacher, which provides a social motivation to perform well; (2) providing opportunities for students to enhance their individual *autonomy* by investigating questions on their own rather than being told the answer, and by exploring issues that dovetail with their own personal interest, background, and goals; and (3) developing students' sense of academic *competence* by setting challenging academic standards and tasks, coupled with targeted support that helps students meet those challenging standards.[71] The typical fully online course does an even poorer job than the typical face-to-face course in developing these three foundations of motivation, with the possible exception of autonomy.

The most obvious motivational challenge for the online classroom is its weakened interpersonal ties. Qualitative studies of fully online community college courses document that online students typically feel isolated from one another and from the instructor.[72] For example, in a CCRC study at two community colleges, even though several instructors spent quite a bit of time and energy encouraging high-quality peer-to-peer interaction, these instructors were rather disappointed at students' lackluster responses. When we talked with students, they explained that peer-based activities in their online courses felt forced and artificial, and did not help cultivate the spontaneous personal connections they enjoyed in a face-to-face classroom.[73] As one student remarked of online group work, "it's just extremely difficult and not really worth it basically."[74]

If interpersonal connectedness is important to motivation, it is clear that professors teaching large-enrollment online courses will face difficulties in motivating students who are not already engaged with and enthusiastic about the material. This observation is important to keep in mind as we consider learning options such as massive open online courses, or MOOCs. Because thousands of students enroll in such courses, it is impossible for faculty to meaningfully connect with more than a few of those individual students.

On the other hand, fully online asynchronous courses do provide somewhat more autonomy to students, at least in the sense of providing more choice and flexibility regarding when, where, and how to access learning materials and complete assignments. Such flexibility represents an advantage for an experienced student; however, if students do not yet feel competent to manage a high level of autonomy and flexibility, then too much autonomy can erode rather than build their motivation to persist in the course.[75] And unfortunately, according to our interviews with community college students and instructors, online instructors tend to *assume* rather than to *build* their students' competence to manage the high degree of autonomy inherent in the online context. For example, students complained to us that their online courses provided little guidance regarding how to prioritize tasks, manage their time, and interpret assignment requirements.[76]

In general, professors in reasonably small face-to-face courses have many verbal and nonverbal cues that help them judge whether a student is engaged in the material, and have a variety of light-touch ways to provide direction if the student seems lost. Without this interplay of in-person cues, online instructors in our study seemed confused and frustrated about how to identify and support struggling students. Online learning enthusiasts hope that by tracking detailed information on student learning (for example, through the recording of students' "clicks" as they work through material), software tools can help instructors pinpoint student problems, intervene to provide guidance as necessary, and thereby help build students' sense of competence. The little research that has been conducted in this area, however, suggests that in order to be helpful, such software would need to be more tailored to instructors' and students' needs than it currently is; moreover, instructors would need intensive professional development and ongoing support to help them use the software effectively— support that is currently lacking in the context of the cafeteria college.[77]

ONLINE LEARNING: NOT A SYSTEMATIC SUPPORT STRATEGY

For the typical cafeteria college, online learning represents a primary strategy to help students manage their external responsibilities. And for some students, the online strategy helps them find time and attention for school. In our interviews with online students, we met several who seemed to manage the near-impossible: they were raising children while working full-time, and were enrolled in a full-time and primarily face-to-face course schedule, with an online course mixed in to create more flexibility. These students balanced multiple roles and constraints not only through online learning, but also through other forms of thoughtful planning, such as taking a mix of easier and more-difficult courses together in the same semester; proactively making arrangements for flexibility with their instructor; negotiating with their spouse or extended family regarding childcare, household, or financial responsibilities; or seeking out specific support services that helped them manage their lives.[78] Creating such an effective "balancing" plan requires students to engage a variety of metacognitive skills. They must identify relevant obligations and commitments, judge the tradeoffs involved in withdrawing from certain activities and investing more heavily in others, develop a strategy that maximizes benefits while minimizing costs, and modify the strategy if it proves less than optimal.

Such students, however, are already well prepared, well organized, and highly motivated before they ever choose to take an online course. For the much larger group of students who do not yet possess such characteristics, online learning is unlikely to be helpful in promoting their academic success. And the cafeteria college has no systematic strategy in place that requires students to develop their metacognition or motivation. In the next section, we contrast the cafeteria college's unsystematic approach with the approach of the guided pathways college, which more explicitly works to build students' conceptual learning and metacognition.

Instruction in the Guided Pathways College

If the cafeteria college reinforces the instructional strategy of knowledge transmission, with little attention to students' metacognition and academic motivation, how would the guided pathways college approach instruction differently? Rather than conceptualizing each individual course as a stand-alone experience, as the cafeteria college does, the guided pathways approach conceptualizes each course as a step along a coherent path. Instruction should therefore focus on building the skills, concepts, and habits of mind necessary for success in subsequent courses.

This framework for instruction may require sacrificing some content within each course—spending less time covering specific pieces of knowledge in order to spend more time building concepts, skills, and habits of mind. At the same time, instruction should motivate students to work harder and persist longer at academic tasks; students' interest in and excitement about learning should be stimulated in their first courses and reinforced in every subsequent one.

These principles are consistent with the learning facilitation approach to instruction, and many books are available on that topic, including the extremely helpful volumes *How Learning Works,* by Susan Ambrose and colleagues, and *Learner-Centered Teaching,* by Maryellen Weimer. These books provide concrete suggestions for building students' competence, cultivating peer connections, and promoting student autonomy within the everyday context of classroom instruction. In the remainder of this chapter, however, we will focus on a larger issue: how can a college integrate this approach to instruction into every course in the curriculum?

We suggest four approaches. First, as part of the process of program mapping, colleges should convene faculty and professional student services staff to define the skills, concepts, and habits of mind essential to each course in a program. Second, colleges can draw on the expertise of professional staff to help support instructional redesign. Third, colleges should create and sustain peer-based faculty development structures to support ongoing instructional improvement. And fourth, colleges should consider how to best leverage instructional technology. We discuss each of these four approaches below.

Emphasize Skills, Concepts, and Habits of Mind

In Chapter 1, we described the process of "program mapping." During this process, faculty first define program-level learning outcomes, based on the competencies needed for successful transfer with junior standing (for transfer-oriented programs) or advancement in the labor market (for occupationally oriented programs), and ensure that these competencies are mapped onto a college-wide set of general education skills, such as critical thinking or global awareness. Next, faculty determine which courses will help inculcate which sets of skills, thus mapping out the process of how students will build each competency as they progress through a given program.

Competencies can be classified into three areas: skills, concepts, and habits of mind. *Skills* include both program-specific procedures (such as writing a solid business plan, creating a compelling website, or setting a patient at ease) and general education skills (such as considering diverse perspectives on a controversial issue). Rather than focusing merely on how to perform a specific procedure, skill-building instruction also focuses on why the procedure is useful and the diagnostic process involved in determining when to perform it. *Concepts* capture how a student understands and experiences discipline-specific content, as we will discuss in more detail later. Finally, *habits of mind* include metacognitive processes (e.g., breaking a large, complex learning task into component parts to be accomplished step by step); behavioral habits (e.g., completing at least some school-related work every day); approaches to learning (e.g., reading text for meaning rather than skimming it for specific facts); and mind-sets (e.g., the "growth mind-set" that hard work, rather than innate talent, is the key to success), all of which students must adopt to successfully learn and apply key concepts and skills.[79]

Importantly, the purpose of the program map is not to specify the content to be taught in each course but rather to determine (1) which skills, concepts, and habits of mind are necessary for program graduates; (2) where each competency will first be introduced; and (3) where each competency will be developed in subsequent courses. For example, if a program requires a capstone project, the map will need to specify where students will learn skills related to academic project management. Once each instructor is clear on the skills, concepts, and habits of mind that are key to a given course, he or she can determine the particular activities and factual content areas that will be most helpful in building those competencies.

Two crucial challenges may arise as colleges consider how to design these program maps. First, this tripartite list of competencies—skills, concepts, and habits of mind—seems to omit the central aspect of a course: its factual content. To help clarify how content fits with the other three competencies, we discuss below how concepts are similar to (and different from) content, and how instructors can effectively teach competencies without an exclusive focus on content. Second, to create useful program maps, leaders must convene an appropriate group of designers. To illustrate how other leaders have done this, we show how Miami Dade College went about the process of program mapping.

CONCEPTS VERSUS CONTENT

Students hear factual information in a lecture or read it in a book, but this new information is not retained unless they can fit it into a relevant mental model or *conceptual representation*.[80] For a given piece of information, some students have no relevant conceptual model in which to fit it; some have a model that *could* be relevant, but seems irrelevant and thus remains inactive; and some have a relevant but incorrect model. Only a few students will already have a relevant and correct conceptual model, will call that model to mind, and thus easily integrate and remember the new fact. For example, earlier we pointed out that algebra students can memorize procedures and apply them when told to do so; however, without conceptual representations of mathematical problems, they forget almost everything they have "learned."[81] Similarly, studies of introductory college physics courses have documented that many students still hold incorrect mental models of basic physical processes at the end of the semester; as a result, any information they memorized for the course is forgotten and does not provide a solid foundation for future science courses.[82]

Thus, an instructor's job is not just to provide information, but also to help build, activate, or reshape students' mental models. To make time for this work, instructors must spend less time covering specific factual content, and devote more time to helping students make conceptual connections. While many instructors fear such strategies will hinder students' learning of key skills and procedures, research suggests the opposite. For example, in a 2006 study of college calculus, researchers randomly assigned students to either conceptually or procedurally oriented sections of the course. On the final exam, the conceptual sections' students scored similarly on procedural items and significantly better on conceptual items. The final exam included a novel problem—a type that none of the students had previously seen—and 88 percent of the concept-based students answered the problem correctly, while only 54 percent of the traditional students did so.[83]

By reducing class time spent on factual content and procedural practice, instructors can spend more time on activities that build students' motivation to learn relevant content, skills, concepts, and habits of mind, whether inside or outside of class. Such activities are often grouped under the rubric of "inductive teaching" techniques, which go by many names: inquiry-based learning, problem-based learning, project-based learning, case-based teaching, and just-in-time teaching. These approaches are typified by an instructor posing an interesting problem or question, and then helping students with the particular issues or barriers they encounter when trying to solve the problem. Inductive teaching tends to improve student motivation and conceptual learning, without impacting students' ability to recall facts and procedures on an exam.[84]

As an example, in a qualitative study of developmental education classrooms, CCRC researchers observed some faculty who believed that rather than teaching content, they should teach students how to approach rigorous, college-level tasks.[85] To help their students persist with these very challenging tasks, the teachers employed activities that helped students feel motivated and exhilarated by intellectual struggle, rather than frustrated and defeated by it. In one developmental English course, students read a chapter from Class Matters, a nonfiction book about social class.[86] In small groups, students were asked to discuss conceptual questions, such as "Explain what the author means that many people believe that higher education is 'the great equalizer.' Does the author believe this? Do you think that education is an equalizer?" The small-group format allowed students to tackle more sophisticated concepts than any one student could tackle on his or her own.[87] As the instructor circulated the room, she did not correct misreadings outright; instead, she pointed the group to a relevant passage, and asked them to reread it and justify their interpretations, which typically resulted in the students realizing their own errors. When students were confused by new vocabulary, she pointed them to contextual clues in the text that allowed them to decode unfamiliar words on their own. As we have noted, research suggests that students are more motivated when they establish interpersonal connections with instructors and other students, develop a sense of competence by successfully engaging in challenging tasks, and enhance their autonomy by finding answers to interesting questions on their own. This teacher encouraged all of these processes, and as a result, her students willingly engaged in intellectual struggle, and were pleased with their ability to reach their own conclusions about the text. In the process, the instructor was also covertly teaching academic content related to reading comprehension strategies. But rather than dedicating class time to teaching these strategies in a dry, abstract, and isolated way, she taught them in the context of an engaging, challenging, and authentic assignment.

WHO SHOULD CREATE PROGRAM MAPS?

Miami Dade College, whose efforts are described in Chapter 1, provides a good example of a college that convened faculty to design program maps: its design group was made up of twenty-seven faculty members who represented all of the college's schools and major disciplines. The group first created maps for the four most-popular disciplines (business, psychology, biology, and criminal justice). Faculty experts took the lead for each discipline, with support from general education faculty drawn from a cross-disciplinary set of members. The planning group members were responsible for vetting draft pathway maps with their respective departments, which resulted in more than 200 faculty members who were engaged in the pathway redesign process. Draft pathways were submitted to student services directors, the implementation council (the initiative's steering committee), and academic deans, all of whom provided feedback. Finally, pathways were presented to the college academic and student support council (which reviews and helps to disseminate new and revised curricula across the college), and they were implemented in the fall of 2013.

While Miami Dade's instructional faculty constituted the heart of the mapping process, college leaders recognized that the final map design would suffer if it did not incorporate insights from student services staff. These professionals work closely with students every day and have a nuanced understanding of their anxieties, frustrations, and aspirations. Similarly, as instructors embark on the challenging work of redesigning courses to support program maps, they may discover the work to be easier, and the final design more effective, if they integrate input from professionals across the college. In the next section, we discuss other ways in which professional staff can contribute to redesigning instruction for the guided pathways college.

Collaborate with Student Services Professionals

Every institution employs a broad array of professional staff whose positions are not strictly instructional, but who work with students daily and thus possess a rich trove of information about how students think, what they care about, and how to help them learn. Examples include psychological counselors, academic advisors, financial aid counselors, career counselors, student life coordinators, teaching and learning center staff, writing center staff, information technology staff, and librarians. Some institutions have recognized the contributions of these professionals to the teaching and learning function of the college by classifying their positions as faculty. Yet regardless of whether they are formally classified as "staff" or "faculty," in most colleges these professionals' expertise remains isolated and rarely informs instructional practice.

In recent decades, some reformers have become interested in blurring the line between instruction and student support, and have issued calls for professional staff to work more closely with instructional faculty, as well as to embrace a more explicitly pedagogical philosophy for their own work.[88] By the 1990s, student affairs professionals began to argue that support services should be embedded in the academic enterprise, that advising should be seen as a teaching activity, and that noninstructional professional staff should collaborate extensively with faculty, in order to improve student success.[89]

Although the idea of a faculty-professional instructional alliance has been slow to spread (no doubt because of the strong cultural change required to make it happen), examples have been documented at multiple institutions. For example, in his 2013 study of developmental education at California community colleges, Norton Grubb details the strong partnerships between Chaffey College's developmental instructors and student services staff.[90] And a recent review provides multiple examples of collaborations between instructional and student services staff on orientation programs, first-year seminars, learning communities, service learning projects, and other curricular and extracurricular activities.[91] Here we consider two examples that are particularly relevant to the guided pathways model: the integration of librarians and other student service professionals into the course design process, and the inclusion of professional staff in instructional teams.

INCLUDING LIBRARIANS IN COURSE DESIGN

When groups of faculty convene to identify key general education skills, they frequently flag the importance of what librarians also call "information literacy."[92] Incorporating these skills into early coursework is important. Empirical research demonstrates that information literacy test scores predict incoming students' later college grades and, in fact, predict them more strongly than do the popular math and English placement tests that most community colleges administer to incoming students.[93] In general, college instructors believe in the importance of these same skills, but few integrate them into their courses because they are complex and challenging both to teach and assess.[94]

Many librarians are eager to partner with instructors to help integrate information literacy into the curriculum.[95] In practice, however, the vast majority of these partnerships result in stand-alone workshops or courses taught by the librarian.[96] Most such activities are voluntary for students, short in duration, and only loosely connected to the partnering instructor's course. That is, they are consistent with the structure of the cafeteria college. A more integrated approach involves librarians working with instructors to design discipline-specific information literacy materials or assignments that can be readily integrated into existing courses.[97] Although the evidence is largely qualitative and anecdotal, such embedded instruction seems to be more effective than stand-alone workshops and courses.[98]

As a further step toward integrating information literacy into the curriculum, some universities are now experimenting with team-based course design, which embeds information literacy instruction into the structure of the course itself. In general, in a team-based course design process, faculty work together with multiple professional staff—possibly including librarians, teaching center staff, student services staff, or technology staff—to redesign an existing course or to design a new course from scratch.[99] For example, at the University of Kansas, psychology and political science professors worked closely with librarians and writing center staff to redesign large-enrollment courses in ways that more explicitly built students' analytical reasoning and writing skills.[100] The positive results convinced faculty to expand the team-based design process to other disciplines. As two faculty members involved in the initial project explained,

> Designing a course collaboratively with a team of specialists is both a valuable and a viable instructional innovation. Gathering the skills of many people is a very good way (and maybe the only way) to meet the challenge of large enrollment lower-division courses. While seminars and some specialized upper-division courses may not need as much input, all instruction will benefit from a larger vision of the skill set of instructional design.[101]

Similarly, Bryn Mawr College brought together instructors, librarians, information technology staff, and students to think through the integration of new technologies into different courses. Professors redesigned their syllabi with the active input of a multi-talented team. According to the program's organizers, these collaborations strengthened relationships and understanding among instructors and professional staff. For example, information technology staff became more interested in understanding how they could proactively support instruction, rather than passively responding to faculty members' technology requests. Faculty were also surprised, and eventually pleased, to discover that professional staff were interested in making their instructional duties both easier and more effective. As one faculty member realized, "all of these wonderful ideas can come to fruition without me doing and being everything."[102]

INCLUDING STUDENT SERVICES PROFESSIONALS IN INSTRUCTIONAL TEAMS

Guttman Community College, which opened in 2012, uses a novel approach: all students are enrolled in a learning community, which in turn is nested within a specific "house."[103] Within each learning community, students take all courses together; and within each house, a group of faculty—known as the house's "instructional team"—teach all the same students.

Each instructional team includes a cross-disciplinary set of faculty, as well as a librarian, an advisor, and a graduate student assistant from the City University of New York (CUNY). The librarian, advisor, and graduate student assistant all participate in instructional roles. The advisor teaches a required student success course, the librarian creates information literacy materials and activities to support the house's curricular content, and the graduate assistant organizes "Studio" (similar to a supplemental instruction session), for which students receive participation grades. The team is led by a faculty member, who facilitates weekly meetings to discuss curricular, pedagogical, and student support issues. In addition, house faculty and advisors are located in the same office space, which results in informal conversations outside of the weekly meeting.

Guttman's faculty members are overwhelmingly positive about the value of instructional teams, claiming that they are "critical to the success of their work."[104] For example, advisors help instructors by shedding light on why certain students might be having academic or behavioral problems, and collaborating on potential supports that may help a given student better succeed. Meanwhile, instructors help advisors by sharing academic challenges and issues that advisors can then address in the student success course. Faculty also recognize the value that non-instructional members of the college community can add to its academic mission. For example, as part of a unit on sustainability, one instructor brought in the college's facilities director for students to interview and learn from.

Guttman is a "greenfield" college, which built its instructional model completely from scratch, and recruited faculty who were enthusiastic about the instructional team approach. Creating such teams in an existing college is more challenging, but many colleges are taking initial steps in this direction nevertheless. For example, in Chapter 1, we introduced Queensborough College and its freshmen academies, which are each focused on a general field of study. Each academy is coordinated by an advisor and faculty member, who collaborate with other faculty and student affairs staff to design cocurricular and extracurricular events that reinforce classroom learning and build community for the academy's students.

Peer-Based Professional Development

Every college already employs at least some faculty who excel at learning facilitation, but how can the college draw more faculty to the model? How might we improve professional development to make it useful for individual faculty members, while simultaneously expanding its scope to serve entire departments—or, indeed, the entire campus? We suggest turning the traditional model of the faculty workshop on its head. Rather than being delivered from the top down, professional development topics and issues would be generated by faculty; rather than being isolated from the classroom context in a one-time, short-term event, development would be intertwined with the everyday practice of teaching and learning; and rather than being delivered to individual faculty, development would be focused on groups of faculty working together across a program. To achieve this vision, professional development must be designed with two key goals in mind: deepening the usefulness of professional development through a process of *faculty inquiry,* and widening professional development across the campus through *collaborative* intradepartmental structures. Together, these two factors comprise what we refer to as "collaborative inquiry."[105] Below, we discuss the inquiry and collaborative components, before ultimately providing examples of how collaborative inquiry can work in practice.

FACULTY INQUIRY

Top-down professional development workshops typically attempt to sell faculty on a "technical solution," or a specific and clear-cut tool for teaching improvement.[106] Technical solutions work well when both the challenge and its solution are well-defined; to meet such a challenge, one must simply learn about the solution and how to properly execute it. Many of the challenges we encounter in our personal and professional lives are technical ones. We learn how to file a tax return to take advantage of the most write-offs, how to prepare clear and concise presentation slides, or how to create a useful rubric for grading essays.

The challenge of supporting student success is not strictly a technical one, however: no single teaching approach or tool works brilliantly to solve the challenges facing every teacher, course, and student. A quick glance at a meta-analysis of any particular instructional technique will show that it varies widely in its effectiveness, based on its implementation—which in turn varies according to the personality of the teacher, the skill levels of the students, and the academic discipline of the course.

Because of the complex interactions among student skills and background, teacher personality, and course content, the challenge of supporting student success is an example of an "adaptive challenge."[107] In contrast to a well-defined technical challenge, an adaptive challenge tends to be new, unique, unclear, or ill-defined. To find the best solution to such challenges, leaders need to investigate, rethink old ideas, and experiment with a variety of potential approaches. Similarly, to identify specific practices and techniques that will be most effective with their unique mix of students, instructors need to experiment with promising new tactics and observe the effects on motivation and the quality of student work. Doing so requires instructors to reexamine their assumptions about a given learning problem, generate new insights, and apply these insights to create new solutions or adapt old ones to the unique context of their classroom. This process, known as faculty inquiry, is the most effective way for an individual instructor to continuously improve his or her own quality of teaching.[108]

Faculty inquiry has some technical components; indeed, it is quite similar to the highly technical research processes with which many instructors are already familiar.[109] Yet it is intrinsically an adaptive approach. In contrast to workshops that predefine instructional problems and prepackage specific techniques to solve them, faculty inquiry relies upon instructors to reframe problems and generate their own solutions. Accordingly, faculty inquiry helps instructors construct a more personally meaningful classroom experience, which allows them to connect even more deeply to their students.[110]

The cafeteria college, however, does not support or encourage inquiry-based instructional improvement in a systematic way. Some faculty will shift toward inquiry or the larger learning facilitation model on their own, after having some sort of "defining experience," as Tamsyn Phifer called it in her qualitative dissertation.[111] In Phifer's study, the defining experience for many instructors occurred at the beginning of their teaching career. Feeling "overwhelmed," "alone," and "lost" in their course as they struggled to help students learn, these instructors turned the lens on themselves, critically examining their own practice, and had insights about how they might move forward and experiment with new ways of teaching. For example, one decided to ask her students for help: "I just decided to ask, tell me what you didn't get! And then I started to find out what they didn't understand."[112]

While some faculty will come to inquiry on their own, many will not, because inquiry is difficult and emotionally challenging, and it requires institutional encouragement and support. Next, we discuss these barriers in more detail, and how peer-based professional development can help address them.

BARRIERS TO INQUIRY—AND HOW PEER-BASED STRUCTURES CAN ADDRESS THEM

When individuals encounter a novel challenge, they tend to frame it first as a technical problem. This approach is rational: if the challenge is indeed a technical one, then solutions will be relatively easy to find (someone else has already discovered the answer) and implement (someone else has already laid out the necessary steps, and the individual must simply follow them). The problem and related solution are clear-cut, and therefore the implementation of the solution is unlikely to create controversy among one's colleagues. And, importantly, following a preexisting and well-accepted recipe does not require adjusting one's own perspectives or values. In contrast, generating an adaptive solution requires seeing things in a new way. It often involves disagreement with colleagues about the best approach, and it implies that one will be trying a new, untested tactic, which is therefore risky. Rather than making things better, the solution might well make them worse.

In their book on how to overcome adaptive challenges, *Immunity to Change,* Robert Kegan and Lisa Lahey point out that people who are authentically committed to change may also harbor underlying fears about the negative consequences that might result if they actually attempt to pursue the change.[113] For example, an instructor might want to spend more class time encouraging critical thinking, but also be worried that this will depress his students' performance on the department's fact-based common final. Another instructor might want to encourage more discussion among her students, but also be worried that she will lose control of the discussion, or be asked a question she cannot answer.

When attempting anything new or risky, it is helpful to have peers who are aware of, support, and encourage one's progress, in part because of the emotional and logistical support such peers can provide, and in part because peers exert some social accountability for continuing to move forward.[114] Moreover, working with one's peers is much more interesting than working alone. Although the instructional culture of the cafeteria college tends to be one of isolation, when instructors are given the opportunity to interact and collaborate around teaching with others at their own college, they consistently report that the experience is both intellectually stimulating and emotionally rewarding.[115] For example, in a qualitative study of teaching at a community college, some faculty members reported that they felt "lonely" in their teaching practice, but one recounted the excitement of connecting with a larger group of instructors around a new instructional reform (known as "Process Ed."):

> But it's hard when you're doing it all by yourself and that's why when Process Ed. was first introduced, it was really neat. . . . We were sharing ideas about things. And it was so neat to find out everybody's kind of doing the same thing. And they're all still struggling with it. And it was just, what a wonderful learning experience![116]

Peer support helps instructors face the initial risks and worries associated with faculty inquiry. After instructors have practiced inquiry for some time, however, they typically find that the process yields its own set of emotional and psychological benefits. As instructors uncover the complex reasons underlying their students' resistance, low motivation, or poor performance, they see that those issues are not solely the result of their own personal failures as an instructor—a realization that brings a strong sense of relief.[117] As they more deeply understand the complexities of students' experiences, thinking, and learning processes, instructors discover ways to positively shape them. These discoveries are empowering and, as instructors begin to see changes in their students' success, deeply rewarding.

In addition to providing emotional support, peers can provide one another with logistical support. To pursue inquiry in a relatively efficient manner, some faculty will need help defining new learning goals for their course; some need new assessments to measure existing learning goals that they never explicitly measured before; some want help designing methods to gather student input or feedback; some need help thinking through how to analyze and interpret the data they gather; some want help figuring out how to manage a productive student discussion; and most need help finding preexisting assignments and materials that can be adapted to their own students and learning goals.

Just as peer collaboration is an effective way to support student learning, it is an equally effective way to support professional learning. In K–12 education, a large body of research unequivocally demonstrates that student outcomes substantially improve when teachers work together in a strong and deep professional community that maintains a focus on student learning.[118] In these communities, teachers provide not only emotional but also logistical support for one another, in large part because they talk with one another about student learning at every opportunity—at lunch, at departmental meetings, in the hallway, in the parking lot, and whenever and wherever they meet. These discussions do not consist of vague complaints or "small talk," but instead are concretely focused on specific activities and assignments, and how various students react to them.[119] Teachers observe one another's classes and give feedback. They continually share their insights, new things they try in the classroom, and what happens as a result.

As an example of how a professional community provides logistical support to individual teachers, consider the story of a researcher who took Italian at a school for adolescents and adults. As a student, she was immediately impressed, in the first course she took, by how effectively the teachers improvised and adapted to unexpected developments in the classroom.

> One day, early in the course, the class had been working in pairs on an activity that the teacher had introduced that morning after going over the homework. He walked around watching and listening to what the students were doing. The activity had several parts, and the class was expecting to go on to the next part after a 15-minute break, but when students came back into the room to begin the second half of class, the teacher passed around copies of something new for them to work on. . . . This analytic activity focused attention on something that students had been struggling with during their work in pairs. How did he so readily come up with this text that was so particularly appropriate to the problems the class was having? Why did he bother to readjust his lesson in this way rather than going on with what he had planned?[120]

After embarking on a formal study of the school's teaching and learning processes, the researchers discovered the school's secret: teachers pooled their materials and assignments, and because of ongoing and concrete discussions about student learning, each teacher was intimately familiar with the array of options available in the pool. When an instructor felt it would be helpful, he or she developed new materials or adapted old ones; but instructors always contributed the new or altered materials back to the pool, and shared reflections on how well (or poorly) the new activity worked to address specific learning issues. As a result, individual instructors did not need to spend hours developing new instructional activities each week. Their familiarity with the vast pool of available resources (and the specific issues that each was helpful in addressing) enabled them to quickly select and implement resources and activities appropriate to their students' needs as they arose.

EXAMPLES OF COLLABORATIVE INQUIRY

In the university setting, two well-known examples of collaborative inquiry are Miami University's "faculty learning communities" and Virginia Tech's "faculty study groups." According to papers published about each initiative, groups are typically one semester or year in length, participation is voluntary, and meetings are frequent enough to support ongoing work.[121] Each group is organized around a specific topic or theme—for example, integrating technology, focusing on critical thinking, or gaining confidence as a brand-new teacher—but all groups focus on inquiry and innovation in the classroom. Because of their voluntary nature and thematic focus, groups tend to be interdisciplinary rather than intradepartmental. Logistical support for the groups, including facilitation of group discussions, is provided by the university; in particular, a professor or support professional experienced in facilitation is appointed to help manage the groups. At both universities, group members feel that participation lessens the sense of isolation, serves as a positive personal experience, improves their own teaching, and enhances their students' learning. For example, in a survey of the Miami participants, 98 percent reported that they were now more enthusiastic about teaching, 94 percent were more reflective about it, 90 percent were more confident in it, and 90 percent felt "revitalized."

In the community college context, the best-known examples of collaborative inquiry come from eleven colleges that created "faculty interest groups" among developmental education instructors as part of an initiative supported by the Carnegie Foundation for the Advancement of Teaching.[122] Each college constructed and supported its developmental education inquiry groups in different ways. Some involved cross-disciplinary groups, while others brought together instructors who taught the same sections of a specific course. Staff from the Teaching and Learning Center, the college's developmental instruction coordinator, or another staff member could facilitate groups. Faculty reported that participation in these groups generated enthusiasm for teaching, helping teachers feel more confident and revitalized.[123]

Earlier in this chapter, we described Guttman Community College's instructional teams, which also incorporated elements of collaborative inquiry into their practice. In the opening semester of the college in 2012, each instructional team was faced with a variety of student challenges. As a report on the college summarizes:

> It came as a shock to many students that they were expected to do the reading in advance of classes and be prepared to discuss it, that reading and writing assignments required considerable work beyond the classroom, and that instructors expected a high level of participation in class. . . . In all courses, faculty needed to learn how to scaffold assignments for students, how to think about grading in terms of student progress and development while maintaining high standards of performance, and how to figure out the amount of effort they would expend in following up with students who were reluctant or disengaged.[124]

The support of their peers within the instructional team made it much easier for faculty to manage these challenges, both logistically and emotionally. To support quality teaching, instructional teams focused on samples of student work, including strong, weak, and middle-range examples. Discussions around these samples helped faculty think about how to structure assignments, identify where students were struggling, and provide feedback and support to help them through those struggles. The Guttman report notes that "these discussions removed the burden of finding solutions from individual faculty members. When presenting a problem, faculty felt a sense of relief that others recognized the issue and had possible solutions."[125] As one faculty member put it, "We are never alone in the endeavor; the instructional team gives us stamina."[126]

In a CCRC study of colleges that were undertaking instructional reforms in developmental education, we saw many examples of more-informal collaborative groups.[127] However, we observed that simply providing time and space for faculty to get together and talk about the reforms was not always helpful. Groups were much more useful when they were grounded in a process of inquiry: defining challenging learning outcomes, working on how to incorporate those outcomes into specific tasks or assignments, examining the result of students' work on those tasks for evidence regarding their thinking, or generating ideas for new activities that could help reshape student thinking. Without an in-depth focus on student work, combined with planning about concrete next steps to try in the classroom, groups could easily devolve into freewheeling discussions that had little impact on instructional practice. Groups also found that an experienced facilitator helped them focus their time in productive ways.

In general, in order to create and sustain such collaborative work across time, institutions must abandon the cafeteria model and move toward a more cohesive and integrated approach to teaching and learning. Collaborative work is difficult to sustain if a faculty member's department and institution do not value it. For example, after the Carnegie Foundation "faculty interest group" grant ended, Norton Grubb followed up with the participating colleges to see if the groups were still meeting.[128] Most had dissipated, and those that remained seemed aimless. Why? In short, most groups had never been integrated into the larger culture of the institution. For example, faculty time for meetings and experimentation was created through special mechanisms, such as temporary reductions in teaching loads, rather than being integrated into ongoing departmental activities. When the funding used to reduce the teaching load disappeared, so did the time. In Chapter 5, we will return to this theme and discuss how institutions can sustain collaborative work across the long term.

LEVERAGE TECHNOLOGY . . . WISELY

If appropriately used, technological tools may help faculty implement learning facilitation in an effective and efficient way. For example, the integration of digital resources into face-to-face and hybrid courses can provide variety and novelty that enliven students' interest in the topic at hand.[129] Technological "bells and whistles," such as games and puzzles, embedded video, or pre-quizzes, can help catch a student's interest; however, unless the instructor exploits the temporary opening in the student's attention to hold interest in a pedagogically effective way, such bells and whistles do not improve learning outcomes.[130] For example, computer-based simulation games (which students find engaging) can be effective in teaching a particular topic or skill when used in a blended-learning approach—particularly when paired with group activities and instruction—but are not particularly effective when used as the sole method of instruction.[131]

In general, as with any other instructional tool or approach, technology can be used well or poorly. In this section, we describe some specific examples of technological tools and approaches that can increase student learning and motivation, while cautioning that these tools must be used thoughtfully to be effective.

USING TECHNOLOGY TO SUPPORT INDUCTIVE TEACHING

Earlier in this chapter, we introduced "inductive teaching" techniques, which generally involve posing an interesting problem or question, and then helping students with the particular issues or barriers they encounter while trying to solve it. Instructors interested in inductive teaching are increasingly using technology to overcome logistical barriers inherent in the process.

For example, one form of inductive teaching that is easily integrated into lectures is "questioning": asking students a question, giving them time to formulate an answer, and then addressing any misconceptions that those answers may reveal. Prior to the advent of "clicker" technology, instructors using questioning techniques did not have a quick or efficient way to gather and summarize answers from the entire class. One study suggests that without this seamless integration, questioning is no more effective than simply lecturing without a break; but the adoption of clicker technology allows instructors to see and respond to students' aggregate responses immediately, resulting in student learning gains.[132]

Of course, a specific technology, in and of itself, is rarely responsible for student learning gains. For example, one can imagine a course in which students submit their answers to a question via a clicker, but the instructor never addresses their responses—or simply says "interesting; 36 percent of you thought the answer was C, but the correct answer is A," without further explanation. To make a given technology useful, then, an instructor must design the course by first considering the types of processes, activities, and assignments that will engage students, and only later determining which particular learning technologies may be most helpful in promoting that design.

In recent years, instructors interested in using technology to support inductive teaching have increasingly gravitated toward hybrid courses. In a thoughtfully designed hybrid course, students can begin to engage with an intriguing problem and formulate questions using online materials, and then class time can be devoted to activities that help address those questions and further build students' abilities to solve the problem. The most-researched example of hybrid learning is a statistics course designed at MIT, known as the Open Learning Initiative (or OLI) statistics course.[133] In the OLI course, students interact with highly sophisticated custom-designed learning software at home, and then receive further scaffolding and support in class, although for only one hour per week. The OLI interface includes a "dashboard" that allows instructors to assess the overall progress of the class as well as the particular difficulties faced by individual students. Rigorous studies of this course at four-year colleges have found that OLI and face-to-face students perform equally well on tests of facts and procedures, despite the decrease in face-to-face class time. However, students in the OLI course also reported that they learned less, and liked the course less, than did their peers in face-to-face versions of the course. As the authors of a recent report explain:

> Students' responses to the open-ended questions on the end-of-semester surveys indicate that many students in the hybrid format would have liked more face-to-face time with the instructor than one hour each week; others felt that the instructor could have better used the face-to-face time to make the weekly sessions more structured and/or helpful in explaining the material and going over concepts students did not understand.[134]

The results of the OLI study provide hope to policymakers looking to cut costs while maintaining the *same* level of learning; however, instructors interested in inductive teaching are much more concerned about *improving* student learning and motivation while maintaining similar costs. Perhaps in part because of the reduction in face-to-face class time, the hybrid nature of the OLI course did not seem to boost students' intrinsic interest or motivation to learn the material. For example, in response to the question, "How much did [this course] increase your interest in the subject matter?" OLI students and face-to-face students gave the course a similar rating.[135]

In addition to the OLI research, other studies of specific hybrid courses suggest that they can have more positive impacts than face-to-face courses, largely because students tend to spend additional time on task in hybrid courses. In these studies, students typically spend a full three hours in face-to-face class sessions while also accessing additional online content outside of class.[136] Of course, this additional time is not at all a bad thing, if it implies that inductive teaching methods and accompanying technological tools engage students more in the course.

USING TECHNOLOGY TO PROVIDE PERSONALIZED FEEDBACK

In addition to supporting inductive teaching and capturing students' interest through fun or novel digital resources, other technological tools are designed to help build students' competence through "personalized" feedback or instruction. Many colleges subscribe to commercial learning software packages that allow students to attempt problems and receive feedback on how well they are doing. There is surprisingly little research on the effectiveness of such tools, and the research that does exist is mixed, with some positive effects and some negative ones.[137] We suspect that the variation in results across studies is due to the software's own intrinsic pedagogy, as well as how the instructor integrates the software into the larger course.

Software programs that merely indicate when a student has solved a problem incorrectly, without providing additional feedback about how to improve, will be less effective than those that provide useful information about where the student went wrong, as well as pointers on how the student might think through the problem differently next time.[138]

A larger problem with software-based pedagogy is that it tends to focus on factual, clear-cut, easy-to-assess skills and procedures. That is, it may promote fact-based knowledge and procedural fluency, but it is unlikely to promote conceptual learning. Accordingly, learning software may be most useful when it is paired with an instructor who can pull reports regarding individual and aggregate student performance, quickly diagnose how well students are performing on different problems, and create ways to support conceptual understanding in areas where students are struggling. For example, in our qualitative study of online learning described earlier in this chapter, we observed a chemistry instructor who used Mastering Chemistry software in this way, and who also had usually strong student outcomes in her courses.[139]

As part of their pedagogical approach, some learning software packages attempt to build student competence through "mastery learning." In this framework, students must complete a particular module at a high level of performance (for example, 80 percent correct) before they are allowed to move on to a new topic. Mastery learning is thought to build students' sense of competence by encouraging them to put forth a stronger intellectual effort and experience the success of performing at a high level, rather than scraping through the semester with minimally sufficient grades. While a large body of research in face-to-face classrooms has suggested positive effects for mastery learning, criticisms of that work have noted that much of the positive effect can be explained away by the instructor's other pedagogical approaches—for example, the extent to which the teacher incorporates student collaboration.[140] It is unclear, so far, whether the incorporation of the mastery approach into online learning software increases its effectiveness. In our own visits to community colleges, both instructors and students have described cases in which students become frustrated and disengaged when they cannot complete a particular online module at a high level of mastery, and never move beyond it.[141]

In an attempt to overcome this problem, one university has incorporated "amplified assistance" into its mastery-based online psychology course software.[142] When the system detects signs that a student is disengaging (for example, by not reattempting a failed quiz), the instructor receives an alert containing a modifiable template for an e-mail. Based on the student's recent activities, the template essentially provides a customized "growth mindset" intervention. For example: "Melissa, you've done well on the previous quizzes, and I believe you can do well on this one; where you really need to focus your work is on the following concepts. . . ." The automated nature of the intervention allows faculty to connect with students quickly and efficiently when the student most needs it. Analyses indicate that students in the "amplified assistance" online course strongly outperformed those in face-to-face courses. But the regular face-to-face course's success rates were so terrible that the online course's success rates were still disappointing: only about 35 percent of the students earned an A or B.[143] That is, instructional software coupled with semiautomated instructor assistance may have upgraded a poor course to a mediocre one, but quite a bit more pedagogical improvement—both for the software and the human instructors—will probably be necessary to transform the course into a motivating and compelling learning experience for most of its students.

In our qualitative study of online courses, we asked students enrolled in courses that incorporated instructional software (including MyMathLab, Mastering Chemistry, WebAssign, and Skills Assessment Manager) how useful they thought the software was. Generally, they told us it was helpful or an interesting change of pace, but it was not sufficient to replace a real instructor.[144] Similarly, in a developmental math class that used the ALEKS software, researchers found that "even though students were positive about ALEKS, they would not want to replace the human contact a classroom instructor provides."[145]

Overall, the message we take away from research on the effectiveness of educational technology is that "technology" is not a method of instruction. Rather, "technology" is a set of tools that can enhance or undermine the effectiveness of a given instructor, depending on how the tools are used. Colleges that wish to use technology to enhance student learning may be best served by supporting team-based course design processes, which allow instructors to draw on the expertise of librarians and technologists to integrate effective technology tools, as well as encouraging collaborative, inquiry-based course improvement efforts so instructors can continuously improve how they leverage the array of tools at their disposal to enhance student learning.

Thus far in this book, we have contrasted two models of college: the cafeteria model is built around individual courses, while the guided pathways model is built around programs of study. In the cafeteria model, the student must choose from a bewildering array of disconnected courses, and instruction and student services are separate and often uncoordinated functions. Like courses, services are available for students who know about them and choose to use them; however, most students do not.

In this chapter, we have argued that the typical college's approach to instruction, curriculum design, and faculty development reflects the structure of the cafeteria model. Pedagogy and curriculum development are focused primarily at the course level, faculty development is organized around episodic and uncoordinated voluntary activities, and student services and other professionals are not systematically integrated into the instructional mission of the college. While every cafeteria college has some excellent teachers and innovative programs, these tend to emerge from the initiative of individuals or small groups of professors and student services personnel, rather than being fundamental to the institutional culture. This cafeteria-style structure reinforces a knowledge-transmission model of instruction, which emphasizes procedural over conceptual learning, pays insufficient attention to student motivation, and makes little attempt to strengthen students' abilities to understand their own weaknesses and develop conscious strategies to overcome them. Instructional technology and online learning, at least as they are often used, further reinforce the underlying cafeteria model.

The structural components of the guided pathways model have the potential to strengthen student outcomes by moving more students into and through more coherent college-level programs. However, we believe these structural changes must be accompanied by instructional changes. In particular, colleges must extend the concept of guided pathways into each classroom, transitioning from a knowledge transmission approach to a learning facilitation approach, which pays more explicit attention to metacognitive skills and student motivation.

However, there is no fixed or "technical" recipe for effective instruction under the learning facilitation model; rather, instructional improvement requires faculty to take an "adaptive" approach. We have argued in this chapter that a process of collaborative inquiry is the most effective strategy for overcoming the challenges presented by a learning facilitation approach. Moreover, peer collaboration is the key to designing program curricula that ensure students learn the concepts, skills, and habits of mind in a given course that will prepare them for the next step on their program pathway.

Well-designed programs that incorporate motivating and engaging instruction will be an excellent thing for students who are academically prepared to embark upon their chosen program or meta-major. But what of students who are poorly prepared for their program of interest? In many community colleges today, the typical intake process does little to help students prepare for, and integrate into, a specific program or even a general area of study. The developmental education system in particular tends to default students into a long sequence of courses that seem (to the student, and often to outside observers) to have little relationship to students' personal goals and professional hopes. Thus, we next turn to the challenges caused by the large number of students who arrive poorly prepared for college and how those challenges can be overcome.

4

Helping Underprepared Students

A PPROXIMATELY TWO-THIRDS of incoming community college students fail to meet their institution's standards for college readiness.[1] To deal with such a large volume of underprepared students, community colleges use low-cost standardized math and English tests to determine whether students need "developmental" coursework in reading, writing, or mathematics. The assumption is that by completing these courses, which do not count for credit toward degrees, students will acquire the basic academic skills they need to succeed in college-level courses—particularly English 101 (College Composition) and Math 101 (College Algebra), but presumably other introductory college courses as well.

However, as we discuss in this chapter, standardized tests cannot clearly distinguish between students who are "college ready" and those who are not. Moreover, among the students who begin on the developmental education track, fewer than half successfully complete it, and even fewer move on to eventual graduation. Meanwhile, of their peers who are deemed "college-ready," many also struggle in college-level courses—not only in English and Math 101, but also in key introductory courses for their majors, such as Psychology 101, Business 101, or Biology 101.[2]

Over the past decade, leading community colleges have devoted a tremendous amount of effort toward reforming the traditional system of developmental education. Some of the most promising reforms eschew the notion that students can be precisely identified as either college-ready or developmental, as well as the idea that developmental students should be remediated *before* they enter college-level programs. Instead, these reforms seek to *immediately* engage all students in challenging college-level material that is relevant to their program of study, while building students' foundational academic skills along the way, often by using the learning facilitation approach. This general reform strategy fits well with the guided pathways model, which views the goal of the intake process as enabling students to choose and successfully enter a program of study.

In this chapter, we first examine the weaknesses of the traditional system of developmental education. We then discuss how colleges redesigning their programs and services using the guided pathways model can instead adopt more integrated and accelerated approaches that provide an "on-ramp" to programs of study. A primary aim of these approaches is to prepare each student to take and pass critical introductory college-level courses in the student's chosen field of study as quickly as possible.

Of course, community colleges will continue to have to deal with large numbers of entering students who are poorly prepared for college, unless efforts are made to improve the preparation of incoming students. While improving college preparation among students in K–12 is a complex issue that is mostly beyond the scope of this book, at the end of this chapter we discuss some promising strategies for improving high school students' college readiness. These strategies share the essential approach of closely connecting basic skill-building to college-level learning requirements and content.

The Developmental Diversion

As we have mentioned, incoming community college students typically take short, standardized placement tests designed to measure their skill levels in reading, writing, and mathematics. Students scoring below a predetermined cutoff are referred to developmental education, which usually consists of one or more semester-long remedial courses that cover precollege material. Many colleges also use secondary cutoffs to sort developmental students into different course levels; for example, while a student scoring barely below the math cutoff may be referred to a developmental algebra course, a student scoring far below the cutoff may need to take and pass a sequence of three or more courses (such as arithmetic, pre-algebra, and algebra) before being allowed to proceed to a college-level math course. For this reason, it makes more sense to conceptualize remediation as a *sequence* of courses rather than as a single course. Indeed data from students entering college between 2006 and 2008 indicate that approximately one-fifth of entering community college students were referred to a sequence of three or more remedial math courses.[3]

Typically, each course in a developmental sequence is one semester in length, meets three to five hours per week, uses a knowledge transmission approach to teach basic content, and costs the student the same as a regular college course.[4] Despite their full-tuition cost, developmental courses carry only "institutional credit"—they count as regular courses for financial aid purposes but do not count toward college-level degree requirements. The annual cost of providing remediation to community college students nationwide may be as much as $4 billion.[5]

At first glance, the conventional approach to developmental education seems simple and sensible: students identified as having weak skills are exposed to the academic content they need to succeed in college-level work, and if they complete their developmental courses successfully, they can move on with confidence to college-level work. This approach also keeps students with very weak skills out of college-level classes, which is believed to benefit both these students (who would presumably perform poorly in such classes) and their peers (as the presence of low-skilled students might slow the pace of the course and be detrimental to the learning of college-ready students).

Yet a variety of research studies conducted in the last decade suggest that the conventional approach to developmental education does not increase an underprepared student's probability of succeeding in relevant college-level courses or of reaching longer-term milestones such as transfer or degree or certificate completion—in large part because most students referred to developmental education never finish their developmental sequence. In a CCRC analysis of approximately 150,000 students from community colleges across the country, we found that just 30 percent of students referred to developmental math completed their sequence within three years, and only 16 percent completed a first college-level math course. Outcomes were even worse for students assigned to lower-level developmental math courses; for example, among those assigned to three levels below college-ready, only 15 percent completed their referred sequence, and 8 percent completed a college-level math course. The numbers for reading and writing sequences were somewhat better but still disappointing.

One important insight from this analysis is that many students who fail to complete their sequences do so without failing or withdrawing from a remedial course. They either never show up for their first remedial course (in the math sample from above, 26 percent) or do not return after completing one of the lower courses in the sequence (22 percent). Additionally, some students complete the sequence but do not enroll in a college-level course (4 percent).[6]

Although these findings hardly suggest that the developmental system is robust and effective, it is still possible that even fewer of those students would have been successful in the absence of developmental education.

Indeed, evaluating the effectiveness of remediation is difficult, since developmental students start out weaker, at least as judged by the assessments, than students who are not referred to remediation. Thus, even if they did benefit from developmental education, they could still end up less successful than students who were initially judged college-ready.

To investigate the question of whether underprepared students perform better or worse in the absence of developmental education, several recent studies have dealt with this methodological problem (that is, that developmental students, on average, begin college with weaker skills than college-ready students) by comparing outcomes for students with scores *just above* versus *just below* a college's developmental cutoff score. Students who score so similarly on placement tests are essentially equivalent to one another in terms of the skills measured by the test, owing to a known degree of measurement error in most tests. Thus, if developmental education is helpful, then students just below the cutoff (who received developmental assistance) should be more successful than students just above the cutoff (who received no assistance). For example, developmental education might allow marginal students to brush up on their skills while gaining confidence in a relatively easy course, providing the foundation for a strong start in their subsequent college-level courses. In contrast, their peers who scored just above the cutoff might struggle in their first college-level courses, and become discouraged by their own poor performance. Under this scenario, the developmental students could overcome the semester lost in noncredit precollege coursework and move ahead, earning better grades and proceeding more quickly toward a degree than similar students who did not receive the benefit of developmental education.

Unfortunately, studies using this above-or-below-cutoff methodology have generally found that students who scored just below the cutoff did *not* have better long-term outcomes than similar students who went directly into college-level courses.[7] This "null" finding is a strike against developmental education: if the service requires time and resources from both students and taxpayers, and yet provides no long-term benefit to students, then it is not worth the time and money invested in it. It is important to note that this conclusion applies only to developmental students who score near the cutoff; however, studies have examined a wide variety of cutoff scores, and in general the conclusion holds even when cutoff scores are very low.[8]

Of course, these findings do not imply that students who place in a three-course sequence in remedial math should instead enroll directly in college-level math with no additional support. Rather, the studies' results imply that students at many points in the developmental continuum are unlikely to be harmed by attempting courses that are slightly more challenging than their placement scores suggest they can handle.[9] For example, students currently referred to three levels of developmental math do not seem to have better outcomes than similar students who are referred to only two levels of remediation; but whether one or two semesters of developmental math, or a college-level math course with additional targeted supports, would be more useful to these students is an open question.

In general, the current developmental education system does not improve the typical student's chances of successfully completing introductory college-level courses. Instead, students earn developmental credits at the expense of earning college-level credits, and never quite catch up to their peers in terms of the number of college-level credits they earn.[10] Thus, rather than facilitating a student's successful entry into college-level programs of study, developmental education diverts students away from such programs.

In the remainder of this section, we investigate broad reasons why the conventional approach to developmental education fails many students: the form and function of the system for assessing and placing students, the lack of alignment between the content of developmental and college-level courses, and the ineffective instruction used in many developmental classrooms. All of these problems have their roots in, and are exacerbated by, the cafeteria structure of many community colleges.

Developmental Assessment

We have argued that an effective intake system should establish students in a coherent college-level program of study as soon as possible. Yet the traditional developmental education assessment system has an opposite purpose: to identify some group of students who will be *kept out* of a college-level program of study, or whose entry will at least be delayed.

From the point of view of many faculty and administrators, one key function of the developmental assessment system is to maintain standards and quality in college-level courses. In CCRC studies of developmental education across several community college systems, researchers found that faculty and administrators often assume that, without the screening mechanism of placement testing, the academic quality of introductory college-level courses would be threatened. For example, one English instructor reported:

> Our vice-president has initiated an excellence crusade—it's all about being excellent. And one of the things that a lot of faculty were talking about was

the fact that you cannot serve everybody *and* be excellent. It's definitely a truth. . . . Our pass rates were atrocious because we were keeping our standards—we keep our standards in the classroom—at college-level rigor. But that means of course that some of the students, in the very first two weeks of class, are already set up for failure. Because they're behind. They don't have the necessary skills. . . . We take anybody that wants to come here, which means we set them up to fail. So we'll have to figure that out. You can't have it both ways. You can't have excellent classes and college-level rigor and every type of student possible in that classroom. They're going to have to have somewhere else to go.[11]

From this point of view, maintaining high standards requires colleges to screen out students who lack the skills to be successful in college-level courses. As another English instructor explained:

Right now there's such a mix that it's so tough to try to address all of these different needs. You don't want to play to your strong students; on the other hand, you don't want to just play to your weak students. But what I find is that when there's such a gap, it's really difficult to know what happy medium to strike. And I do think it's a matter of placement. Sometimes you'll get into a class and you'll think, "How can all of these students be here?" . . . And I do wonder whether raising some of the [placement] standards a little bit might help with that.[12]

For many colleges, then, the traditional purpose of developmental placement tests has been to screen out students who cannot succeed in college-level courses. This approach reflects a "knowledge transmission" rather than a "learning facilitation" orientation to instruction—a point to which we will return later in this section. But leaving aside the validity of the approach for the moment, if we take at face value the notion that placement tests should indeed separate "developmental" from "college-ready" students, then we must acknowledge that the tests do not even do a good job at that task, for two reasons.

First, there is no consensus about what it means to be "college-ready."[13] For example, in a study of Ohio community colleges in the late 1990s, researchers found that colleges varied widely in their placement cutoffs.[14] A prospective student with a given level of high school performance and ACT/SAT score might have a very small chance of taking developmental education (perhaps a 15 percent chance) at one community college but a very high chance (perhaps 90 percent) at another community college. Some state systems have moved to create consistent cutoff scores across community colleges, but these efforts have often met resistance from faculty in individual colleges who believe that college readiness standards for one college or program are inappropriate for other colleges or programs.[15]

Second, placement tests are unable to provide a clear and obvious cutoff—a point below which students will fail and above which students will succeed. Instead, the relationship between placement test scores and the probability of success in a college-level course is a continuous and shallowly rising function. Figure 4.1, taken from a study by CCRC researcher Judith Scott-Clayton,[16] illustrates the challenges inherent in using a single placement test score to separate college-ready from developmental students. Three lines represent the relationship between an algebra placement score and the probability of earning at least a grade of B (the bottom line), a grade of C (the middle line), or a grade of a D (the top line) in one's first college-level math course. The vertical line represents the cutoff score in the community college system from which these data were obtained. Students who scored below the cutoff were assigned to developmental math, and Scott-Clayton, based on other information about those students, estimated what grade they would have received had they enrolled in the college-level course. Note that almost 70 percent of the "developmental" students who scored just below the cutoff, and more than half of all students assigned to math remediation overall, would have passed the college-level course with a D or better. Of course, most colleges would like their students not just to pass math with a D but to perform more respectably, perhaps with a B or better. Still, at the cutoff margin, over 30 percent of the "developmental" students would have earned a B or better had they been allowed to enroll directly in college-level math.[17] Scott-Clayton termed these students "severely underplaced."

Overall, Figure 4.1 shows that some students who were referred to developmental education do not need it. In a simulation (drawing on a variety of student achievement predictors) designed to estimate how many students are severely underplaced, Scott-Clayton estimated that 18 percent of students who took the system's math placement test fell into this category. On the other hand, Figure 4.1 also suggests that some "severely overplaced" students are deemed "college-ready" but nevertheless fail their first college course in math. Scott-Clayton's analyses suggest that about 6 percent of the students who took the system's math placement test fell into this category. Misplacement rates were even worse in English. Among students who took the reading and writing placement tests, 29 percent were severely underplaced and 5 percent were severely overplaced.[18] And

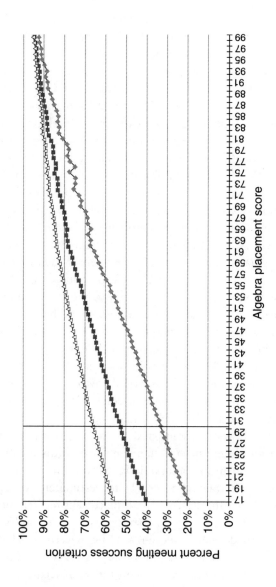

FIGURE 4.1. The lack of a clear cutoff.

the misplacement rates for both subjects would be even higher if we counted a grade of C as adequate.

There are at least three reasons why developmental placement tests, when used in isolation, have such high misplacement rates. First, most incoming students are unaware of the purpose and consequences of the placement tests, in large part because colleges do not want to discourage students from enrolling and thus tend to downplay the tests' importance.[19] Students may be told that they cannot fail the test, or that the test is intended only to match them to the best possible courses.[20] Without understanding the potentially high-stakes consequences of the tests, students do not generally prepare or "brush up" ahead of time and often rush through the test session, and may earn scores that fall below their actual level of academic ability.[21] Second, placement test content is often poorly aligned with the academic standards and expectations of college-level coursework, an issue we will discuss in more detail below. Third, and perhaps most important, the skills that can be tested on a short multiple-choice test represent only a small subset of those needed to be successful in college. For example, students' metacognitive skills, critical-thinking skills, and levels of academic motivation may be more important to their success than the mechanical reading, writing, and math skills measured on placement tests.

In general, given the cafeteria college's emphasis on access to courses rather than on completion of programs, it may seem entirely rational to prevent underprepared students from entering college-level courses and instead assign them to skill-building prerequisite courses. In contrast, however, the logic of the guided pathways model suggests that the goal of assessment should be to gather multidimensional information on each student that will help the college integrate appropriate curricular and extracurricular supports into the student's experience, while at the same time helping the student learn about and become successfully established in his or her chosen program of study.

Developmental Instruction

Instruction in remedial courses contrasts with what would typically be expected in a college course. According to Norton Grubb's recent observational study of 169 classes in twenty community colleges, most developmental courses have a very similar pedagogical approach:

> The approach emphasizes drill and practice (e.g., a worksheet of similar problems) on small subskills that most students have been taught many times

before. . . . Moreover, those subskills are taught in decontextualized ways that fail to clarify for students the reasons for or the importance of learning these subskills.[22]

For example, a developmental writing course might use a checklist for essay writing, which requires students to create a formulaic and error-free product, with little opportunity for creativity in form and with little relevance to the student's larger personal, academic, or career goals. Students are expected to master these subskills before they can move on to college-level materials or activities. It is not surprising that many students find this knowledge transmission approach boring. There are of course exceptions, some of which we will discuss later in this chapter, but based on his fieldwork, Grubb concludes that innovative exceptions are the result of initiative taken by individual instructors, not the result of broader institutional support and policy.

In addition, the curriculum of developmental education tends to be focused narrowly on math and English skills, which may or may not be well aligned with the content of subsequent courses that students will take in their program of study. For example, in a CCRC study of one community college system's developmental education curriculum, we observed that many of the colleges' degree programs allowed students to fulfill their college-level math requirement by taking a course that did not rely extensively on algebra (such as introductory statistics or quantitative literacy, or a course on mathematics history and culture). Yet the system's upper-level developmental math course, which was required of all developmental math students regardless of their program of study, was designed to prepare students for college-level algebra. Thus, many students are blocked from advancing because they do not complete a noncredit course that is irrelevant to their college-level program of study. As we concluded in that report, "many students could probably skip the top level of developmental [math] education and do no harm to their chances of success in courses that fulfill their own program's college-level math requirement."[23]

If the developmental curriculum is aligned with college-level content at all, it is usually aligned only with the content of freshman composition and algebra. The assumption underlying this arrangement is that the general math and English skills emphasized in developmental coursework will help students succeed in other courses. For example, students may need strong reading skills to parse a History of Western Civilization textbook. Yet most developmental courses are not designed to build the type of reading, writing, and quantitative skills necessary for success in disciplinary coursework, such as assessing an argument, writing research papers, or understanding statistical tables and figures.[24] Even if a student does learn such skills in developmental English or math, she may have no idea how to apply them to her history class. Identifying which skills she should make use of in her history assignments, how to apply those skills, and when to do so, is a complex task requiring metacognitive abilities that developmental students—as well as many "college-ready" students—may lack.[25]

Developmental studies also tend to focus on math and English because freshman composition and algebra are stumbling blocks for many students. But they are not the only major hurdles in the introductory college curriculum. For example, in one study of community college dropouts, CCRC researchers found these students had indeed performed poorly in college-level math and English (with failure rates of 17 and 14 percent, respectively), but they performed even worse in other key introductory courses, including History of Western Civilization (where the failure rate of eventual dropouts was 18 percent), Introduction to Business (18 percent), Principles of Accounting I (23 percent), and Beginning Spanish I (18 percent).[26]

Overall, the traditional system of developmental assessment, placement, curriculum, and instruction delays students' entrance into college-level programs and, in many cases, diverts them from those programs entirely. Even when its success is defined in terms of an overly narrow goal—preparing students for initial college-level courses in math and English—the conventional approach fails to help most developmental students enter and succeed in these courses. To help developmental students enter and succeed in not just English and Math 101, but also in the other introductory courses critical to success in their program of study, we need to re-think remediation as an "on-ramp" to each student's program of study.

Rethinking Developmental Education as an "On-Ramp" to Programs of Study

The goal of the intake process under the guided pathways model is to help students choose and successfully enter a program of study as quickly as possible. For developmental education to play an effective part in such a process, colleges must redesign three key elements of their approach to remediation: assessment and placement, curriculum, and instruction. Below, we discuss each of these components separately, although all three should be pursued together for maximum effect.

Customizing Assessment and Placement

Colleges across the country are already involved in three types of assessment and placement reform. First, some states and colleges are creating customized tests that are more closely aligned with the expectations of the college's own college-level programs of study (unlike the standardized tests common on the market). Several states are including diagnostic components in their mathematics tests, which allow students to meet specific standards of readiness that differ between STEM programs, liberal arts programs, and occupational programs. Customized tests are in use or under development in California, North Carolina, Oregon, Texas, Virginia, Washington State, and Wisconsin, among other states.[27] Such efforts may be particularly useful when readiness standards and their related assessments are designed with input not only from English and math faculty but also from social science, science, and other disciplinary faculty. In the cafeteria college, disciplinary faculty are often entirely unaware of developmental assessments and coursework; in contrast, by drawing on the expertise of an interdisciplinary group of faculty, collaborative design processes can ensure that tests are tapping more than the narrow skills represented in freshman composition and college-level algebra.[28]

Second, an increasing number of colleges are providing clearer and more explicit information to students regarding placement tests, and they are encouraging students to prepare for them. For example, a North Carolina college has created online review courses for its reading, writing, and math placement tests, which students can access and complete from any computer at their convenience.[29] For each subject, the review includes approximately eighty minutes of content: a diagnostic pretest, information on areas in which the student is weak, instructional videos that cover the test content, a post-test, and additional resources to help the student prepare for the placement test, such as PowerPoint presentations created by faculty and links to supplementary online practice materials. The college's internal research provides some descriptive evidence that use of the reviews improves placement accuracy. Among students who took the review courses before retesting in 2010–2011, 60 percent tested at least one level higher in the developmental reading and English sequence than they previously tested, and about 35 percent tested at least one level higher in the developmental math sequence. These students performed well in their new placements, having pass rates similar to or higher than their counterparts who placed directly into the courses. While the review courses required some time and expense to create, administrators described it as "relatively" low cost and easy to scale up.

Third, many colleges are experimenting with using multiple measures to assess entering students. Currently, few colleges use multiple measures, in part because doing so is time-intensive. For example, one small Wisconsin two-year college gathers a wide array of information on each student (including ACT scores, high school grades, class rank, math placement scores, TRIO eligibility, high school curriculum information, length of time since high school, and home language). An English faculty member spends about ten minutes reviewing each individual's profile before referring the student to an English course (first- or second-semester college composition, developmental English, or a course for English language learners) and, if needed, one or more supplemental support courses.[30]

To support a more automated and efficient multiple-measures approach, some colleges are working to execute data-sharing agreements with local high schools that would allow them to access students' high school records, including their grade point averages. In general, a student's high school GPA is a much stronger predictor of success in college than ACT or SAT scores. In explaining this phenomenon in their 2009 book *Crossing the Finish Line*, Bowen, Chingos, and McPherson speculate that "high school grades reveal much more than mastery of content. They reveal qualities of motivation and perseverance—as well as the presence of good study habits and time management skills—that tell us a great deal about the chances that a student will complete a college program."[31]

Indeed, in a study described earlier in this chapter, CCRC researcher Judith Scott-Clayton performed a simulation comparing two conditions: assigning students to developmental education on the basis of either placement test scores alone, or the "best of" the placement test or the student's high school performance in the given subject area. The simulation suggested that under the "best of" criterion, the rate of students referred to developmental education would fall substantially: from 75 to 67 percent in math, and from 81 to 69 percent in English. That is, more students would be able to enroll directly in college-level courses. Moreover, this tactic would not increase placement error. On the contrary, the rate of placement errors would also fall: from 24 to 22 percent in math, and from 33 to 28 percent in English.

Long Beach City College (LBCC) has also implemented a multiple-measures assessment and placement system. In 2012, LBCC worked with the Long Beach Unified School District to access information on students' high school course taking and grades and high school standardized tests, and placed students into developmental education using a combination of this transcript information plus placement test scores, rather than using the placement test scores alone. They did not use this system for students from other districts, which allowed a comparison between students placed under the new and the old systems. Under the old placement test system, 13 percent of first-time students from the school district who entered the college tested into transfer-level English, and only 9 percent tested into transfer-level math. After the introduction of the new assessment system, 60 percent tested into transfer-level English and 30 percent into transfer-level math. After this change, there was no statistically significant difference in transfer-level math and English course pass rates between students placed via the new assessment system and students who were placed via the previous method or who had advanced through the institution's developmental sequence. These descriptive data suggest that students who were placed using the new system were more than three times as likely to pass the transfer-level courses than students under the old system.[32]

While all three of these assessment reforms may help colleges more accurately identify students who need extra help and assess their readiness for success in particular fields of study, an improved assessment and placement system alone will not go far toward improving the success of underprepared students in college-level coursework. To be effective, reformed assessment processes need to be coupled with efforts to redesign curriculum structures and teaching methods.

Accelerating Developmental Curricula

The majority of students referred to developmental education drop out before completing their assigned sequence—either because they fail a course or because they simply do not enroll in the next course in the sequence. As a result, only a small proportion of developmental students ever enroll in college-level math or English.[33] To address these high rates of attrition, many community colleges have begun experimenting with "accelerated" models of developmental education, which are designed to help students complete remediation within a shorter time frame.

Proponents of acceleration believe that it can mitigate two problems that plague students' progress in developmental education: too many opportunities to quit in the developmental course sequence, and poor alignment with college-level curricula. First, lengthy developmental sequences give students multiple opportunities to drop out. Many students—even those who perform well in their developmental courses—leave before they reach college-level courses.[34] Acceleration strategies are designed to minimize exit points and limit the time students spend in developmental education, reducing the likelihood that outside commitments or events will pull them away from college before they complete their developmental sequence.[35]

Second, developmental courses sometimes teach skills that are not clearly relevant to the tasks and assignments given in college-level programs of study.[36] Many acceleration strategies solve this problem by tailoring the developmental curriculum to the skills required for success in introductory college-level courses, which has the happy side effect of eliminating unnecessary topics and allowing students to move through the course material more quickly. Some also employ assignments that approximate college-level expectations, including a quicker pace of instruction, along with pedagogies designed to support students' efforts to meet these challenging expectations—a point we will discuss in more detail later.

Most acceleration models include one or more of the following features: paired courses, compressed courses/sequences, or mainstreaming students into college-level courses with added academic supports. Under the *paired* or *combined* course model, two sequential developmental courses are paired in a single course with the same overall number of contact hours. The curriculum remains the same, but the paired structure strongly encourages students to complete the equivalent of two courses in a single semester. Assuming they successfully complete the course, students are then poised to move quickly to the next course in the sequence. For example, at the Community College of Denver, students who place into the lowest level of mathematics must complete three developmental math courses. Under the college's FastStart program, however, students have the option to take two of those courses together in one semester.

In a *compressed* developmental sequence, the total number of contact hours in the sequence is reduced. In some cases, this reduction results from aligning the curricula among developmental courses and eliminating redundancies. In other cases, the course covers the same quantity of material at a faster pace. For example, Chabot College in California offers a one-semester, four-credit developmental reading/writing course as an alternative to a two-course sequence totaling eight credits. While some colleges restrict entry into compressed courses, at Chabot any developmental student may enroll in the accelerated course, regardless of his or her score on the reading and writing placement tests.

Finally, under the *mainstreaming with supports* model (also referred to as the *co-requisite* model), students who fail to meet the college's placement test cutoffs are nevertheless allowed to enroll in a college-level English or math course, while receiving supports designed to help them succeed in that course. This model comes closer than other acceleration strategies to blurring the distinction between college-ready and developmental students and to integrating remedial supports into college-level coursework. The best-known example is the Accelerated Learning Program (ALP) at the Community College of Baltimore County. Students at this college who test into upper-level developmental writing may enroll directly into college-level English 101, provided that they co-enroll in a special ALP section of developmental writing. Only ten ALP students are allowed to enroll in any given twenty-student section of English 101; after each class, these students meet with the same 101 instructor in the companion ALP section, where the instructor helps them build the learning strategies and skills necessary to succeed in the assignments they encounter in English 101.

CCRC research suggests that accelerated models allow students to complete college-level English and math more quickly.[37] Our study of the ALP program found that 73 percent of ALP students completed English 101 with a grade of C or higher within three years, compared to 45 percent of similar non-ALP students, a difference of 28 percentage points. Most of this boost was due to ALP students' much higher enrollment rates in college-level English; but once enrolled in the college-level course, ALP students were just as likely to pass the course as their college-ready peers.

To help students succeed with an accelerated course's faster pace and more challenging expectations, most acceleration programs integrate student supports of some type. At the Community College of Denver, accelerated students have a case manager, and many participate in a special student success course; at Chabot College, many of the original accelerated courses were offered in the context of a learning community; and at the Community College of Baltimore County, the ALP course itself serves as a support (although the ALP course confers developmental credit, it does not reproduce the content of the traditional developmental course; rather, it consists of a flexible curriculum designed to help students build the context-specific skills they need to succeed in their concurrent college-level course). This concept of connecting remediation with the learning demands of college-level coursework is also a key component of Chabot College's philosophy, where students in developmental reading and writing receive the same types of assignments they will receive in college-level English. Importantly, rather than teaching discrete basic skills in isolation, Chabot instructors teach them within the context of challenging and interesting college-level tasks. Moreover, all three acceleration programs support their instructors in the development of a learning facilitation approach to teaching, an issue we will discuss later in this chapter.

Especially since the growth and spread of the ALP program, the co-requisite model of acceleration has become increasingly popular. Complete College America (CCA), an organization that as of 2014 was working with more than thirty states to help them increase their number of college graduates, has made the co-requisite model one of its "game changer" strategies—strategies CCA believes will help dramatically improve success for underprepared students. Since 2011, more than one hundred colleges have adopted a strategy similar to the ALP model. However, some practitioners are concerned about whether acceleration is appropriate for all developmental students or only for students who score near the cutoff of college readiness. For example, highly controversial reforms in Connecticut and Florida seem based on the assumption that most or all developmental students could be successfully served either in a co-requisite model or a one-semester remedial course.[38]

Can students with very low scores on assessment tests benefit from the co-requisite model? CCRC's studies of the ALP and Chabot programs provide suggestive evidence that many students who score near the bottom on placement tests benefit from acceleration strategies.[39] However, both the ALP and Chabot programs provide a high level of intensive in-class supports, consistent with the learning facilitation approach. It seems unlikely that very poorly scoring students would benefit from a co-requisite or one-semester accelerated prerequisite approach without such strong support.[40]

In general, our inclination based on our research is to lean toward a policy in which the majority of developmental students are referred to a co-requisite program with an integrated student support section, such as ALP. For the minority of students who score very poorly, some may still be able to handle the co-requisite model, but others may not. Assessments using multiple measures, combined with in-person advising, should help determine which low-scoring students need a more sustained and intensive developmental education program. For students who fall into this category, we need further research to determine how best to accelerate them into a college-level program of study. One model is the City University of New York's Start model, an intensive full-time program designed to bring students with very weak academic skills quickly up to a level in which they can participate in college courses. Preliminary internal analyses by CUNY staff suggest the program has strong potential.[41] In 2014, CCRC partnered with MDRC to begin a more rigorous study of the program and its outcomes.

Integrating Academic Support into Programs of Study

As we have noted, increasing developmental students' completion of college-level math and English courses is helpful, but students' evolving numeracy and literacy skills should also be relevant to (and contextualized with) students' chosen area of study, in order to help students succeed in critical introductory courses in their program. Thus far, full integration of basic numeracy and literacy skill-building into specific programs has proven elusive, for two reasons: this strategy would require students to choose a program of study before they embark on their first semester, and it would require coordination between program and developmental education instructors.

We are aware of only one program that has fully integrated basic skill-building into college-level programs of study: Washington State's I-BEST program. I-BEST (Integrated Basic Education and Skills Training) is focused on adult basic education (ABE) students interested in career-technical education, who have already determined their program of interest but do not meet their program's readiness standards. Most I-BEST programs are in fields such as health care, education, clerical work and office management, and manufacturing. Under I-BEST, career-technical faculty work together with basic-skills instructors to design and team-teach courses, with the basic-skills curriculum contextualized and tailored to the needs of the occupational program. As of 2012, when CCRC carried out a study of I-BEST, approximately 150 such programs operated across the state's thirty-four community and technical colleges.[42]

To receive formal funding for I-BEST courses, colleges must show that these courses are part of a "career pathway" that leads directly to credentials and jobs that are in demand in the local labor market. Students who complete only the I-BEST coursework (which is typically only a few months in length) earn a certificate providing them with a slight advantage in the labor market, but most programs encourage students to continue their studies and pursue longer-term certificates, associate degrees, or bachelor's degrees. For example, one I-BEST health care program gradually transitions students from intensive basic-skills support into a regular college-level nursing program. Students start with an intensive, one-week pre-I-BEST course that introduces various health careers. They then enroll in a yearlong I-BEST program that integrates basic skill-building into college-level courses that are foundational to any health care field. Students also learn more about health career options, allowing them to choose among several different subfields. In their second year, students interested in nursing enroll in a lighter version of the I-BEST basic skills program, while completing additional nursing course prerequisites. And in their third year, students begin the nursing program without any additional support.

I-BEST shows encouraging results. Basic-skills occupational students in colleges that adopted I-BEST were about 10 percentage points more likely to earn college-level credits and 7 percentage points more likely to earn a certificate within three years than similar peers in colleges without I-BEST.[43]

However, I-BEST programs are designed for students who have decided to pursue a particular career field. Most community college students have only a general idea of their goals and interests and need help exploring and identifying their specific program of study over the first semester or two of enrollment. We have proposed that enrolling students into broad "meta-majors" constitutes the most feasible way to accomplish this goal. Of the colleges we discuss that have instituted the meta-major approach, none has yet tackled the issue of how to integrate developmental education into each meta-major.

As a step forward, however, some states and colleges have introduced different developmental mathematics pathways for students with broadly different goals, in order to avoid blocking students' progress with math courses whose content they do not need. In one example, Virginia's community colleges have developed a modular placement test system with different developmental prerequisites for students with different goals. Students seeking to enroll in science and technical fields are required to pass nine math modules, while other students only need to pass five, or in some cases, fewer. After the introduction of the new test, the share of tested students who completed college-level math within one year increased from 5 to 18 percent.[44] A second example is the Statway and Quantway models (developed by the Carnegie Foundation for the Advancement of Teaching) and the Mathways model (developed by the Dana Center at the University of Texas at Austin). These models design different pathways through mathematics developmental education for students with broadly different program objectives (for example, STEM versus liberal arts). By eliminating content that is unnecessary to the student's broad area of study, the curriculum can reduce the time students spend in developmental education and accelerate their entry into college-level math in their program of study. The approach appears to be effective: descriptive outcomes for Statway and Quantway found a substantial increase in the proportion of students who complete a college-level math course in one year.[45] The positive outcomes for these math pathways are likely due in part to the acceleration and contextualization of their developmental content, and in part to their revised approach to teaching and learning, as we will discuss below.

Engaging Students through Improved Instruction

In Chapter 3, we discussed some principles for improved instruction, which colleges could develop and implement through a collaborative inquiry process. The same general principles apply to developmental education, but two particular pedagogical concepts may be especially useful for developmental instructors: college-level rigor, and the cultivation of "productive persistence."

First, the ALP and Chabot acceleration models both use college-level materials and college-style pacing in their developmental coursework, even for students who fall far below the English developmental cutoff. At the same time, they systematically support students' ability to meet those college-level standards. This "high-expectations, high-support" approach is in stark contrast to the typical developmental curriculum and instructional style, which repeats the content and pedagogy that most students experienced in high school. In addition to the impressive quantitative results we cited above, qualitative investigations of the ALP and Chabot programs reveal that students enjoy these courses more. For example, surveys of the Community College of Baltimore County found that, in comparison to students in the traditional developmental English course, ALP students were 10 percentage points more likely to have felt positive about having taken the course, and 9 percentage points more likely to have felt that the content they learned was useful.[46]

Similarly, an in-depth qualitative study of two upper-level developmental English courses—one focused on making strong, well-supported arguments of the type expected in college-level courses, and a second focused on grammar—found that students were much more engaged in the first course.[47] That course's instructor chose to contextualize the material with the topic of sociology, drawing on readings from challenging texts such as Marx's *The Communist Manifesto,* MacLeod's *Ain't No Makin' It,* Mills's *The Power Elite,* Rose's *Lives on the Boundary,* and Kozol's *Savage Inequalities,* and with student essays focused on issues of race, class, and gender. Students in this course found it much more compelling and useful than similar students in the grammar-based course.

Second, the notion of "productive persistence," which emphasizes the value and rewards of persisting through difficult problems, is a key component of the Mathways, Statway, and Quantway reforms. The productive persistence approach is built on the work of Stanford psychologist Carol Dweck, who points out that if students initially fail at a challenge, they can come to two different types of conclusions. They may think the challenge is beyond their natural ability and therefore not worth attempting again, or they may think it will *eventually* be within their ability if they work hard enough at it. Dweck has dubbed the two approaches as a *fixed* mind-set ("I'm not smart enough for this") versus a *growth* mind-set ("I haven't figured it out yet, but maybe I will if I keep trying it in different ways").[48]

Empirical studies have demonstrated that helping students realize that their academic abilities are not fixed results in improved motivation, task persistence, and eventual success. For example, one random-assignment study that focused on helping black students understand the malleability of their academic abilities found that the students later reported enjoying and valuing academics more; they also earned higher GPAs in the next term (3.32 versus 3.05) in comparison to similar students who did not receive the intervention.[49] And in a recent random-assignment study of developmental math students, researchers assigned students to a very limited intervention: a onetime exercise, which could be completed online in approximately thirty minutes, and communicated the basic precepts of the growth mind-set approach.[50] Preliminary evidence from the first semester indicated that only 9 percent of the intervention group withdrew from their developmental math course, whereas 20 percent of the control group did so.

Connecting to College Learning in High School

In most localities the connection between community colleges and their feeder high schools are weak. As a result, it is difficult for the two sectors to align readiness standards and curricula, leading to a large volume of students who graduate from high school but are nevertheless deemed unready when they arrive at college. The Common Core State Standards (CCSS), which are currently being adopted and implemented by many states' K–12 systems, theoretically should align high school graduation and college entrance expectations. However, CCRC research suggests that the development of the CCSS was dominated by the secondary school sector, and the involvement of postsecondary representatives has been surprisingly inconsistent. It thus remains unclear how the standards will interact with college entrance standards or with assignment to developmental education.[51]

Better preparing students before they enter college, especially for low-income students, is a large and complex topic that we cannot address in a comprehensive way here. Any thorough solution to the problem would involve significant reforms within high schools, adult education programs, and other feeder organizations. Earlier in this chapter, we discussed the I-BEST program, which represents a promising collaboration between colleges and adult basic education feeder programs. In addition, below we highlight two promising strategies that colleges are undertaking in partnership with high schools and that are particularly relevant to preparing students to enter college-level programs designed according to the guided pathways model: the use of transition curricula and of dual-enrollment or "early college" high school programs. While they differ in their specific designs and targeted range of participants, the two strategies share the approach of more clearly connecting instruction to college learning requirements and content.

Transition Curricula

As states begin to implement the CCSS, they are considering how to leverage the CCSS final assessment, which high school students will take in their junior year. If a junior is not on track to be college-ready, the high school could theoretically design the student's senior year to bring him or her closer to college-ready standards.

Prior to the advent of the CCSS, several colleges had already experimented with assessing students in their junior year of high school (or even earlier). A well-studied example is the Early Assessment Program in California, in which the California State University (CSU) system collaborated with state education agencies to set standards for college readiness (which reflected CSU's entrance standards in reading, writing, and math) and to revise the California high school standardized test (CST) to measure these standards during the junior year of high school.[52] If students score below college-ready on the CST, they can take special English or math courses jointly designed by CSU faculty and California high school teachers. Thus far, the program has had a modest effect on lowering the proportion of students enrolling in remedial classes on CSU campuses.[53]

Other programs that assess students in their junior year and provide coursework in the senior year, or that assess students in their senior year and provide workshops or "boot camps" during the summer before college matriculation, typically reduce the proportion of students who are referred to developmental education when they enter college, sometimes dramatically; however, the broader effects of these programs (such as whether students enroll in and succeed at greater rates in college-level courses) tend to be small and fade over time.[54]

In 2013, CCRC embarked on a study of high school transition curricula in several states to explore the factors that seem to lead to stronger outcomes for students who are deemed underprepared in their junior year. As of this writing, our work is still preliminary, but we have observed that a strong working relationship between the K–12 and higher education sectors is critical to effective implementation and to maximizing the benefits that can derive from early college readiness assessments and transition curricula.[55] Simply putting into place a transition course, without deep dialogue and strong collaboration between the two sectors in order to help shape the student's entire senior year, is unlikely to improve student outcomes. Moreover, transition curricula may be most helpful when they help students begin the process of academic and career exploration—for example, by exploring programs or meta-majors available at local community colleges and state universities, which could allow students to transition more quickly into a specific program of study when they enter college.

Dual Enrollment and "Early College" High School

Dual-enrollment programs, which allow students to enroll in college courses while still in high school, seem to improve both college enrollment and graduation rates.[56] Qualitative evidence suggests that these courses have positive impacts because they help at least some students understand some aspects of college academic life more clearly. For example, in one CCRC study, some dual-enrollment students told researcher Melinda Karp that they learned to use different study skills in order to succeed in a "college-like" course.[57] By the end of their dual-enrollment experience, most students in Karp's study were able to identify at least some of the ways in which college is different from high school (in terms of academic experiences, expectations, and effective strategies for success), although some students were unable to do so.

As with any program, quality and implementation matter in dual-enrollment programs. But to the extent that dual enrollment helps students understand what to expect in college and how to deal with essential issues, then student success courses and other college resources can focus less on those problems and more on helping students solidify goals and develop academic plans. Furthermore, dual enrollment has the potential to increase the institutional interactions among colleges and high schools, which are critical to the development of more effective high-school-to-college transitions.

In most dual-enrollment programs, students can take any course that will fulfill their high school graduation requirements, and for which the college deems the student ready. While such "à la carte" course-taking can help students understand what might be expected of them in a typical college classroom, it may not do much to help them develop goals or enter a specific college-level program of study. With this in mind, North Carolina recently instituted a policy in which high school students can only take dual-enrollment courses that are part of a program of study.[58] One could envision a context in which high school students would only be allowed to take courses that are part of an exploratory major or meta-major, in order to ease the transition into a program of study when they arrive at college as a "real" student. Indeed, a model quite similar to this is "early college" high school, which already exists in several places across the country.

Early-college models, which tend to be built around occupational themes, provide high school students with an opportunity to take a coordinated set of college courses accompanied by systematic support services. A 2013 study of ten early-college models in North Carolina found modest positive effects for high school completion but stronger positive effects for college enrollment.[59] Indeed, 20 percent of the students in the study actually completed an associate degree by the end of high school.

The Pathways in Technology Early College High School (P-TECH) is an even more structured model that has received a great deal of attention, especially after President Barack Obama visited it in 2013. Based on a partnership between the New York City Board of Education and the City University of New York (CUNY), the P-TECH model completely integrates high school and the first two years of college into one institutional structure, with career exploration and college readiness development incorporated throughout the curriculum. The student's program of study spans six years, starting in ninth grade and ending with a CUNY-awarded associate degree in applied science. The school benefits from a significant partnership with IBM, and the company has pledged that P-TECH graduates will be first in line for job openings at IBM.

In principle, the P-TECH model has great potential; it certainly strengthens the institutional relationship between high schools and colleges, and helps establish students in a college-level program. On the other hand, it seems unlikely that a model depending on significant support from a high-profile company would be a realistic mainstream approach, and in any case the model is too new to have been evaluated. Nevertheless, this type of close institutional connection between high schools and colleges is worth studying and expanding.

In general, strengthening community college partnerships with feeder institutions has the potential to play an important role in improving the readiness of incoming college students. Given the growing consensus that every student needs some postsecondary education, it is important for high schools and colleges to help students transition from eleventh and twelfth grade to college, and from adult basic education into college-level programs. Colleges' efforts to work with their feeder high schools and adult education programs could be greatly facilitated if each college would first clarify and strengthen pathways within the institution, including creating on-ramps to college-level programs for underprepared students. Clearer paths to programs of study for new students would give high school and adult education counselors and students a better target for which to aim.

———————

While it was certainly not planned as such, the approach to remediation that characterizes the cafeteria college serves more to divert students into a developmental track than to help them enter and succeed in a college-level program of study. Thus colleges that are redesigning their programs and services according to the guided pathways model need to rethink their approach to developmental education. Rather than attempting to identify students who are not college-ready and requiring them to take long sequences of developmental courses focused on college composition and algebra, colleges can take inspiration from the models described in this chapter and consider how to integrate or otherwise connect developmental skill-building into college-level courses that are critical to broad meta-majors or to specific programs of study. In short, colleges need to redesign developmental education to be an integral part of the broader on-ramp to a program of study. As part of this process, developmental assessment and placement processes also need to be rethought and customized to help better gauge students' readiness for success in particular programs of study. Similarly, promising models for better preparing students in high school and adult basic education for college-level programs of study share the approach of more clearly connecting instruction with the requirements and content of college-level coursework in particular fields.

Thus far in the book, we have set forth our research and recommendations redesigning programs, intake and support services, instruction, and developmental education in order to help students successfully enter and complete a program of study as quickly as possible. In Chapter 5, we turn to the issue of how to engage college stakeholders in the design and implementation of these various dimensions of the guided pathways model.

5

Engaging Faculty and Staff

To develop and sustain an effective guided pathways model, a college needs a critical mass of faculty and staff excited about the process, ready to collaborate with one another to achieve larger goals, and willing to engage in inquiry, reflection, and ongoing improvement. The culture of the cafeteria college tends to discourage such deep and broad engagement, however. In this chapter, we discuss how leaders can reshape institutional culture—including a college's approach to governance, professional development, and hiring and promotion—in ways that cultivate the collaborative and inquiry-oriented spirit crucial to the success of guided pathways. We also discuss specific types of professional development that are particularly helpful to faculty and staff as they engage in the development of guided pathways.

Governance

At the typical college, the relationship between faculty and the administration tends to be a reactive one: when a new challenge faces the college, the administration develops a proposal to meet that challenge, and the faculty reacts to that proposal.[1] Similarly, other campus bodies, such as the student senate or various collective-bargaining units, may actively engage in governance only when they object to an administrative proposal. Finally, the vast majority of the college's students, faculty, and staff, who are not involved in any particular governing body, remain disconnected from institutional discussion and decision making. These members of the community may become engaged only when a crisis emerges, and their ideas and feedback come too late to affect the administration's response.

In many colleges, the disconnection between administration and faculty is exacerbated by faculty mistrust, which in turn is rooted in a sense that the administration does not understand the issues and challenges that students and faculty face every day. For example, in a qualitative study of a large community college, faculty were skeptical of the administration's ability to separate useful knowledge from educational "fads," and felt rather insulted by the administration's presumption of expertise. As one faculty member explained, administrators

> have no, or very little, experience in education; so that makes them maximally subject to fad acquisition and becoming enthusiastic about fads. . . . I don't think that most people in community college administration as a whole realize how ridiculous they look when they're talking about education from an educator's point of view. . . . If you're not overwhelmed by the bells and whistles, and you listen thoughtfully and critically, most of it is just silly. And what happens is that it puts off serious people.[2]

Similarly, at a community college in North Carolina, one faculty member told us that he joined a working group to map out default programs of study because when the administration pushed the notion of "structured pathways," he thought it "sounded suspicious." Thus, he wanted to be at the table "to find out what it was about and make sure it wasn't a bad idea."

The divide between administrative and academic governance bodies reinforces a corresponding divide between student services professionals and teaching faculty, who often report to distinct and disconnected parts of the college and rarely interact with one another. To make matters worse, the academic side of the college may itself be fragmented: faculty are frequently organized by department rather than program, with limited communication across departments. Moreover, even within a given department instructors rarely feel they can discuss curricular and instructional challenges candidly with their peers.

The status quo of fragmented governance does not lend itself to a guided pathways approach. To design educationally coherent programs that build skills across the curriculum, faculty must communicate across departments, academic and nonacademic staff need to find common ground, and the larger college should adopt a more collaborative approach to governance. As part of this process, faculty must move from a reactive to a proactive stance, and the administration will need to encourage and support this move.[3] As one faculty leader argues, such a shift could have strong positive consequences for the college as a whole:

Beyond the traditional, political senate focus of guarding against the errors and misdeeds of administrative others rests a powerful and generative faculty role—the opportunity to initiate, propose, and lead campus change. How, for example, can faculty draw on their intimate campus knowledge to propose bottom-up strategies for increasing university revenues rather than automatically lock into opposition to what they see as unfair and administrative-proposed budget cuts? Or how can faculty design ways to support and enhance administrative effectiveness, not just mechanisms for questioning or evaluating it? And equally important, how can faculty senators engage their campus constituents in the same kinds of proactive leadership?[4]

In this section, we discuss two ways in which college leaders can move toward these goals. First, leaders need to understand the concept of *relational trust* and actively cultivate this quality across the college. And second, leaders can reshape existing governance structures to focus on *practice rather than politics*.

Relational Trust

In a 2002 study of K–12 schools that strongly improved their student outcomes over time, Anthony Bryk and Barbara Schneider identified *relational trust* as a key element in each school's success.[5] The researchers defined relational trust as distinct from *organic trust,* which is granted unconditionally among those who have strong personal or moral bonds (for example, among staff members who happen to be close friends), and from *contractual trust,* which is granted on the basis of an implicit or explicit contract (for example, faculty tenure agreements). Most faculty and staff relationships occupy a middle ground between these two extremes, in which trust is granted only after strong evidence of professional competence, personal integrity, and collegial respect. Yet as Bryk and Schneider point out, in most educational settings there is little opportunity for teachers to experience the depth of one another's trustworthiness in terms of these criteria. As a result, there is only a shallow depth of trust. As the researchers put it, "Social exchanges may appear respectful, but little of consequence happens in them."[6]

Bryk and Schneider argue that a strong and deep level of relational trust is important for organizational improvement because it encourages risk taking and innovation, facilitates problem solving, and motivates teachers to work more energetically toward collective goals.[7] For example, when K–12 teachers hold a common set of goals and trust in one another to make efforts toward those goals, each individual is more likely to make contributions beyond his or her own formal job requirements, even without any other recognition or compensation.[8] Moreover, when relational trust is strong, reforms are more likely to take hold broadly and deeply across the organization, rather than being implemented superficially.[9] Bryk and Schneider's findings about relational trust in K–12 schools are relevant in higher education as well.

At many colleges, faculty and staff do not *mistrust* one another, but neither do they *trust*—primarily because they have not had the opportunity to connect with one another on a personal level, nor have they worked together on problems of mutual concern. In contrast to this neutral lack of relational trust, faculty and staff may be actively distrustful of the administration. Accordingly, for many college leaders, a critical first step in implementing a guided pathways model will be to demonstrate their own trustworthiness. Recall that when *relational* trust is in question, it is best built and reinforced through evidence of professional competence, personal integrity, and collegial respect. Leaders need to realize the importance of publicly displaying the latter two of these. Below, then, we provide additional research and examples of how leaders successfully demonstrate personal integrity and collegial respect to cultivate relational trust.

DEMONSTRATING INTEGRITY

In Bryk and Schneider's study, K–12 teachers judged one another's integrity based on whether there was "consistency between what they say and do."[10] We have observed similar dynamics at work in community colleges. For example, at Macomb Community College, a staff member told us that the culture of the institution helped support a sense of sharing and trust. When asked to provide an example, she said,

> I can at any time call the president. . . . This is a big place; we have over 20,000 students. But the president and the provost, they are just always the same. So I could go to a meeting where the community is there . . . and they are the same. It's not like they have to wear a hat that says "I'm different today." . . . And guess what? I want to do things for these types of leaders. I want to give as much as I can, because they respect me. And you will hear this across the board, I don't think I'm the only one. I've heard clerical say, "oh, just saw the president, we just had a little conversation out in the vestibule." That's how we are. . . . It's like a family environment.[11]

This sense of consistency is important because it provides evidence that the leadership does not have a hidden agenda. Similarly, in their study of universities with successful collaborative cultures, Adrianna Kezar and Jaime Lester noted that such colleges often have "open" leadership meetings.[12] Allowing any and all comers to witness the leadership's deliberations represents incontrovertible evidence that they are not plotting something in secret.

In contrast, a leader lacking integrity may pay lip service to a proposal endorsed by faculty and staff, while simultaneously working to undermine the same proposal. In such cases, a leader can hide his or her true agenda in at least two places: behind an opaque budgeting process, or within a contentious college climate. More often, leaders are simply poor communicators—they may not intend to be duplicitous, but they lack the communication skills necessary to reassure others of their good intentions. These leaders can show strong evidence of their integrity by implementing more transparent budgeting processes, while directly tackling and working through contentious campus issues related to guided pathways.

Transparent budgeting.   An opaque budgeting process may seem attractive to leaders because it allows them flexibility. Studies of organizational budgeting, for example, suggest that unit managers inflate their budgets to protect against unexpected problems (for example, the possibility that a critical project will require more staff time than anticipated). To retain these extra resources, however, managers must keep the budgeting process fairly obscure, and ensure that any leftover resources are spent by the end of the year—knowing that, otherwise, the larger organization will cut that amount from the unit's budget next year.[13] Similarly, institutional leaders may wish to keep the budget process as opaque as possible to allow maximum flexibility in case of crisis. A leader can leverage this opacity to cut resources for a service or project that he or she believes to be a low priority—even while touting it as a high priority—by claiming that sufficient resources simply were not available.

In the short term, hiding behind an opaque budget may protect leaders from faculty and staff ire. Over the long term, however, campus constituencies will begin to observe that the leadership's purported priorities do not match the institution's actual spending patterns and conclude that the administration lacks integrity. Moreover, paying lip service to an idea without creating the conditions that allow for it represents a spinelessness that members of the community find difficult to forgive.

To demonstrate that their budgetary actions match their purported priorities, leaders may wish to take a more transparent approach to budgeting, sometimes known as *strategic budgeting*. In the business research literature, the term "strategic budgeting" has two somewhat different meanings. The first meaning is quite general, implying that one's budget reflects a collaboratively created and highly actionable strategic plan. Theoretically, because faculty and staff have been involved in the process of creating a shared vision, and understand exactly how the budget reflects it, they are more likely to support difficult budget decisions.[14]

While this general style of budgeting has not been extensively studied, a second and more technical form of strategic budgeting has been the focus of several recent studies. Under this process, the organization trims each unit's budget by an agreed-upon amount and pools the trimmed money into a shared pool.[15] For *any* unit to withdraw money from the pool, the heads of *all* contributing units must meet together, consider each request in light of their shared priorities and larger vision for the organization, and mutually agree to the withdrawal. These discussions, together with the resulting transparency in spending, create stronger organizational cohesion and focus the organization more closely on its strategic priorities. For example, when a municipality in the Netherlands adopted strategic budgeting, researchers found that the process "seemed to shift the focus from *short-term justification* of the status quo to *long-term solutions.*"[16] As an additional benefit, the process seemed to result in financial savings of 24–38 percent over several years.[17]

Tackling contentious issues.   A leader can often undermine a project simply by stepping back and allowing internal disagreements among stakeholders to mire the process in argument and acrimony for years. In contrast, community college leaders who successfully help to develop guided pathways tend to demonstrate their integrity by facing up to, and helping constituents work through, such difficult disagreements and conversations.

For example, at Guilford Technical Community College in North Carolina, some faculty members began to resist the program redesign process when they realized that their own courses might not be included in the default program pathway. As one faculty member on the program redesign committee recounted, the committee's leadership did not ignore the problem or shy away from a difficult conversation. Instead, they sat down and had a face-to-face conversation, communicating that "you won't lose your job, but you will probably be teaching something different," which was "an easier pill to swallow." This faculty member added, "But it was important to educate ourselves and to have face-to-face communications with those who might be affected." After these meetings, the concerned faculty were much more supportive of the reform.

Leaders who display integrity do not "shut down" dissenters, but rather openly consider their concerns. For example, leaders of the program redesign process at Guilford Tech told us that in order to create more clearly defined program pathways for students, it was important to include all points of view. As one administrator said, "We wanted the naysayers on the program redesign committee, so they could voice their opposition out loud in public; otherwise they'd be complaining in private." A similar sentiment was expressed by the president of Davidson County Community College in North Carolina, who told us, "If you don't include everyone in the decision-making process, those who are excluded will be skeptics." According to several people we interviewed at Davidson, some faculty initially resisted the idea of redesigning program pathways, but by including them in open conversations on difficult issues, most came around and became strong supporters. Based on this experience, an associate dean of academic affairs at the college advised: "Don't shy away from uncomfortable conversations. Let them happen as early as possible so that faculty don't have the impression that the decisions have already been made."

SHOWING RESPECT FOR OTHERS

In addition to the trust-building power of integrity, Bryk and Schneider found that K–12 teachers were sensitive to whether leaders and fellow teachers showed respect for others, which was demonstrated by "a genuine sense of listening" to others' concerns, "taking others' perspectives into account," and signaling that "each person's ideas have value."[18] Across the colleges profiled in this book, we have observed three ways in which leaders showed such respect for their faculty and staff. The first is openly and respectfully addressing opposing points of view, as we have already discussed.

Second, respectful leaders consider listening a key leadership activity. For example, at Queensborough Community College, the idea of organizing programs into "academies" came from the college's president. Originally, the president proposed redesigned programs that would be highly structured and block-scheduled, with students moving through together in cohorts. This idea met strong opposition from the faculty and advisors. In response, according to an academic administrator and former faculty member, the president "led by listening":

> The president really took time to listen to faculty and advisors and understand the concerns they had. There were academy planning groups with faculty. He allowed others to have input, and the idea that emerged was different—and he himself said, and in many ways better—than the idea that the president originally proposed.[19]

Third, leaders at these colleges did not attempt to shape the redesign themselves, but rather gave stakeholders the responsibility to do so. For example, at Guilford Tech, college leaders made an explicit decision to ask faculty members rather than department chairs and deans to lead the development of the program maps. Leaders were concerned that, otherwise, there could be suspicion that administrators were driving the changes. With faculty leading the effort, according to one faculty member, "It didn't seem like a scheme." A social science faculty member told us that it was a smart strategy to start with a small group of respected faculty and let them come up with a plan for redesigning program pathways and present their ideas to peers in their departments—thus, the message was coming from peers, not from administrators.

Similarly, the faculty at Davidson reported that, in the past, decisions affecting their courses had often come down "from above" with little faculty input, which contributed to low morale.[20] When college leaders realized it was necessary to redesign program pathways, they created cross-divisional teams made up of faculty and advisors, and charged them with designing the pathways. Faculty said the program redesign process went well because they were asked to shape the outcomes, given time to discuss the redesign, and encouraged to voice their disagreements. According to a humanities professor, "One of the smartest things about the process was that it gave faculty a voice." A psychology professor said that the experience was "unusually empowering."

As leaders work to build bridges with faculty through transparency, respectful listening, and power sharing, they can also begin to reshape old governance structures or create new structures that are more focused on practice than politics.

Structures That Focus on Practice, Not Politics

In most colleges, governance meetings—including those of departments, committees, unions, and faculty senates—often become bogged down in administrative or political topics rather than tackling challenging issues of practice. For example, in their book on organizational change, Kegan and Lahey quote an administrator at a social services agency, who explained that in his leadership team meetings

> we struggled over what to put on the agenda. We tended to discuss administrative and political topics only. And one of the fundamental rules I have is that most organizations like this spend about 80 percent of their time on politics and administration and about 20 percent of their time on practice. And a kind of core rule I have is you've got to flip that. You've got to make it

80 percent of the time on practice and 20 percent of the time on politics and administration.[21]

Why are governance meetings so often focused on politics and administration? Kegan and Lahey suggest the problem is rooted in the distinction between *technical* and *adaptive* challenges. When given the choice between a cut-and-dried technical issue versus a complex and emotionally challenging adaptive issue, a group's focus invariably defaults to the technical issue, because it seems more manageable. For example, in a study of K–12 teachers who were trying to adjust to new state curricula and learning requirements, researchers found that

> collaborative time was spent resolving problems that appeared to be more immediate and feasible (i.e., following the guidelines and identifying materials) rather than working on the less agreeable and difficult issues that teachers were experiencing in using constructivist pedagogy. . . . Technical work provided a mechanism that allowed teachers to incorporate external requirements without substantially modifying their norms or beliefs.[22]

In this study, teacher groups spent the bulk of their time analyzing administrative and technical issues in intensive detail, rather than engaging in inquiry—asking bigger-picture questions, gathering information that would yield insights as to the adaptive challenges of the new curricula, and beginning to tackle those larger problems. Of course, political or technical issues were necessary to work through in some cases, but exclusive focus on these issues tended to create busy-work without pushing real progress.

How can a leader determine whether a particular governing group tends to be overly focused on administrative and technical issues? Kegan and Lahey suggest that the litmus test is participants' affect when they exit the meeting. If participants feel bored and exhausted, the group may need to rethink its purpose and agenda. If participants leave the meeting energized and ready to act on the next steps, then the group is probably doing productive and worthwhile work.[23]

To refocus governance on substantive problems of practice, should leaders work to reshape existing governing bodies, or create new ones? In most cases, leaders may wish to do both. Below, we first discuss how leaders can engage with existing groups of faculty and staff to help them understand the importance of improving current practices, and then we discuss how leaders can create new governance bodies known as *cross-functional teams,* which can more directly address the design and implementation of guided pathways.

ENGAGING EXISTING FACULTY AND STAFF GROUPS

To help faculty and staff recognize the necessity of improving curriculum, instruction, support, and intake practices, leaders can encourage these groups to discuss and connect to a commonly shared value of student success, and provide data that help them question how well current practices are living up to that value.

Connecting to values.   In their study of four universities that successfully integrated collaboration into many areas of the institution, Kezar and Lester note that colleges are ultimately driven by the personal values of the individuals who make up the organization. Thus, successful collaborative efforts do not occur because leaders change hearts and minds, but rather because they clarify and emphasize how these efforts will promote individuals' preexisting values.[24]

Happily, many of the values that faculty and staff already hold are deeply compatible with the guided pathways model. For example, Kezar and Lester find that most faculty and staff believe in being student-centered, innovative, or egalitarian; and a study of community college faculty found that most endorsed the values of learning-centered teaching without being aware of it.[25] In the latter study, only after the researcher explained how the instructors' preexisting values were consistent with learning-centered teaching were the instructors interested in hearing more about learning-centered methods.

In our experience, faculty and staff choose to work at community colleges because they believe in the open-access mission and are passionate about improving students' lives. That is, most place a strong emphasis on the value of "student success." Faculty and staff forums that allow discussion and articulation of the group's shared values can help reconnect participants to the goal of student success, and spark new thinking about how the college might better live up to it.

When clearly articulated, the shared value of student success can help motivate faculty and staff to initiate change and persevere through difficult challenges; it can also serve as a touchstone to which groups can continually return throughout the design and implementation process. As an example, we return to the case study of Macomb Community College, the Detroit-area college that worked to redesign its intake and advising process. After researchers presented dismaying information to the college's administration and advising staff regarding student frustration and confusion, Macomb's leadership convened two "work teams" that were charged with recommending changes to the process and moving forward with implementation. In initial interviews with team members before the work began, we found that they were excited about the opportunity to make real improvements to the student experience, but some felt trepidation about working with unfamiliar people from other units. Sixteen months later when we reinterviewed the team members, they were immensely pleased by how well the team had functioned. All emphasized that a key driver of their success as a team was their common goal of improving student success.[26]

Team members reported that when they disagreed, they were able to recenter the group's conversation on the question "What would be good for students?" which allowed team members to "let go" of their own preconceived notions and consider other options. Once individuals realized that other team members had valuable information about students' needs and perspectives that could strengthen the team's ability to promote student success, they were willing to listen to and integrate that information. The work teams' leaders encouraged members to focus on student success as the primary driver of the redesign and implementation—to stop focusing on "what can't be done" and instead envision the best process or product to help students achieve their goals. This values-based approach supported the team in designing and executing an ambitious agenda for meaningful change.

In the Macomb example, the shared value of student success was important to help people stay focused and work together effectively, but the initial impetus to pursue change was also spurred by something else: data.

Using data to question current practice. To highlight the gap between individuals' preexisting, value-driven goals and the reality of how well those goals and values are being met, some form of data is necessary. Without data, the gap is easy to deny or ignore. (Which, recalling Chapter 3, may be why faculty teaching under the knowledge transmission model often say that critical thinking is important, yet they assess their students using quizzes and exams that focus only on factual outcomes.)[27]

As an illustration, we turn to Davidson County Community College. Although college leaders believed that ill-defined transfer pathways were posing a barrier to student progress, faculty in liberal arts and other transfer programs were not convinced. At an initial meeting of a faculty committee that had been asked to streamline associate of arts programs to be more clearly aligned with university transfer requirements, some faculty resisted based on their deeply held value of student exploration and freedom. They argued that students should be allowed to choose from among a wide array of courses to explore and develop a range of ideas and interests. To highlight the value of exploration, one longtime faculty member recounted how she decided to become an English professor because of a positive experience in a Romantic poetry course in college. Others argued that unfettered exploration did not pose a barrier to student success; as evidence, they cited a statewide articulation agreement established in the 1990s, which guaranteed the transfer of courses in a forty-two-credit general education core curriculum from the state's community colleges to the University of North Carolina universities. Given that most of the popular courses at the community college fell within the bounds of that articulation agreement, they felt it was unlikely students were taking courses that would not transfer to their chosen destination.

To clarify the reality of the situation, the group was presented data from a series of student focus groups, which were conducted at their college and other community colleges in the North Carolina system. Focus-group students expressed confusion and frustration over transfer requirements and the transfer process, and said that being in a program with a well-defined pathway would improve their chances of completing an associate degree and transferring. To reinforce the message, the group reviewed a spreadsheet compiled by faculty members at nearby Guilford Technical Community College. The spreadsheet showed that of all the general education courses offered by Guilford Tech (which were generally the same as those offered by Davidson County), only one course—freshman composition—was accepted at all sixteen University of North Carolina institutions for core general education credit, as opposed to elective credit. Thus, depending on the university and the program within it, some transfer students might be required to retake many of the courses they had already completed at the community college to earn credit toward a bachelor's degree in their major.

By the end of the meeting, one faculty member who had strongly endorsed the value of exploration exclaimed, "Oh my god, I've been misadvising my students all these years!" In essence, faculty realized that their deeply held value was not about exploration per se; it was about helping students succeed in their further studies as well as in their larger lives. While exploration is certainly a component of that success and should be built into the student experience, it is not the only component of student success: guidance and clarity are also vital. Three months later, interviews with group members indicated that, having gone through the exercise of mapping out default paths for students in associate degree programs, the group now believed in the usefulness of creating more-structured pathways and felt their students would benefit when the maps were implemented in the coming fall.

At Guilford Tech, the transfer data highlighted the pathway problem in ways that connected to the faculty's sense of "what matters," and thus motivated efforts to address the problem. According to a biology faculty member, "Once departments were able to visualize the [course articulation] problem in the spreadsheet created by the program redesign committee, other faculty were able to see the problems." What made this piece of evidence so compelling was it showed that a system many assumed was working—in part because it had the backing of state law—was in fact not operating as intended, and students were being harmed as a result.

The process of articulating shared values, and using data to identify where and how the college is not living up to those values, will tend to dispose faculty and staff groups more positively toward the notion of guided pathways. Yet to move forward with a guided pathways approach, it will be insufficient merely to persuade these groups, or even to reshape their work to focus more strongly on practices that improve student success. Regardless of a given group's effectiveness within its own area of responsibility and expertise, each existing governance group operates within an organizational silo. In contrast, the design and implementation of guided pathways must draw on expertise from a diverse array of roles and perspectives across the organization. Accordingly, most community colleges implementing guided pathways have begun the process by creating an additional governing structure known as the cross-functional team.

CREATING CROSS-FUNCTIONAL TEAMS

Cross-functional teams are a very popular approach in industry; they are formed for a limited time to bring together people with different areas of expertise, and who report to different areas of the organization, to create more innovative and integrated products and solutions.[28] In community colleges embarking on guided pathways, cross-functional teams typically include a mix of faculty and professional staff from across the organization, and serve as a de facto additional governing body during their limited life span (in most of the community colleges implementing redesigns, cross-functional teams seem to last for one, two, or three years). Unlike a standing committee, cross-functional teams have a clear set of inquiry-driven goals to accomplish within a specified time frame.

Numerous examples of cross-functional teams have appeared thus far in the book. All of the colleges that we have described that are implementing elements of the guided pathways model are using cross-functional teams that are collaboratively designing new program pathways. These include course design teams, which bring together the expertise of faculty and professional staff to create more innovative methods of teaching and learning. And we have described Macomb Community College's work teams and their shared value of student success. In general, all of these cross-functional teams have yielded the additional benefit of building relational trust across departments and divisions.

As a more specific example, at Sinclair Community College in Ohio, a psychology professor and an academic advisor co-led the process of helping each academic department develop default curriculum maps for its programs of study. The leaders assigned an advisor to work with each department—a new strategy, given that faculty and advisors had not worked closely together before. According to the faculty co-leader,

> It is imperative to bring student services staff and faculty together any chance you get. We've existed in silos for too long. . . . As a faculty member, understanding what advisors do was important. I'm now more appreciative and empathic about what they do. Now I'm thinking more from the advisor viewpoint. This is also true for advisors who can see things from the faculty viewpoint more clearly now. It's amazing what great work can come from putting faculty and staff together.[29]

The advisor co-leader agreed: "It's not us versus them now; it is both of us working together to improve student completion."

In order for a cross-functional team to have a positive impact on the organization, the team must be empowered to make decisions that will be accepted and supported by the administration.[30] Based on our observations of the colleges we describe in these pages, leaders felt most comfortable turning over decision-making power to cross-functional teams when the team's charter was based on a well-understood and generally endorsed set of boundaries. For example, Macomb's cross-functional teams were formed to redesign the college's intake and advising process—but only after a full year of collaborating with CCRC to investigate and understand the problem, generate a broad set of recommendations, and gather feedback on those recommendations. The final versions of the broad recommendations set the boundaries for the team's work, and the team was empowered to imagine and implement the best possible solutions within those boundaries. This strategy accords with effective practices in industry: when team members are not "spinning their wheels" about the boundaries of their work, they are able to work more efficiently and effectively within those boundaries.[31] They can also be confident that, if the team creates a thoughtful best-case solution, senior leadership will indeed support its implementation.

In addition, to operate successfully and build relational trust, cross-functional teams require an adept team leader who helps the team set goals and stay on track, while facilitating an environment of cooperation. We discuss this issue, as well as other professional development needs of cross-functional teams, in the next section.[32]

Professional Development

Professional development activities at colleges and universities are typically designed to enhance the skills and knowledge of individual full-time faculty and staff, rather than to support collective efforts to strengthen programs and processes.[33] For example, we have argued that pedagogical development activities typically consist of top-down, one-time workshops that are disconnected from faculty experiences in the classroom and that faculty generally regard as a waste of time. We suggested that colleges instead adopt a professional development approach rooted in "collaborative inquiry," in which faculty work together to identify challenging problems of practice, gather data that help them reexamine their assumptions and generate new insights, apply these insights to create potential solutions, and experiment with those solutions in the classroom.

A similar spirit of collaborative inquiry is necessary for cross-functional teams to design high-quality guided pathways, for rank-and-file faculty and staff to implement pathway elements successfully within their own area of responsibility, and for the college as a whole to continuously assess and improve its guided pathways model. The colleges appearing in this book that are implementing elements of the guided pathways model have all treated inquiry as a foundational activity of each cross-functional team, and have used professional development resources to ensure that the team's process of inquiry and design is both productive and high-quality. Beyond the professional development of cross-functional team members, guided pathways colleges also need to ensure that professional development is strategically designed to support faculty and staff as they work to implement and improve the guided pathways elements that fall within their own daily work.

In the sections below, we first discuss three areas of professional development that are critical to the success of guided pathways, and next we discuss how colleges can repurpose existing time and resources to support these development activities.

Critical Areas of Development

Based on the experiences of the colleges profiled in this book, we have identified three professional development areas that are useful to faculty and staff working to improve programs and instruction: team facilitation, advising, and assessment and inquiry strategies.

First, team facilitation is critical to the success of cross-functional teams and collaborative inquiry groups because collaboration can initially be quite difficult. For example, in a qualitative study of cross-functional teams in technology organizations, researchers summarized their findings thus: "We find that building collaborative teams, even among highly qualified and technically savvy people, is challenging because it requires participants to shed dated views, unlearn old habits, develop new theories of action, and adopt new behaviors."[34]

In order for a collaborative team to operate successfully and have a positive impact, the team needs at least one individual who is adept at facilitating an environment of cooperation, and who can help the team explore innovative ideas, work through disagreements, and make decisions.[35] If the team has a formal leader, this individual often takes on that role; however, in faculty teams, it is more common for a faculty peer to serve as facilitator—a strategy that is effective only if the person is well trained and comfortable in the role.[36] Miami Dade College recognized the importance of facilitation as it began the process of redesigning its program pathways. The college engaged Public Agenda, a firm with experience in engagement and change management, to train members of the many teams involved in the college's multiple interrelated initiatives. Public Agenda staff provided advice and hands-on practice in how to facilitate effective meetings and frame difficult discussions, which participants found highly useful.

Second, advising skills are an important area of development for both faculty and staff. Among the colleges with which we work, several decided to create a formal role for faculty in the academic advising process, by shifting students from generalist professional advisors to discipline-specific faculty advisors at a given milestone in the student's studies. To serve as effective advisors, faculty needed training in how to use the college's advising software and systems, as well as in how to access and understand program-specific degree and transfer pathway requirements. To prepare program faculty and academic program staff to take on specialized advising roles, Miami Dade college provided six hours of training that included role-playing in situations that participants would likely encounter with students. Prospective faculty advisors also spent two to four hours shadowing student services professionals who would serve as liaisons to their program.

If faculty members take on program-specific advising roles, professional generalist advisors can focus more strongly on helping new students understand the qualities, costs, and benefits of the college's programs of study, as well as on explicitly teaching students how to make informed academic decisions. This "advising as teaching" approach represents the ideal of most advisors; however, many have not had the opportunity to practice this ideal in their everyday work. Accordingly, advisors may benefit from collaborative inquiry groups that focus on improving their own teaching practice.

Finally, instructional faculty participating in inquiry groups need principles and examples that will help them design assessments to measure complex learning outcomes (such as critical thinking), and that will help them think through how to use the results of learning assessments to improve instruction. For example, as part of its "academies," Queensborough Community College encouraged instructors to assess more complex forms of student learning and use the results to inform instructional improvement. To support faculty in this effort, the college provided extensive training on assessment and inquiry methods through the college's Center for Teaching and Learning.[37]

Faculty peer groups can be quite effective in providing support to one another as they work to improve their own assessments, explore how the assessments reflect students' thinking, and generate insights about potential instructional activities that might influence that thinking. If no members of the group have participated in such an inquiry process before, however, they may not be sure where to begin. As a result, the group may quickly devolve into sharing ideas or strategies without grounding the discussion in concrete practice. While faculty find these freewheeling discussions interesting, they rarely change the group members' classroom teaching.[38] To help jump-start an effective inquiry process, several groups have found it helpful to begin with a highly structured, step-by-step method of inquiry such as "Japanese lesson study."[39] Under the lesson study method, faculty who teach sections of the same course collaborate on a new lesson plan. One member of the team then teaches the lesson, while the other members observe. After seeing students' reactions and analyzing student work, the group discusses how the lesson went and revises it, and then a second teacher implements the lesson and brings back input on how the revision fared in the classroom. While the structured nature of lesson study may be too constraining for some groups, others have found the structure comforting as they venture into risky new territory.

It is not only faculty inquiry groups that need help with inquiry and assessment processes; cross-functional teams involved in pathway redesign also need data to help them understand the problems they are facing, generate ideas, and evaluate the effectiveness of those ideas in practice. As part of Miami Dade's program redesign process, the college provided training to implementation teams on topics such as what questions to ask as part of an effective evaluation, and how to develop an evaluation plan. To assist with ongoing learning, the college also embedded institutional researchers into each major implementation team to help members evaluate the team's progress and impact.

Overall, faculty and staff are likely to be resistant to professional development unless they perceive a need for it as they struggle with new tasks, and unless the training or support is contextualized to the particular tasks they are attempting. To make the training less top-down and more classroom-applicable, some colleges eschew external consultants and instead rely on local faculty or staff who have experience in the given area of desired development. Kezar and Lester note that the institutions they studied "found that [practices involving] tapping the local expertise of pioneering collaborators, who understood the organizational contexts and how collaboration unfolds on campus, were the most successful approaches to learning."[40] Indeed, they argue that "one of the most important roles of change agents and senior executives is to monitor and be aware of various collaborative projects and to know when ones have gone particularly well. These projects are sources of learning for the campus."[41]

Similarly, at Virginia Wesleyan College, leaders of a college-wide effort to integrate critical thinking into the classroom reported that outside experts were not always helpful:

> Among our [initial] six sessions, two featured outside experts. Both offered worthwhile know-how, the one on inspiring and evaluating student class participation, the other on constructing and employing evaluative rubrics. Yet both also tended to presume too little expertise among our own faculty.... Subsequently, we developed an annual series of spring workshops based on issues that arose in the fall delivery of the course and in previous workshops. Instead of the big-school model in which professionals affiliated with an institutional teaching center design and facilitate workshops, we tapped primarily our own faculty to lead their peers. Our faculty led sessions on such topics as developmental learning theory, Bloom's taxonomy, teaching critical reading practices, developing problem-based learning assignments, using journal writing to promote critical reflection, teaching without talking, creating service learning projects, and structuring the exploration of academic majors as mini research projects.[42]

In general, faculty are more interested in learning from their peers rather than from a consultant;[43] however, research from the K–12 sector also cautions that outside expertise may still occasionally be necessary. In particular, K–12 teachers typically do not have experience with research, and thus one review found that when professional development on inquiry methods was conducted in-house, "school staff members paid lip service to the use of research" and "were more interested in designs that drew on research about practices that they already felt were 'good' than in designs that were producing results."[44] Of course, in the college context, many faculty members will have deep expertise in both formal research and informal classroom inquiry methods; however, the K–12 experience illustrates the point that organizations should remain open to bringing in the occasional outside experts. Indeed, the leaders from Virginia Wesleyan added,

> Although we have especially depended on in-house expertise, we have also continued to benefit from the occasional guest expert whose outside experience could contribute perspectives we could not supply as well on our own. We have been careful, however, to seek outside expertise only where it answered an authentic faculty need and from experts who could promise to engage our faculty in an active and collaborative workshop process.[45]

Of course, professional development is expensive. If it is designed and delivered by a third party, the college incurs out-of-pocket costs; but even if it is designed and delivered internally, the college must bear the costs of faculty and staff time. In the next section, we discuss how colleges might find the time and resources necessary to support critical development activities.

Time and Resources

Community college faculty and staff already feel overworked and stretched too thin; adding more hours to their working days to incorporate the demands of cross-functional teamwork, collaborative inquiry activities, and additional professional development seems impossible. The good news is that such activities help faculty and staff find *more* time in their day, but the bad news is that this time-saving process unfolds over the long term. Thus, in the short-term, colleges may need to find resources to start the process.

THE LONG-TERM PAYOFF IN TIME AND ENTHUSIASM

While the activities that contribute to the development and implementation of guided pathways are time-consuming and sound potentially exhausting, paradoxically those who engage in such activities begin to feel reenergized and find that previously existing feelings of exhaustion and burnout fade away. This phenomenon has been observed in several studies of faculty inquiry, and we heard similar messages from faculty and staff in the community colleges discussed in this book.[46] The same paradox has been observed in the business world. In a study of employees at thirty-five companies, researchers found that many employees were working long hours and felt exhausted, yet at the same time felt underutilized.[47] Why? Because their skills, ideas, and interests were being ignored by management. These employees worked to carry out instructions from above, and although they had ideas about how to make their own work more effective and improve the company, the leadership seemed entirely uninterested in those ideas. In such companies, researchers found that employers were taking advantage of only 48 percent of their employees' true capacities. In contrast, when companies recognized the value of their employees' ideas and put them into practice, employees became twice as productive—and far from feeling exhausted, they felt exhilarated. Given the research on motivation, this finding is not at all surprising: when companies repress employee autonomy, their workers feel depressed and depleted, but when companies encourage autonomy, people feel motivated and even excited by their work.[48]

Similarly, Kegan and Lahey discuss the case study of a faculty member who felt overworked and burned out. After reexamining her priorities and removing less-important activities from her plate (such as attending mind-numbing departmental meetings that focused primarily on technical, political, and administrative issues), she was able to pursue more challenging and risky—but also more personally fulfilling—projects. Interestingly, she worked longer and harder than before; yet, as she told the researchers,

> If you knew me even a few years ago you'd understand that this is a complete turnaround. Instead of being miserable and grumpy all the time, I am excited. And it has a positive impact on the rest of my life. I eat better, I exercise. Everything has fallen into place.[49]

However, such effects are felt only *after* faculty and staff begin to invest time in activities such as collaborative inquiry groups. Those who have not embarked on these activities have not yet felt these emotional impacts, and therefore are likely to remain skeptical that they are worth the additional time and effort. Accordingly, colleges need to find ways to support the initial investment of time and energy required. We suggest that before expending new resources in this regard, colleges reexamine existing time and resources to determine whether they can be usefully repurposed to better support guided pathways activities.

REPURPOSING TIME AND RESOURCES

As we discussed earlier in this chapter, valuable faculty and staff time is often wasted in unproductive meetings or workshops. We provided a rule of thumb for determining whether this time could or should be repurposed: do participants leave the meeting feeling drained and annoyed, or energized and excited to move forward?

In the professional development arena, one pocket of time that may be ripe for repurposing are "flex days"—time devoted to professional development in which faculty are required to participate. In his book on developmental education in California community colleges, Norton Grubb notes that most of these colleges required a day or two of professional development each semester, but that nobody thought these days were particularly effective. Grubb quotes one instructor: "Usually, people find the flextime activity just a waste of time. So, I would have to say that, professionally— all around from every possible angle—the school actually has no professional encouragement. I haven't gleaned anything from [this college] whatsoever."[50]

In a few departments within a few colleges, however, flex days were useful. That was because the department had decided to repurpose the time, as Grubb put it, to support "collective discussions of teaching approaches, assessments, alignment, and curriculum development," which helped faculty move forward with improvements to their pedagogy.[51]

A few flex days each semester are insufficient to provide faculty and staff with the logistical and technical support they need to effectively implement the guided pathways elements discussed in this book. But other pockets of time may be available for repurposing, such as those spent in faculty committee and departmental meetings. To identify these pockets, departmental chairs and administrative leaders might consider surveying faculty and staff about the activities that take up their time, and ask respondents to rate the usefulness of each activity for improving their own practice.

In addition to repurposing time, colleges can also consider how to repurpose existing money. All colleges have a pool of money dedicated to professional development, but much of this money is spent on a myriad of individual activities that may or may not relate to student success. For example, a physics instructor might attend a conference to learn about the latest research in her field, but this new knowledge may not directly influence her teaching or the pedagogical approaches of her larger program. Hence, colleges might consider redirecting at least some resources currently spent on individual professional development toward collaborative efforts.

One step in this direction would be to set aside professional development funds only to groups of faculty and staff rather than to individual faculty members, based on proposals for collaborative work to improve programs and instruction. For example, the physics department might strategically select a set of conferences, each with a specific purpose related to improving teaching and learning (for example, one faculty member may attend a scientific conference to keep tabs on new cutting-edge research findings, while another attends a practitioner's conference to learn about new pedagogical techniques in the field). To be funded, such a proposal would build in a mechanism for attendees to share their learning among members of the department, including discussing how faculty might build that learning into their teaching practice.

By repurposing existing time and money, leaders can provide most faculty and staff with sufficient resources to engage in guided pathways activities. However, faculty and staff who are leading such activities—including the chairs of cross-functional teams and the facilitators of collaborative inquiry groups—will need to devote much more time to these activities. For faculty who lead such work, departments should consider reducing their teaching loads by at least one course per year; while for staff leaders, some duties should be reassigned to allow for their full participation.

Finally, leaders can help faculty and staff reorganize their own time in more effective and efficient ways by emphasizing activities related to key institutional priorities, while deemphasizing other activities. In order to communicate and reinforce this emphasis, colleges need to reexamine their hiring, promotion, and recognition practices.

Hiring, Promotion, and Recognition

When it comes to hiring, promotion, and other forms of recognition, most colleges dole out rewards for efforts to reach or maintain individual goals. For example, at a given college, a faculty member may be assured of tenure if he or she is reasonably well liked by departmental colleagues, has student course evaluation ratings that are consistently above 3.5 or 4.0 on a 5.0-point scale, and has published an acceptable number of academic articles.

Yet in order to design, implement, and continuously improve a guided pathways approach to education, a college must encourage faculty and staff to engage in *collaborative* efforts to improve student pathways, using inquiry-based approaches to move forward into unknown territory and toward goals that may change. To create incentives for faculty and staff to engage in this difficult and challenging—even if intrinsically rewarding—work, colleges need to rethink their hiring, promotion, and recognition processes. In particular, institutional leaders need to reconsider incentive processes for part-time faculty and staff, who in many community colleges constitute a majority of the campus constituency.

Collaboration and Inquiry

To revise hiring and promotion processes in ways that will support guided pathways, the first step is for academic and professional units to redesign their own job descriptions and consider how they can be refined to emphasize within- and across-unit collaboration and inquiry.[52]

An example from Valencia College, a community college in Florida, illustrates how a college can incorporate inquiry into its faculty hiring and tenure process.[53] The process began in the late 1990s with a college-wide examination of student learning problems, which led the broad majority of faculty to the conclusion that inquiry was a key leverage point to improve student learning, and that the tenure process might need revision in order to focus it more squarely on inquiry. In 2000, the college appointed a five-member multidisciplinary faculty team to design the new tenure process. As a report on the process describes,

> The design team began its work by discussing the goals of the tenure process, agreeing that preparation for tenure should be a welcoming induction that was supportive rather than adversarial, should invite growth, and should be rooted in the idea that candidates who care about improving their teaching should be given tenure. The design team did not work alone in fleshing out these ideas. To determine how the final tenure decisions would be made, the team helped organize a tenure summit, led by the Faculty Council president.[54]

Today, Valencia's tenure process is designed around a three-year individual learning plan, which is designed to help each faculty member develop teaching excellence. Every learning plan includes at least one "action research project," a formal version of the inquiry process we discussed in Chapter 3. Tenure-track faculty who clearly demonstrate a commitment to improving their teaching are awarded tenure. Part-time adjunct faculty are also given the opportunity to create individual learning plans and conduct action research projects, and those who do so strengthen their probability of being hired into a full-time position. Indeed, 60 percent of Valencia's tenured hires have come from the ranks of the college's own part-time faculty.[55]

In order to incorporate within- and across-unit collaboration into the incentive structure, colleges may wish to require faculty and staff to engage in some type of collaborative service as part of their job descriptions. At most colleges, full-time instructional faculty are already expected to participate in departmental service, including attending regular departmental meetings. Converting some departmental meetings into practice-based inquiry sessions that focus on intradepartmental improvement of curriculum and instruction would certainly be helpful; beyond that, however, departmental faculty need incentives and support to collaborate with colleagues in other units and departments. For example, contracts could allow faculty temporary release from intradepartmental service to join cross-functional teams.

More broadly, job descriptions might include cross-departmental collaboration as a baseline expectation for both faculty and staff. Such formal expectations could encourage faculty-staff collaborations such as a project at Virginia Commonwealth University, where English faculty collaborated with student services staff to create fifteen prompts for reflective essays, which were assigned weekly in every freshman English class. Prompts dealt with students' adjustment issues, learning experiences, and other facets of college life. Student services staff worked with faculty to code over 10,000 individual essays, the results of which helped the college better understand the personal, social, and academic struggles of first-semester students, and triggered a variety of changes to the university's approach— including the creation of the position of an associate dean for student affairs who, among other things, is responsible for helping student affairs and academic faculty work more closely together.[56]

To the extent that a college's current tenure process emphasizes research, faculty may also consider revising the description of research to encourage classroom-based, inquiry-oriented research, as well as community-based research that is integrated with service learning activities.[57] In general, campus values of collaboration, inquiry, and student success should blend with academic tenure and professional promotion requirements, rather than clashing with them.

Finally, in addition to formal hiring and review processes, colleges can also communicate the importance of collaboration and inquiry by recognizing faculty and staff who are exemplars in each area. When the recognition is formal—for example, awards for individual teaching excellence, or awards for an individual program or department's efforts at improvement—it can sometimes discourage others who believe that the honored individual is "naturally talented" and cannot realistically be emulated. To avoid this mind-set, it can be helpful for honorees to publicly discuss their own struggles and challenges along the path toward excellence.[58] Recognition can also be informal. For example, the president of Montgomery County Community College in Pennsylvania takes the time to have lunch with different groups of faculty who are working together on teaching and learning issues. These types of respect, recognition, and integration are particularly important to extend to part-time and adjunct faculty.

Roles of Adjunct Faculty and Staff

Part-time faculty now make up the majority of faculty appointments at community colleges.[59] In addition, in our visits to colleges, we have observed that most rely heavily on part-time advisors during peak enrollment periods. If part-time faculty and staff are not involved in efforts to design and improve guided pathways, they cannot be expected to fully understand and successfully implement the underlying principles in their own work. It seems obvious, then, that part-timers should be included in the college's collaborative inquiry process. Yet at some colleges, part-time faculty and staff are isolated and poorly incentivized to participate in such processes.

In a 2013 study of part-time and full-time adjunct faculty's working conditions in four-year institutions, Kezar found that departments varied in their treatment of adjuncts along a continuum from destructive or neutral to inclusive or learning-oriented.[60] Of the twenty-five departments Kezar examined, 64 percent fell into either the "destructive" or "neutral" categories, in which adjunct faculty were explicitly disrespected or simply ignored. In both cultures, adjuncts were not recognized as faculty on websites and other official documents; they were excluded from departmental meetings, professional development, and governance; they received no orientation, mentoring, serious evaluation, or direction; their classes were scheduled without giving them adequate time to prepare; and they often had no place to store student files or meet with students. As a result, adjunct turnover was high. Moreover, adjuncts were frustrated and had no particular loyalty to the institution, were unwilling (and indeed unable) to advise students, were unwilling to hold office hours unless they were paid for them, were unsure how to connect their course to the larger curriculum, and had little opportunity to improve their own teaching.

Kezar's qualitative findings accord with research in industry, which indicates that part-time knowledge workers are more likely to act in ways that support organizational functioning when they have close relationships with peers inside the organization.[61] If the typical departmental attitude toward adjuncts is indeed one of isolation or outright disrespect, that might explain why the larger literature finds that adjuncts hold fewer office hours, use less innovative teaching methods, and are less able to advise their students—and, therefore, why part-time adjunct teaching is correlated with less-positive student outcomes.[62]

In contrast, some departments in Kezar's study openly welcomed adjuncts and respected their contributions. In "inclusive" cultures, adjuncts were included in meetings and governance, were treated as professional peers, and had courses scheduled reasonably far in advance. Departmental chairs also typically made an effort to improve adjuncts' salaries and benefits, although these perks were still well below the level of their tenure-track peers. Departments with "learning-oriented" cultures were similarly inclusive, but also emphasized professional development, mentoring, and useful evaluation processes for adjuncts. For example, adjuncts teaching the same course sometimes shared office space, allowing them to support and learn from each other. In inclusive and learning cultures, adjuncts were more attached to the institution, their colleagues, and their students. They were willing to advise students and conduct office hours even without additional pay, to participate in professional development, and to talk with their colleagues about teaching. Moreover, adjunct turnover was low, allowing the time and opportunity for ongoing professional development.

The research literature on adjunct faculty suggests that if colleges want to improve teaching and learning, they cannot afford to exclude adjuncts from the process. Kezar's study also suggests that the leverage point of faculty cultures lies within individual departments, and is deeply influenced by the department chair. Accordingly, if the larger institution wishes to be inclusive and respectful of adjunct faculty, then the college's leadership needs to work with departmental chairs to develop policies for part-time faculty employment. These policies might indicate the resources to which adjunct faculty are entitled (including office space, administrative support staff, and professional development), require the scheduling of courses reasonably far in advance, and outline a path to promotion that emphasizes collaborative, inquiry-based professional development and teaching improvement. For example, one community college with which we work is considering creating a new category of "associate adjunct" for both part-time and full-time non-tenure-track faculty, which would include a pay raise and provide recognition for improvements in teaching and learning. A recent study of adjunct faculty at Northwestern University suggests this tactic may be a good one. In contrast to studies showing that adjuncts negatively affect student learning, this study found more positive student outcomes for adjunct compared to tenure-track lecturers—but the majority of adjuncts at Northwestern are long-term, full-time lecturers who have a career ladder at the university.[63] In the wake of the Affordable Care Act, we have seen some colleges convert well-respected part-time faculty into full-time non-tenure-track faculty; but other colleges are cutting adjuncts' hours to avoid increased health care costs.[64] We suspect that the return on investment to the successful implementation of guided pathways and related improvements in student outcomes will be much stronger for colleges that pursue the former tactic.

While several studies have exposed the plight of part-time and non-tenure-track faculty, we have little hard data on adjunct advisors and other part-time student services professionals, who are frequently hired as temporary workers during peak registration periods. In CCRC's recent work on electronic advising systems, we have informally observed that part-time advisors have little understanding of the college's programs, curricula, and transfer options. It is, of course, not realistic to expect that temporary workers would have a clear or nuanced understanding of these larger processes, even if a given worker were rehired every semester. Yet without such an understanding, part-time workers can function only as registration assistants, who help students select a slate of courses based solely on requirements laid out in the catalog, or who help students navigate the online registration system. While this type of assistance is certainly helpful to confused students—particularly within the context of cafeteria-style program and course offerings—it does not contribute to the ultimate goal of teaching students how to make well-informed academic decisions. As colleges shift toward clearer program pathways, course maps, and e-advising systems, the need for minimally trained registration assistants should dwindle. Accordingly, colleges may be able to convert several part-time positions into a new full-time advisor, who could more actively engage in and support the college's guided pathways approach.

In this chapter, we have suggested a variety of ways in which leaders can engage faculty and staff in the design and implementation of guided pathways. In general, we have attempted to outline approaches that are no-cost or low-cost, allowing colleges to absorb much of the costs of guided pathways into their existing budgets. However, as we have pointed out, some elements of the guided pathways model may demand new resources. In Chapter 6, we discuss the types and sizes of resources that are typically required, and how colleges can think through the process of acquiring and deploying these resources.

6

The Economics of College Redesign

I N REDESIGNING programs and services according to the guided pathways model, colleges are seeking to improve the rates at which students persist and complete programs, while preserving access and quality. What implications does such a redesign have for the economics of a community college education?

This question is a critical one, as the high cost of college is believed to be a growing barrier to completion for many students. Governors and state legislatures are calling for public colleges to provide cheaper associate and bachelor's degree programs; at the same time, higher education commentators posit that the high cost of college is opening the door to lower-cost online providers that are seeking to "disrupt" postsecondary education and fundamentally reshape the sector.[1]

The traditional community college—the cafeteria college—has always been sensitive to costs; indeed, community colleges are considered the low-cost alternatives to state universities. To keep costs under control, community college administrators and policymakers have sought to minimize the *cost per student in a given course or semester,* which in turn minimizes the amount of tuition and public subsidies necessary to fund student enrollment. In contrast, the guided pathways model focuses on the *cost per high-quality completion.* In economics, the costs or expenditures per desired outcome can also be defined as efficiency. If completion of a credential is the desired outcome of postsecondary education, then cost per successful completion can be considered a measure of efficiency. In this chapter, we argue that the drive to reduce the cost of an immediate outcome—enrollment—has paradoxically led to an increase in the cost of the desired longer-term outcome—completing a high-quality credential that enables students to advance in the labor market and pursue further education. In particular, existing state and federal funding formulas make it difficult for colleges to make the necessary investments to retain students over time and thereby increase the proportion of those who earn high-quality credentials.

Thus, guided-pathway reforms raise important questions about community college finances and funding. For example, what are the initial and ongoing operating costs of moving from a self-service cafeteria model to a guided pathways model? What are the implications of such reforms for college affordability? Is the guided pathways approach economically sustainable? How should public funding of two-year and four-year colleges change to motivate them to move toward guided pathways? And if new investments are indeed needed, are they justified by the expected returns?

In this chapter, we examine the economic implications of the guided pathways approach. We begin by exploring how the cafeteria college has successfully sought to cut the cost of enrolling a student each semester, but how this strategy at the same time has hurt student outcomes. We then discuss how efforts to improve student completion affect institutional operating costs as well as revenue and cost per completion (or efficiency). We also examine the up-front or transitional investments that may be required to successfully implement guided pathways within a college. Next, we explore the potential of state policy to motivate colleges to change their practices. And, finally, given the costs required to strengthen pathways to success for students, we ask whether such reforms are worth the student and taxpayer investments. In particular, we contrast the evidence for a guided pathways investment against that of a competing innovation—the "unbundled" approach of new delivery models to teaching and learning, which some see as the future of higher education.[2]

The Cafeteria College: Affordable . . . But at What Cost?

Community colleges are designed to provide broad access to higher education, and thus state legislators and college administrators have worked to keep these colleges' costs low. In contrast to selective four-year colleges, many of which charge extremely high tuition, community colleges have maintained low tuition. The average tuition and fees for a full-time student at a community college in the United States totaled just $3,264 per year in 2013–2014.[3] Moreover, after taking into account financial aid from all sources, the average full-time community college student *received* $1,550 over and above the costs of tuition and fees (to cover the costs of college-related expenses).[4] As a result of community colleges' low tuition, their students take on a relatively low debt burden. Sampled at a single point in time, only 30 percent of community college students have any student loans, and only 2 percent of students at community colleges default on student loans within six years of starting their studies, compared to a default rate of 21 percent for students at for-profit two-year institutions.[5] Thus, while policymakers and middle-class parents fret over the explosion in costs in higher education generally, they may fail to notice that community colleges remain a remarkable bargain.

Nevertheless, community colleges have come under increasing financial pressure over the past two decades as state appropriations for higher education have declined—both as a share of total revenues, and in absolute terms. Measured in constant dollars, state appropriations per full-time student were 25 percent lower in 2009 than in 1999.[6] To keep tuition and fees low in the face of funding cuts, community colleges have reduced their operating costs. Between 2000 and 2010, community colleges cut per-student spending by over 9 percent, and expenditures on instruction by nearly 11 percent.[7] Despite these cost-saving efforts, cuts in state funding resulted in an average increase in community college tuition and fees of over 40 percent (approximately $1,000) between 2002–2003 and 2012–2013, although increases in federal financial aid offset that increase for low-income students.[8]

Unfortunately, research suggests that two primary ways community colleges have reduced costs—relying on part-time instructors and increasing student-to-faculty ratios—have hurt completion rates and may also have reduced the quality of the education provided. Several studies have shown that greater reliance on adjunct faculty lowers student completion and transfer rates at both two- and four-year institutions.[9] This research does not suggest that adjunct instructors are inferior teachers per se; indeed, adjuncts who are strongly connected to the labor market may be superior instructors for some occupational areas. However, adjunct instructors are paid only to teach courses, not to assist students outside the classroom or participate in program development. Thus, colleges that rely heavily on part-time instructors have fewer full-time faculty who can focus on improving programs and instruction.

A similar logic applies to increases in student-to-faculty ratios: one study estimated that every 1-percentage-point increase in the ratio would decrease community college degree completion rates by half a percentage point.[10] Over time, increasing student-to-faculty ratios may also reduce the quality of the instructor pool.[11] Thus, short-term cost reductions would be offset by long-term declines in quality.

A third cost-cutting strategy, expanding fully online instruction (as opposed to hybrid-online or technology-enhanced face-to-face instruction), also undercuts community college students' academic success and progression (as we showed in Chapter 3). And to the extent that online faculty reduce the time they spend on campus and in interaction with peers, fully online instruction may discourage faculty engagement in the collaborative activities that are crucial to the design and successful implementation of guided pathways. Moreover, later in this chapter we will argue that it is not clear that online courses actually do cut costs.

It is difficult to measure the impact of these cost-cutting strategies on educational quality and student learning in particular, and no studies we know of do so adequately. However, it is clear that these strategies can do little to remove the barriers to student progression and learning that we have discussed throughout this book—barriers that are endemic to the cafeteria model. For example, developmental education poses a key barrier to many students, and this barrier is unlikely to be reduced by greater reliance on part-time faculty, larger classes, or online learning options.[12] In contrast, the guided pathways approach is explicitly designed to remove or minimize such barriers to completion. As we will argue later in this chapter, guided pathways should therefore decrease a college's cost per successful completion. To better explain why, we first set forth a new way to measure the costs incurred (and revenue generated) by students as they progress through college over time.

Costs and Benefits of Guided Pathways

Throughout this book, we have described the cafeteria college's focus on providing easy and relatively affordable access to college *courses* (as opposed to a focus on *completion of programs*). Given this focus, and the related fact that colleges are typically funded according to current enrollment levels rather than students' eventual outcomes, community colleges have traditionally calculated costs on a per-credit-hour (or per-student-enrolled) basis rather than on a per-credential-completed basis. Moreover, colleges generally view student costs in cross section (or during a particular "snapshot" of time, such as a given year), despite the fact that students' progression through college unfolds over multiple terms and years. Even when calculating the cost per completion, the most common approach is to divide the total annual cost by the number of graduates that year.[13]

Traditional models based on cost per enrollment encourage colleges to take a shortsighted approach to spending. Rather than helping colleges consider how to allocate resources in order to maximize student outcomes over the long term, traditional models pressure colleges to focus on immediate cost cutting. As we have emphasized throughout the book, the guided pathways approach seeks to support students along their entire path into and through a program of study. Thus, to help colleges and their funders better understand the costs and benefits of the guided pathways approach, a new cost model is needed.[14]

In this section, we first introduce a new approach to calculating institutional costs that fits within the guided pathways perspective and that provides new insights into how colleges' operating costs shift as their students' persistence improves. We then turn to cost issues that are more specific to the implementation of guided pathways (particularly, the up-front or "transitional" costs).

Student Pathway Costs

To help colleges assess the economic effects of their efforts to improve student progression through programs over time, CCRC researchers developed the concept of "pathway cost," which is an institution's spending on an individual student as he or she takes courses over time. To calculate pathway costs in the example discussed below, we use longitudinal transcript data on cohorts of first-time-in-college students at one large community college linked with data on instructional and noninstructional costs per credit hour for each course students took.[15] (Note that the pathway cost is relevant to any pathway a student takes through college, whether it is "guided" or not.)

Traditional cross-sectional cost and funding models are based on the cost per student enrollment during one semester. In contrast, the pathway cost model conceptualizes college completion as a longitudinal process, based on students' course-taking patterns and a college's related costs over multiple terms. Pathway costs cannot be accurately captured in a single semester, in large part because enrollment patterns are not stable over time. Many community college students drop out or transfer after a term or two, and among those who stay, there is great variation in the intensity of their enrollment, with many studying part-time or stopping out for one or more terms over several years.[16] Moreover, new and advanced students take different courses (each of which may have different instructional costs), and students vary in their use of services at different points in their college careers.[17]

In Figure 6.1, we provide an example of pathway cost calculations, by taking into account these across-time variations in cost, and we illuminate important information about "cost per completion" that would otherwise remain obscure.[18] The figure uses real data from a community col-

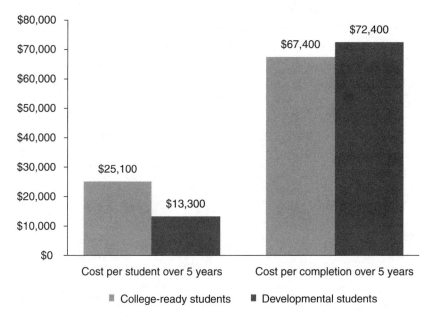

FIGURE 6.1. Five-year average pathway costs "per student" versus "per completion" for first-time college students in selected subgroups at one large community college.

lege to calculate pathway costs across five years for two groups of first-time-in-college students: those deemed college-ready and those referred to developmental education. The pathway costs per student who were considered college-ready are calculated by adding up the total pathway costs for five years for every student in the cohort who tested directly into college-level courses with no remediation.[19] That sum is divided by the total number of college-ready students in the cohort to yield the pathway cost per college-ready student. The pathway cost per *completion* of college-ready students is calculated by dividing the sum of the pathway costs for all of the college-ready students by the number who completed. Note that in this model, a "completion" is defined in terms of "associate degree equivalents," which include associate degrees, occupational certificates weighted by the number of credits required to attain them, and credits earned toward an associate degree by students who transfer to a four-year institution.[20] All of the costs for those who did not complete are also included in the calculation for the cost per completion.

The bars in the left half of Figure 6.1 compare the five-year pathway cost per student of college-ready and developmental students. In their first year, developmental students took cheaper developmental courses, while college-ready students took more expensive courses. And by the second or third year at this college, many developmental students had exited school, resulting in zero additional costs to the college, while many college-ready students persisted in more expensive courses. Accordingly, the college's average five-year spending per student for those deemed college-ready was nearly double that for developmental students.

In contrast, the right half of the figure shows average costs *per completion* for the same cohorts of students over the same five-year period. The "pathway cost per completion" is much higher than the "pathway cost per student" because the former takes into account the institution's expenditures on students who accumulated some credits but did not complete a credential: these students absorbed institutional resources but provided no payoff in terms of completion.

While the cost-per-student calculation shows that colleges spend less on each remedial student over the course of that student's college career, the cost-per-completion calculation shows that remedial students are more expensive to graduate. Two interrelated reasons explain why. First, developmental students are more likely than college-ready students to drop out, resulting in high institutional costs for a relatively low number of completions. Second, the few developmental students who do complete credentials take more courses (given that they are required to finish an entire developmental curriculum before embarking on college-level courses) and may use more support services than their college-ready peers.

Importantly, Figure 6.1 illustrates a perverse incentive inherent in traditional enrollment-based funding models and associated cost-per-student calculations. Because students are cheaper to educate at the outset of their college careers and become more expensive as they persist in school, colleges that are paid on the basis of enrollments have stronger incentives to enroll first-semester students than they have to retain students in later semesters. In contrast, cost-per-completion models incorporate the financial costs caused by factors that delay or block completion. Thus, for example, if a college can accelerate the rate at which academically underprepared students enter college-level courses without extensive remediation, or if it can increase retention rates and the pace at which students complete their programs, it will lower its cost per completion. Removing barriers to progression—by redesigning developmental education in a way that accelerates students' progress into a program of study—is therefore a crucial way to reduce the cost per completion. At the same time, even if colleges can lower costs per student per semester—for example, by cutting expenditures on advising—if this tactic leads to reduced completions, it may cause an increase in cost per completion.

Operating Costs, Revenue, and Cost per Completion

In addition to calculating pathway costs per completion, the pathway cost model also allows colleges to simulate the effects of improving intermediate milestones toward completion. For example, Table 6.1 shows how a 20 percent improvement in selected milestones would affect pathway costs, completion rates, pathway costs per completion, and net revenues over a five-year period.[21] Note that the calculations in this table do not take account of the up-front or transitional costs of reforms, and assume that instructional and related costs per course will not change. We will discuss the transitional costs in the next section of the chapter.

We can draw a number of important conclusions from this simulation. First, as we have already noted, increasing rates of student persistence *increases* pathway costs because students take more courses, as shown in the "Pathway cost" column. At this particular college, for example, increasing by 20 percent the number of students who earn at least twelve college credits in their first year would increase total pathway costs by 6.9 percent over five years. This increase in costs is accompanied by an expected 11.1 percent increase in the completion rate ("Completion rate").

Across various milestones, the extent of increase in pathway costs and completion rates depends in part on two factors: the number of students affected by the change in the milestone, and the milestone's distance from eventual completion. In terms of the number of students affected, consider the first two milestones. Only about one-third of first-time college students at this school earned at least twelve credits in their first year, while nearly half persisted from year 1 to year 2. Accordingly, a 20 percent increase in the first milestone would affect fewer students than would a 20 percent increase in the second milestone. Thus, improving the first milestone by 20 percent requires fewer pathway costs, but it also results in smaller improvements in completion rates, compared to the second milestone. Comparisons of the two improvements would also have to take account of the transitional and longer-term costs of the policies needed to bring them about. These costs are assumed to be equal in this simulation.

In terms of the milestone's distance from completion, colleges often consider students who are close to graduation to be "low-hanging fruit." That is, the college has already invested quite a bit in these students, and they will require only a few more courses and services as they persist to completion. Even if the number of such students is small, efforts to push them forward may have a large payoff. For example, in Table 6.1, "lingerers" (those still enrolled after five years who have earned at least thirty college credits but who have not yet earned a degree or certificate) are quite close to graduation compared to students who are just transitioning from year

Table 6.1 Simulated effects of a 20 percent improvement in intermediate milestones on pathway cost, completion rate, pathway cost per completion, and revenue over five years for first-time college students at one large community college

Improvement in intermediate milestone	Pathway cost (percent change)	Completion rate (percent change)	Pathway cost per completion (percent change)	Net revenue (percent change)
20 percent increase in students earning 12+ college credits in year 1	6.9	11.1	-3.7	-1.0
20 percent increase in students persisting from year 1 to year 2	11.9	14.5	-2.7	-2.8
20 percent decrease in students earning 30+ credits but no degree or certificate ("lingerers")	0.5	14.5	-12.2	0.0
20 percent decrease in students transferring without earning associate degree (vs. transferring with associate degree)	2.4	9.0	-6.0	-0.3

1 to year 2. Implementing reforms that "converted" 20 percent more lingerers into graduates would trigger only a 0.5 percent increase in instructional and related costs, but would yield a substantial 14.5 percent improvement in completion rates. While improving persistence from year 1 to year 2 would result in similar improvements in completion, it would also result in a much greater increase in subsequent operating costs, because students transitioning to their second year still have many more courses to take and services to access before completing their programs.

By combining information on costs and completion improvements, the "Pathway cost per completion" column shows that reforms that improve student outcomes on any of these milestones will eventually decrease the college's cost per completion; that is, the college will devote fewer resources to students who eventually drop out (since fewer will drop out), and thus the college will become more "efficient" in graduating students. Given the substantial resources that have already been spent on students who are close to graduation, colleges will gain more efficiency by spending a little more on these advanced students, rather than by spending the same amount on new students. This is not to say that colleges should only focus on reforming students' experiences at the tail end of college—after all, substantial reforms, and their associated instructional and noninstructional costs, will be necessary to increase the number of students who reach this advanced stage. However, this line of reasoning does suggest that focusing only on the front end of the college experience is shortsighted, and that colleges should work to improve persistence across the entire scope of the student experience.

Finally, the "Net revenue" column shows how this particular college's revenues would change under its particular traditional funding-by-enrollment model if more of its students attained intermediate milestones. An improvement in each milestone reflects an underlying increase in the number of students persisting and taking additional courses, which in turn provides more enrollment revenue. However, because these persisting students will enroll in more advanced courses taught by more expensive faculty,[22] additional revenues will not entirely cover additional expenses.[23] The good news from this analysis, however, is that even in cases where net revenue is negative, the difference is small as long as the instructional costs per course do not change. Moreover, the net revenue is spread over five years in this simulation. Nevertheless, the table clearly illustrates how current funding models penalize colleges for increasing graduation rates rather than rewarding them for improvements in cost per completion. Thus, postsecondary funding entities need to rethink the traditional funding-by-enrollment model. Before turning to that discussion, however, we consider an additional set of cost implications for colleges: the costs of transitioning to a guided pathways approach.

Transitional and Ongoing Costs

Thus far, we have discussed how improvements in intermediate milestones and eventual completions—regardless of whether these improvements are achieved via a guided pathways approach or some other type of reform—may affect colleges' ongoing operational costs. In addition to these basic ongoing costs, guided pathway reforms typically require additional up-front and transitional costs. Based on our observations of the colleges described in this book, common transitional costs include: (1) faculty and staff time to review and redesign programs, instruction, and support services; (2) professional development in key areas; (3) administrative time to coordinate, communicate, and engage college stakeholders in the process; and (4) upgrades to computer and student information systems to improve the tracking of student progress. Some colleges that have implemented guided pathways have also chosen to invest in additional ongoing costs such as hiring additional advisors (both to help students choose a path at the front end, and to provide targeted support along the pathway—for example, when the college's tracking system signals that a student is not making progress).

As we discussed in the previous chapter, many of the costs associated with the first three items can be covered through strategic reallocation of existing time and resources. Among the colleges with which we have worked, some of these costs were also defrayed by foundation grants. The tactic of pursuing grants to support reform is not unusual; as one recent report put it, effective community college leaders are ever more focused on finding "entrepreneurial ways to raise revenue to support strategies for improving student success."[24] Yet all grants are short term, and if they are the only source of support for "special" activities such as targeted professional development, inquiry group meetings, and cross-functional redesign teams, then it is far too easy for a college to revert to its former behaviors and structures when the grant money runs out. It is important, then, for colleges to determine which activities need to remain in place after the grant concludes, and to consider how to reconceptualize these as everyday, normal processes rather than "special activities."

In his 2013 study of developmental education at California community colleges, Norton Grubb cites the example of how various colleges handled monies from the state's Basic Skills Initiative, which was meant to support improvement of developmental education. Most colleges disbursed the money internally based on a Request for Proposal process. As Grubb explains, the typical process was "to invite the submission of individual ideas for funding, and then to support a number of individualized programs—what someone called an 'ATM model' of handing out money—rather than supporting one or two large objectives."[25] One of Grubb's informants lamented that the result was "a lot of talk and still not a lot of coordination. On paper, it may sound like there's a lot going on, but I think nothing really substantial and significant has gone on, even though all this money has been thrown in during the last couple of years."[26]

In contrast, Chaffey College used its Basic Skills Initiative funding as seed money for an interrelated set of initiatives with the common goal of integrating student support services in developmental classroom instruction. The college already had a clear vision for this integration, and planned to find a way to fund any ongoing expenses through its base budget. But the Basic Skills Initiative money helped smooth the initial path, and interestingly, once the integrated structures were in place, the college found it did not need any additional money to sustain them, in large part because the integrated structures were more efficient than the previous stand-alone structures.[27] Grubb explains:

> At first glance, the system of student supports at Chaffey—four Student Support Centers, a Faculty Support Center, different types of tutors and apprentices, and training for all these individuals—seems expensive. However, although we did not audit spending on student services, college personnel insist that they do not have additional funds for student support compared to other colleges; indeed, their discussions were remarkably free of references to foundation or government grants for any of these services. . . . Instead, services seem to be funded by using existing resources more intelligently and less wastefully.[28]

The colleges profiled in this book have attempted to take a similar approach by making additional expenditures, such as the hiring of new advisors, part of the college's larger cost-per-completion investment strategy. For example, as part of its effort to redesign the new student intake experience, Miami Dade College assigned all new students to an advisor to help them develop academic plans.[29] In the fall of 2012, the college launched the new intake system with existing advisors, who reached out to the approximately 9,000 students entering directly from high school. According to the college's internal analysis, students who met with advisors and developed plans were 8 percentage points more likely to persist, resulting in higher overall levels of persistence and increased revenue generation. These positive results persuaded the college's senior leadership to approve the hiring of twenty-five new full-time professional (master's degree–level) advisors, who would enhance the support services offered to new students, while freeing up existing advisors to better support returning students. The new hires required an additional annual investment of $1 million (over and above reallocated resources), which the college incorporated into its operating budget.

To the extent that the cost increases associated with guided pathways reforms exceed revenues, some colleges may choose to reallocate resources away from particular programs or groups of students in order to increase efficiency. Limiting access for disadvantaged students is contrary to the open-access mission of community colleges and thus is an unattractive strategy. Similarly, colleges are reluctant to restrict enrollment in high-cost programs because demand—and economic returns—for such programs is generally high. For example, many community colleges fill a critical need in their community by providing nursing programs, even though the high cost of instruction and equipment for such programs requires extensive cross-subsidization from other, lower-cost programs. However, as they consider reallocating resources, colleges might take a hard look at programs with weak employment and transfer outcomes, particularly if such programs are relatively expensive to maintain. Institutions might also consider combining similar programs to gain efficiencies in scale. For example, the North Carolina State Board for Community Colleges recently approved a major restructuring of career-technical education programs, which consolidated more than eighty curriculum standards into thirty-two, and grouped similar program majors into larger programs that now share a common academic and technical core.[30]

While community college leaders can seek out grants, streamline programs, and reallocate resources to support the design and implementation of guided pathways, they can do only so much with the limited resources available to them. Thus, legislatures, policymakers, and other funders must also play roles in supporting these colleges' efforts, as we discuss below.

Policy Incentives to Redesign Colleges for Success

While implementing guided pathways is sensible from the standpoint of long-term efficiency, many college leaders are much more concerned about their institution's near-term operating stability and thus may be wary of the costs and risks associated with moving toward a guided pathways model.

In this section, we examine how state policymakers can provide incentives for college leaders to invest in redesign strategies that lead to long-term improvements in student outcomes and reductions in cost-per-completion. First, we discuss performance funding models, which—when well designed and implemented—may be necessary (but not sufficient) incentives to improve completion rates. Next, we discuss other policies that may support colleges in their attempts to improve long-term student success.

Performance Funding

Performance funding differs from traditional enrollment-based funding in that it shifts the basis of funding from *educational inputs* to *outputs that reflect policy priorities*. Under such policies, states fund colleges and universities based not merely on how many students they enroll but also at least in part on how many students they graduate, transfer, or place in high-quality jobs. In addition to providing incentives for colleges to improve, performance funding is also intended to make college outcome measures more transparent, comparable, and readily available to the public (a strategy known as "performance reporting").

Tennessee was the first state to adopt performance funding and reporting policies for higher education, in 1979. As of late 2013, thirty states were considering or had enacted performance-funding formulas.[31] The earlier policies provided a "bonus" over and above an institution's base funding from the state if the college performed well across a variety of performance measures. Researchers refer to these policies as "Performance Funding 1.0" (PF 1.0) models, in contrast to newly emerging "Performance Funding 2.0" (PF 2.0) models, in which performance indicators are used to determine colleges' base budget funding. The following states have enacted PF 2.0: Pennsylvania (2002), Indiana (2009), Ohio (2009), and Tennessee (2010).[32]

In an extensive 2013 review of the impacts of performance funding, CCRC researcher Kevin Dougherty found that these policies improve colleges' awareness of both institutional performance and state policy goals. Many colleges have also made changes to academic and student services practices in response to performance funding. However, there is no clear evidence that the PF 1.0 models in place during the early 2000s improved student outcomes (and it is too early to determine the impacts of PF 2.0 on outcomes).[33] Researchers have advanced two key explanations for the disappointments of PF 1.0: such policies may not provide an appropriate mix of financial "carrots" and "sticks," and they may rely on inadequate measures of performance.

In terms of financial incentives, performance funding policies have often been financially unstable and unsustainable, and therefore have been not lasted long enough to change institutional behavior.[34] Similarly, the share of state appropriations tied to performance funding has generally been less than 5 percent, an amount that institutional leaders consider too small to motivate wide-scale institutional change.[35] As a result, some states have recently begun to allocate much larger shares of the total appropriations by institutional performance. As of this writing, Indiana, Louisiana, Ohio, and Tennessee each tie at least 20 percent of their appropriations to measurable outcomes such as degrees completed, credit milestones reached, remedial success, and others.[36] Indeed, in Tennessee, by 2014, *all* unrestricted state funding is now allocated based on performance rather than enrollment, such that performance-based funding accounts for about 25 percent of the overall revenue for universities and 32 percent of revenue for the state's community colleges. A preliminary analysis suggests that completion rates increased by nearly 20 percent in the first three years after the policy was enacted, although it is unclear how much of those increases was due to performance funding, how much was due to a larger set of reforms passed through the Complete College Tennessee Act of 2010, and how much was due to factors independent of public policy.[37] In the future, policymakers and college leaders will surely look to Tennessee and these other states to see if "more money matters" as an incentive to change practice in ways that improve performance.

Regardless of the amount of money tied to performance funding, such policies are unlikely to be effective if they lack valid and credible measures of institutional outcomes. Most performance funding policies suffer from at least one of three flaws in this regard.

First, performance funding policies generally do not take into account the fact that colleges differ from one another in the demographics of their student bodies and in the mix of programs they offer; yet much of the variation in both completion and transfer rates across colleges is due to differences in the student populations that each college serves. After controlling for such differences, the authors of a 2013 study of North Carolina's community colleges concluded that it was difficult to distinguish most of the system's colleges from one another in terms of their performance, although the highest-performing institutions could be differentiated from the poorest-performing ones. The authors analyzed two outcome variables: attainment of an applied diploma or a degree and completion of coursework required for transfer to a four-year university. After taking into account differences in student characteristics across colleges, the outcome measures showed little correlation to the metrics used by the state to measure colleges' performance.[38]

Outcome-based funding systems that fail to adjust for student characteristics penalize colleges that serve large numbers of educationally and economically disadvantaged students. Moreover, such policies could discourage colleges from serving students who are poorly prepared for college and therefore less likely to succeed. In an attempt to avoid such a scenario, the Tennessee funding system provides a 40 percent bonus for credit and degree completion by low-income students.[39] Whether this is sufficient to counterbalance the disincentive for colleges to enroll more disadvantaged students remains to be seen.

Second, to measure a college's effect on student progress and completion accurately, systems must track student cohorts over a period of years. But this sort of longitudinal cohort tracking is difficult to reconcile with state and system budgeting cycles, which typically disburse funding to colleges on an annual basis. It is much easier to use point-in-time measures or year-to-year changes than it is to rely on longitudinal measures, which are generally subject to a lag. For example, the state of Washington's 2006 performance funding policy was designed to reward colleges that increased the number of students attaining key milestones or achievement points (for example, completing a college-level math course, or earning fifteen and then thirty quarter-term credits).[40] As the policy was originally designed, college performance on each milestone was measured by simply calculating changes from one year to the next in the absolute numbers of students who attained the milestone. Yet an analysis of the state's performance funding system found no positive correlation between these calculated point gains and the rates at which individual students progressed over time.[41] Based on the recommendation of a group of presidents who reviewed the implementation of Washington's performance funding system over its first five years, in 2013 the state's college system added measures based on the rates at which individual students advance from one milestone to the next.[42] Planners hoped this measure would create clearer incentives for colleges.

Third, many performance funding measures do not fully capture community colleges' success in supporting student transfer to four-year colleges. Indeed, a 2013 review of performance funding in eight states found that only two—Missouri and Tennessee—include measures related to successful transfer from two- to four-year institutions.[43] Yet, preparing students to move on to and succeed in bachelor-degree programs not only helps to further students' own stated goals, but also has economic value for both individual students and taxpayers.[44]

More broadly, it is very difficult—if not impossible—to assess the performance of complex institutions with just a handful of measures. Defining a set of metrics for performance funding requires a tradeoff between the most accurate approach (a complex suite of longitudinal measures that control for student characteristics and program types and that are rich enough to capture college performance in a meaningful way) and the most practically useful approach (a small set of metrics that are simple, feasible to compute, and widely understood by educators and other stakeholders). While accuracy may seem to be more important, the opaqueness and inherent complexity of the most precise measures could undermine the entire system. If college leaders and faculty do not clearly understand the measures and how they relate to their daily jobs, they are unlikely to embrace them or actively work to improve the institution's performance in terms of them.

The available research to date has analyzed the effects of Performance Funding 1.0 models. Tennessee and other states have implemented PF 2.0 models that future research may find more effective. Based on extant evidence, however, it seems that performance funding plays an important symbolic role in communicating state priorities—and may be necessary to help colleges and their funding entities shift perspectives from a traditional cost-per-student model to a cost-per-completion model—but it may be insufficient by itself to improve college performance. Additional policy incentives may be necessary for colleges to make systemic changes that can dramatically improve student progression and success.

Policies for Strengthening Transfer and Career Pathways

In addition to providing financial incentives for colleges to improve outcomes, a growing number of states have implemented policies that encourage, if not require, colleges to create clearer and more coherent pathways that are aligned with further education and employment in specific fields. In particular, over two-thirds of states have adopted some sort of statewide policy designed to facilitate the transfer of community college students to in-state four-year institutions.[45] Some states, such as Ohio and Texas, have transfer policies that allow for the transferability or "equivalency" of individual courses in a general education core curriculum. Other states—including Florida, New Jersey, Massachusetts, Oregon, and Virginia—award "junior standing" to students who complete a transfer-oriented associate degree.

However, these policies do not guarantee that general education courses or other associate degree credits will be accepted for credit toward junior standing in a *particular* major. Thus, even students who have completed the general education core or an associate degree may have to take additional lower division courses upon transferring to satisfy major requirements. To ensure that students' community college credits count toward bachelor's degrees in particular fields, several states have adopted "major pathways transfer policies," which stipulate both general education and pre-major courses that are guaranteed to transfer toward junior standing in a given major. Washington was an early adopter of such policies, and some research suggests that these policies have improved transfer outcomes in the state, although the evidence is by no means definitive.

The state of Washington has a forty-year history of public two- and four-year institutions working together to facilitate the transfer process for students.[46] However, in the mid-1990s, community and technical college presidents became concerned that, as the state's universities recruited ever-larger numbers of high school graduates to enter as freshmen, there would not be enough room for transfer students from two-year colleges. Ensuing negotiations led to a "proportionality agreement," which stipulated that each university would maintain the proportion of students entering as transfers based on 1992 levels. This agreement helped address a problem that transfer students face in other states: a lack of open slots at public universities.[47]

By the early 2000s, the state's employers and policymakers began calling for more STEM graduates. To address this issue, the two-year and four-year systems came together to create an associate of science transfer (AS-T) degree with two tracks: one for biological and earth sciences, and the other for engineering and computer science. An internal 2006 study suggested that students with AS-T degrees who transferred to in-state public universities completed fewer excess credits and were more likely to earn bachelor's degrees than were students who followed the more general Direct Transfer Agreement with a science-related concentration.

Building on the AS-T work, the two systems again came together in the early 2000s to create "major-related pathways," with a focus on improving transfer in fields with many students such as nursing and information technology. An internal 2009 study found that the three-year graduation rate for students transferring to one of the state's public universities increased from 63 percent in the late 1990s to 71 percent in 2006–2007. The researchers speculated that this increase could have been the result of the major-related pathways, although they were not able to demonstrate this definitively. An internal 2013 study found that university graduates who had first earned an associate degree in business (a specific pathway within the Direct Transfer Agreement) or one of the AS-T fields took fewer excess credits than transfer students who did not follow these specialized tracks.

Key to the collaborative relationship between Washington's two- and four-year systems has been the presence of organizational structures such as the Joint Transfer Council, which includes key decision-makers from both systems. The state's legislature also understands the importance of having well-functioning articulation agreements, and it closely monitors transfer and completion rates.

More recently, other states—including California, Connecticut, Indiana, Maryland, and Tennessee—have adopted major-related transfer pathway policies. These policy efforts are being encouraged by advocacy groups such as Complete College America, which cites research from CCRC and others in promoting the creation of clearer pathways to transfer and occupational advancement. For example, at the urging of Complete College America, the Indiana legislature recently required the state's community colleges and public universities to implement degree maps and "macro-majors." And in 2013, Maryland adopted even more comprehensive legislation that is well-aligned with the guided pathways model.[48]

Yet despite the momentum around pathways policies, research to date provides little empirical evidence that state transfer policies improve transfer rates.[49] Some researchers speculate that such policies are meant to prevent loss of credits among transfer students rather than to increase transfer rates per se, and thus should not be expected to increase the number of students who successfully transfer.[50] We have a different theory, based on research on policy implementation, which suggests that simply passing laws or regulations is not sufficient to change institutional behavior.

The policy implementation literature sets forth a number of explanations for why the effects of policies related to transfer (or performance funding, for that matter) may fall short of policymakers' visions, including unclear policy goals, policy incoherence, and outright rejection on the part of those responsible for implementation.[51] In general, as they examine why policies are (or are not) effective in motivating change, scholars are paying more attention to the cognitive processes of those responsible for implementing policy reforms. For example, implementers may not be hostile to a particular policy, but their understanding of the policy may differ significantly from the understanding of those who crafted it.[52] Alternately, their level of competence and professional experience may limit their ability to implement the reform, resulting in a policy that in practice differs from the original conception.[53]

Overall, research suggests that in order to ensure that policy reforms are implemented as intended, policymakers and college leaders should seek to educate faculty and staff on the goals of a particular policy.[54] Policymakers may need to engage college personnel through their professional communities as well as their institutional roles, because professional communities allow instructors in particular to make sense of new policies in a broader context, which can result in different interpretations of policy based on professional or disciplinary differences.[55]

Transfer policy is no exception; to ensure effective implementation, states need to build an infrastructure for ongoing communication among faculty across two- and four-year institutions to establish and continually update agreements. Without such regular communication, laws by themselves are unlikely to lead to the development of strong pathways. A case in point is North Carolina, which in 1997 established transfer legislation calling for the creation of a common general education core and "pre-major" diploma programs that guaranteed junior standing to transfer students who completed the requirements. However, by 2011 it was clear that the system was not working. Most students who transferred were not completing the pre-major diploma programs, and the few who did may actually have taken longer to graduate than students who transferred without the diploma.[56] As we noted earlier, faculty at one North Carolina technical college were astounded to discover that, of the many general education courses offered by the college, only English composition was accepted for core credit (not just elective credit) at all sixteen University of North Carolina institutions.[57] Frustrated by the lack of alignment between the two systems, the North Carolina legislature passed a measure in 2013 requiring public universities to abide by the 1997 law. This prompted the North Carolina Community College System and the University of North Carolina System to establish a new statewide articulation agreement, which was signed by leaders of both systems in February 2014. That agreement included a provision for updating and refining specific programmatic articulation agreements.

On paper at least, North Carolina's 1997 transfer policy resembled the one described earlier in the state of Washington. Yet in Washington, there was an infrastructure for ongoing communication among faculty across community colleges and universities, which helped keep agreements current and maintained a level of understanding and trust among faculty across the two sectors. In contrast, according to officials in North Carolina, there had been no systematic effort to update the agreements established in 1997 until 2013, when it became clear that the system was dysfunctional. In Chapter 5, we discussed the ways in which communication and collaboration among departments and divisions are essential to building guided pathways within community colleges. Similarly, ongoing communication and engagement are critical to creating both pathways to transfer between community colleges and universities and (in concert with employers) to career advancement.

Are Guided Pathways Worth the Cost?

We have suggested that community colleges will require somewhat more resources to design and implement guided pathways successfully, increase efficiency without jeopardizing educational quality, maintain access for disadvantaged students, and remain responsive to community needs. This observation raises the question of whether such reforms are worth the cost. In this section, we examine the research on the economic returns to a community college education, and discuss the implications for guided pathways policy and practice.

On average, the earnings premium for an associate degree (compared with a high school diploma) is 13 percent for men and 21 percent for women.[58] Short-term returns for students who transfer and then complete a bachelor's degree are even larger, with rapid earnings growth in the years following college graduation, which puts students on a trajectory toward even better long-term returns.[59] While the evidence on short-term certificates (awards that take less than a year to complete) is mixed, long-term certificates also appear to have positive returns for most students.[60] Of course, the size of the return for *any* credential varies by field. Earning gains are higher for those in quantitative or career-technical fields, particularly those related to nursing and other health professions, and more modest for associate degrees in the liberal arts (the latter finding is not surprising, given that most liberal arts students in community colleges intend to transfer, and thus associate degrees in liberal arts are not designed to be terminal, occupational-oriented degrees). However, the majority of student pathways through community college lead to positive economic returns.[61]

There has been little research on the benefits of a community college education beyond labor market returns. However, evidence from studies of the benefits of higher education in general shows very large returns on many health measures, even after controlling for income, health insurance, and family background. Other benefits from higher education include less involvement in the criminal justice system and less reliance on welfare.[62]

Community colleges produce favorable returns for taxpayers as well. One analysis from 2010 found that for each associate degree from a community college, taxpayers gain an additional $142,000 in revenue.[63] Two-thirds of the gain comes from increased income tax payments (as a result of higher earnings of students who earn degrees), but there are also substantial savings in government-funded programs, including those associated with health care, welfare, and crime. On average, taxpayers invest approximately $54,800 per associate degree, resulting in total taxpayer returns over two and a half times greater than the initial investment.[64]

If the economic returns on a community college education were low, that might justify the focus on cutting the cost per student enrolled, which has dominated community college funding and finance over the past decade or more. However, the returns are high; accordingly, they are worth current investments, and justify further investments that would result in additional degrees with similarly high returns. While increasing retention and completion may increase net operating costs modestly and involve additional transitional costs, colleges that have implemented guided pathways reforms seem to have been able to cover most of these costs by reallocating existing resources. Still, guided pathways may require somewhat more state investment to cover the added costs some colleges may not be able to support through reallocation. To the extent that these investments help colleges improve their cost-per-completion by reducing the number of students who drop out (and who thus "waste" the taxpayer investment), a modest increase in public funding would be justified by the further returns on an already high-yield investment.

Are "Unbundled" Models More Cost-Effective?

As we discussed in the introduction, a great deal of excitement has been generated by efforts to "unbundle" instructional and credential-granting activities, by using low-cost online instructional resources (including freely available "massive open online courses," or MOOCs), adaptive learning software, and online "success coaches" that guide students through individually tailored competency-based programs, which are defined in terms of competencies to be mastered rather than time spent in class.[65] Proponents of such an approach, exemplified by Western Governors University (WGU) and Southern New Hampshire University's College for America (CFA), argue that it is potentially more effective not only in expanding access to higher education but also in offering quality education at a lower cost.[66] Research on the effectiveness of this approach is just beginning, with most of the relevant evidence based in the research on online learning. Thus, we will first review the research on online learning (including MOOCs) and then discuss the little evidence we have about features of the unbundled models other than online learning.

Traditional online courses (that is, fully online courses offered by accredited colleges) seem to be just as effective as traditional face-to-face courses for well-prepared and highly motivated students, but tend to be less effective for weaker students who attend open-access and less-selective colleges. Although fully online courses continue to generate interest from policymakers, research does not indicate that these courses are cheaper to develop or sustain over time.[67] Indeed, a 2010 study of the University of North Carolina found that online courses cost more to develop than on-campus courses, and afterward remain similarly expensive to provide.[68] A similar cost analysis conducted by Indiana, Purdue, and Ball State Universities on their combined efforts at distance education programming found that online courses produced a savings of $8.68 in classroom space for each student per credit hour. However, citing research that recommends reduced class sizes for online courses (20 to 35 percent smaller than face-to-face courses, in order to ensure effective engagement among the students and instructor), the study's authors noted that classroom space savings may well be offset by the increased costs associated with smaller classes.[69]

Thus, if we are looking for substantial improvements in learning outcomes, lower costs per completion, or both, then traditional forms of accredited online coursework may not be the solution. In recent years, elite universities hoped to improve on the traditional online course by creating freely available, noncredit MOOCs, which featured "star" university professors. The MOOC phenomenon initially raised hopes that low-income students could use these courses to access and complete high-quality curricula for little or no cost. However, so far, most MOOC enrollees already have college degrees—and even so, their course completion rates are quite low.[70] These findings ought not to be surprising: given the importance of the student–instructor interpersonal connection to student motivation, professors teaching large-enrollment online courses will always face difficulties in motivating students who are not already engaged with and enthusiastic about the material. Even smaller-enrollment MOOCs may struggle to serve underprepared students well: an attempt by San Jose State University to use a relatively small MOOC for a developmental math course resulted in completion rates in the 20 percent range, compared to 45 percent completion rates for the face-to-face course. The effort was abandoned after two semesters.[71]

Even so, Stanford economist Caroline Hoxby argues that MOOCs could offer a financially sustainable substitute for at least some courses offered by broad-access institutions like community colleges.[72] In making this judgment, Hoxby draws on data from a variety of sources to contend that in nonselective institutions the course material is fairly standardized,[73] assessments tend to be multiple-choice or in other easily graded formats,[74] students attend part-time and drop in and out of college, there is little cohort cohesion (that is, classes do not progress or graduate together), and interactions among students and instructors are limited.[75] These characteristics accurately describe the cafeteria college model. Yet, as we have argued throughout this book, this model—with its emphasis on student self-service, self-direction, and self-motivation—is not well-suited to facilitating learning and program completion among the types of students usually served by community colleges. One can interpret Hoxby's argument as implying that since nonselective institutions have been able to sustain themselves despite having an educational model that does not work very well, then that model can be replaced by a cheaper model, even if the replacement model is also not very effective. Such a strategy, however, is unlikely to substantially increase the proportion of Americans with high-quality degrees or credentials.

In an attempt to improve the quality of teaching and learning using MOOC content, some colleges are experimenting with a hybrid or "flipped" classroom model in which students learn material on their own from a MOOC, and then attend small-enrollment face-to-face class sessions to review and apply the material with an instructor. If flipped MOOCs consistently yield substantially stronger outcomes, or cost substantially less but yield the same outcomes, then they could certainly be more cost-effective than traditional classroom models. Thus far, however, their cost-effectiveness remains unclear. The most comprehensive and rigorous study to date of flipped MOOCs found that these courses yield results similar to those of traditional face-to-face courses in terms of pass rates, final grades, and exam scores, but require less instructional time—which would suggest that they are somewhat more cost-effective.[76] On the other hand, the flipped MOOC courses garnered substantially lower student ratings, including students' assessments of how much they learned, compared to face-to-face courses on the same subject matter. Many students complained that they had too little time with their instructors; and instructors invested so heavily in course development that researchers speculated that "faculty members are likely to need incentives, such as relief from other parts of their work load," to engage in such development activities.[77] Accordingly, the researchers could come to no clear conclusion about the current or future cost-effectiveness of these courses. Moreover, by 2014, the enthusiasm for MOOCs had begun to fade, but among educators and policymakers, interest in online instruction continues to grow.

Beyond the research on online learning, we have little information regarding the costs or effectiveness of the larger landscape of unbundled competency-based models. It is possible that models based on demonstrated competencies rather than "seat time" would offer significant cost savings, for several reasons. First, if such models are non-campus-based, they can avoid the overhead associated with a physical campus and extracurricular programs and services. Second, if they are non-course-based, they can minimize the use of instructors and save students on the costs of textbooks, relying on coaches to guide students to learning resources available on the Internet. Third, and most important, non-course-based models could save students time and money by accelerating their progression through degree requirements: such models do not require students to sit through classes (or pay for them) in order to learn things they already know, and programs could potentially be individually tailored to students' career goals, allowing them to skirt any general-education content not directly relevant to those goals. This hoped-for acceleration of program completion, and its associated cost savings, forms the foundation of unbundled competency-based programs such as those offered by WGU and CFA. And, indeed, both institutions charge relatively low tuition. WGU charges $2,890 for a six-month term, and CFA charges $2,500 per year, compared to $3,264 for a thirty-credit year (or $1,632 for a fifteen-credit, four-month semester) at a typical community college.[78]

But do such programs accelerate student progression and completion? Thus far, we have no evidence that they do; the completion rates of most competency-based programs are unavailable and difficult to determine because many are embedded in the completion rates of a larger institution in which the program is housed. Interestingly, however, the six-year graduation rate for first-time, full-time degree-seeking students at WGU is 24 percent, below the national average even for less-selective public universities.[79] Of course, models such as WGU's may be most useful for older adults returning to school, who are not captured in the "first-time, full-time" category. These students may be highly self-motivated and self-directed, able to move quickly through their education by certifying competencies they garnered through years of career and life experience. Indeed, referring to a competency-based education model developed in Wisconsin, a 2014 *Chronicle of Higher Education* article noted that "administrators in Wisconsin say they are screening applicants for those who are likely to succeed in the largely self-guided model of learning: students who are highly motivated, self-disciplined, and mature."[80] Because outcomes for adult students who are returning to college after being in the workforce for some time are not captured in federal databases, we have no information about these students' success rates at WGU or other unbundled programs at traditional institutions. Even if these older returning students' success rates were quite high, however, it is important to note that unbundled programs designed to serve students with focused workforce goals, preexisting career-related competencies, and strong self-motivation are unlikely to address the needs of the much larger population of students who have unclear goals and interests, little preexisting work experience and associated competencies to be certified, and varied levels of motivation. In contrast, the guided pathways model is explicitly designed to meet the needs of the latter population.

In general, if the nation's goal is to improve every student's chance of completing a high-quality degree or credential at a reasonable price, the available evidence suggests that the unbundled approach is unlikely to achieve that goal—or, at least, not for the typical underprepared and unfocused community college student. This observation does not imply that colleges should avoid technological innovations such as online instructional materials or e-advising systems. Rather, such technologies should be integrated into redesigned programs and support services within the guided pathways model, in ways that enhance the capacity of colleges to effectively teach and support students.

Community colleges are committed to serving all members of their local communities who can benefit from higher education, including students who are poorly prepared for college. As part of this commitment to access, community colleges have worked hard to restrain tuition by keeping their per-student cost low. Indeed, community college tuition remains relatively affordable, and community college students generally do not incur large debt. Moreover, both society and individuals reap significant gains from their investments in community colleges. To the extent that there is a cost crisis in U.S. higher education, community colleges are not contributing to it.

Nevertheless, community colleges are experiencing fiscal pressure and continue to look for ways to lower costs. Yet the ways in which they typically cut spending—by an increased reliance on part-time instructors, increased student-to-faculty ratios, and growing use of fully online instruction—reduce completion rates and likely hurt quality. In general, the strategy of cutting per-student costs may weaken the capacity of community colleges to provide well-documented labor market returns and other benefits to students and society.

Successful implementation of the guided pathways model promises to improve student outcomes—but it may also increase colleges' per-student costs, in part because more students will persist and thus incur more costs, and in part because implementing the reforms may involve significant costs. Improvements in student retention and progression will also increase revenue, but our models suggest that any revenue increase may not entirely cover the increase in costs. And, unfortunately, current funding policies tend to serve as a disincentive: they discourage investment in reforms that improve retention, thus undercutting colleges' abilities to lower the cost per completion of high-quality credentials and to maximize returns on investment in higher education.

To resolve this problem, policymakers must think more seriously about how to create incentives for the development of guided pathways. Well-designed and appropriately implemented performance funding strategies seem poised to provide a necessary but insufficient foundation for change. States should therefore also consider enacting policies designed to encourage two- and four-year institutions to work together to improve transfer outcomes, as well as other policies that strengthen pathways to degree completion and labor market advancement. Finally, state policymakers should recognize that community colleges produce high returns on investment for students and taxpayers; thus, rather than focus single-mindedly on cutting costs, they should encourage colleges to use their scarce resources more efficiently. Moreover, states may need to provide a modest level of *additional* resources to cover the costs necessary to implement guided pathways and thereby substantially improve the completion of high-quality credentials. The evidence suggests that these additional investments will be justified by the resulting increases in the returns on an investment that already yields high dividends for both individuals and society.

Conclusion

THROUGHOUT THIS BOOK we have argued that community colleges are designed and operate according to a cafeteria or self-service model. While colleges organized in this way do an excellent job of providing affordable access to college courses, they are not well configured to help students enter and complete high-quality programs of study—programs that prepare them for success in further education and advancement in the labor market. Cafeteria colleges rely on students to find their own paths through college and to seek out supports when they need them, but most students are not well equipped to do either. In fact, many students, particularly those without clear goals for college or careers, are confused and overwhelmed, and often make poor choices.

Despite more than a decade of determined reform in community colleges, much of which has focused on the intake system and developmental education in particular, few colleges have "moved the needle" on overall rates of student completion. Evaluations of major reform initiatives such as Achieving the Dream have found that it is insufficient to pilot and attempt to scale up discrete programmatic interventions. In this book, we have argued that a major reason such reforms have not succeeded is that they attempt to make incremental improvements to a model of college organization that is incompatible with their larger reform goals. If colleges are to improve outcomes for their large numbers of disadvantaged students, they need to redesign their practices and policies in fundamental ways.

We have argued that instead of expecting students to find their own way through college, colleges need to create clear, educationally coherent program pathways that are aligned with students' end goals, help students explore and select a pathway of interest, and track and support students' progress along their chosen pathway. In the introduction and Chapters 1 through 4 we described how this guided pathways model transforms key functions of the college, including program design, student intake and support services, instruction, and developmental education. We recommended key redesign features that research and experience suggest will improve the effectiveness of each function, and cited examples of colleges that are incorporating these key features on a large scale with their students. In Chapter 5, we argued that successful implementation of the guided pathways approach requires active engagement of—and indeed leadership from—a college's faculty and staff, and we provided some suggestions for creating that level of engagement. In Chapter 6, we discussed the costs of implementing the guided pathways model, and emphasized that while such a redesign will have some additional transitional and long-run costs, the added costs will be worthwhile if they substantially improve the rates at which students complete high-quality credentials—thereby lowering costs per completion, increasing college efficiency, and increasing the return on investment in community colleges by students and taxpayers.

In this conclusion, we describe how two similar students might experience the guided pathways model versus the cafeteria model at each stage of their progression through college. Next, we offer some concrete steps that faculty, student services staff, institutional researchers, and administrators can take to initiate and advance the redesign process on their campuses. Finally, we discuss the prospects for guided pathways reforms to spread more broadly among community colleges nationally, highlighting both the promise and some of the challenges in the work ahead.

The Student Experience

A student's progression through college can be divided into four phases: connection, entry, progress, and completion.[1] To illustrate the differences between the cafeteria and guided pathways models, we compare the experience of two hypothetical students—a cafeteria college student and a guided pathways college student—across these four phases.[2] Both are from first-generation, lower-income families; both worked hard and performed well in high school; and both dream of earning a bachelor's degree and pursuing a career in business, although neither has any relatives or acquaintances who are business professionals. Neither student has immediate family members who have a college degree. Both enter higher education through a community college, but the first student's local community college is designed and operated in accord with cafeteria model, while the second student's local community college has redesigned its programs and services following the guided pathways approach.

As the Connection phase figure (Figure C.1) shows, the experiences of the two students diverge well before they apply to their local college. The cafeteria college's connections with local high schools are weak; thus the first student has limited awareness of the programs offered by the college and receives little assistance to explore options for college and careers. She does learn about the local college's dual-enrollment program, but the course she decides to take (photography) is based on personal interest rather than on her career goal. In contrast, the guided pathways college has forged stronger connections between its programs and its feeder high schools. For example, the college's recruitment staff work with high school counselors to organize college and career exploration activities, help students identify a potential college major or exploratory major, and encourage students to participate in dual-enrollment courses fundamental to their field of interest.

With a better understanding of her pathway to a degree in business, and already having earned credits related to her program of interest through dual-enrollment courses, the guided pathways student graduates from high school motivated and prepared to immediately enroll in college full-time. Without a clear sense of the path ahead of her, the cafeteria college student decides to take time off before attending college (a "delayed entry"

Cafeteria college student	Guided pathways college student
• Attends high school that is poorly informed about the local community college's program offerings and readiness standards	• Attends high school that aligns senior-year curriculum to the local community college's readiness standards in its main program areas
• Not helped to explore career and college options while in high school	• Participates in pre-career assessment and exploration offered in collaboration with the community college
• Takes dual-enrollment course in photography	• Takes dual-enrollment courses in field of career interest: business
• Graduates high school, gets a low-wage job, delays enrollment in college, enrolls later part-time	• Graduates high school, gets a low-wage job, but enrolls full-time in community college in the fall with credits toward business degree
⬇	⬇
No clear direction *Enrolled part-time*	*On a program path* *Enrolled full-time*

FIGURE C.1. Connection phase: from interest to enrollment.

Cafeteria college student	Guided pathways college student
• Skips optional orientation, meets with advisor to select first-term courses	• Based on required orientation, career assessment, and advising, selects business meta-major and begins degree plan
• Despite interest in business, takes no business courses; unaware of college career center	• Takes prescribed first-year sequence, including a business course and a business-focused student success course
• Placed in remedial math based on standardized test, will need 2 semesters to get to college-level math	• Takes statistics-oriented math course that enables her, despite not having liked math in high school, to complete college-level math in 2 semesters
• Disengaged by lecture-based courses	• Engaged particularly in social science course, based on topical readings and participation in class projects
Lacks direction *Getting discouraged*	*Has program goal and completion plan* *Gaining early momentum*

FIGURE C.2. Entry phase: from enrollment to entry into program of study.

that is associated with significantly lower degree completion rates),[3] and then when she does enroll, she takes three courses in her first semester rather than a full course load.

In the Entry phase (Figure C.2), the cafeteria college student skips an optional new student orientation and begins her college experience by meeting with an advisor to register for her first-semester courses. Based on her placement test scores, the advisor registers her for a developmental math and English course, and also recommends a student success course; but because she performed relatively well in high school, the student feels she does not need the course and asks for something more "interesting." She and the advisor settle on a psychology course. As the term progresses, the cafeteria college student begins to feel overwhelmed by the volume of information in the psychology lectures and readings, and is not sure how to approach the course's term papers. Her developmental English course, which focuses on writing compositions, does little to help her navigate the reading and writing assignments in psychology. And she is very discouraged by the fact that she has been placed in a pre-algebra developmental math course, a full two levels below college-level math. She disliked math in high school. She still dislikes it and does not understand how pre-algebra, in particular, is relevant; and she dreads having to complete three semesters of math in college. By the end of her first term, she is beginning to feel disillusioned and discouraged. Although she passed all of her courses, she did not find any of them compelling, and she would rather not take yet *another* semester of math and English next term. Her dream of getting a bachelor's degree in business still seems very far away.

In contrast, the new student at the guided pathways college attends a required business program orientation, in which faculty describe how the business meta-major's first-semester course requirements are designed to help students explore the field before they commit to majoring in it. The initial coursework includes an introductory business course and a success course that helps students explore careers, specific programs, and transfer options in business. The success course also requires students to lay out an academic plan (based on faculty-created program maps) that will enable them to complete a selected program in two years and, if desired, transfer their credits toward junior standing in a business major at a selected university.

Because of her high school's alignment of the senior year with community college entrance standards, the guided pathways student is placed directly into college-level English, but she still scores somewhat poorly in math. Based on her interest in business, the guided pathways college places her in a statistics-oriented developmental math course that will allow her to complete a college-level statistics course (fully transferable to state university business programs) by the end of her second semester. Following the default meta-major pathway, she also enrolls in the college's social science course for business majors: a multidisciplinary blend of psychology, sociology, and economics that examines how consumers make decisions, using engaging class projects and readings. The course gets her interested in marketing and advertising; as part of her student success course, she reviews related program and transfer plans, and the instructor connects her to the college's business program advisor to discuss her transfer options in more depth. Going into her second semester, the guided pathways college student is picking up momentum.

The Progress phase figure (Figure C.3) shows that the cafeteria college student continues to struggle in subsequent semesters. Even though she is weak in math, she enrolls in Economics 101, but fails it and fears having to take it again. None of the courses she has taken—including her business courses—have given her a sense of what working as a business professional is like. And given her difficulty with Economics 101, she begins to further doubt whether she can get a bachelor's degree in business. Even so, she does not visit the transfer center and indeed does not know about it. Neither does she connect with other business-oriented students through clubs or other activities; she is not aware of some of these opportunities and feels too busy to take advantage of others.

The guided pathways student performs poorly on her first Economics 101 quiz, but thanks to the college's early alert system, the business program advisor reaches out to reassure her and push her to attend supplemental instruction sections led by peer tutors and managed by the Economics 101 instructors; doing so improves her performance in the course. The advisor also encourages her to participate in a young entrepreneurs club, which eventually connects her to a summer internship. After her third semester, the e-advising system reminds her (and her advisor) that it is time to apply for admission to university business programs, which she does.

As the Completion phase figure (Figure C.4) illustrates, the cafeteria college student is still enrolled part-time in community college after five years. She has not yet earned a degree, in part because she has occasion-

Cafeteria college student	Guided pathways college student
• Poor self-advising leads to extra courses / excess credits	• E-advising system enables student and her advisor to monitor progress on student's degree plan
• Fails Economics 101, considers retaking it	• Early alert initiated by Economics 101 instructor leads advisor to recommend tutoring, which enables her to pass the course
• Does not participate in clubs or activities	• Participates in young entrepreneur club suggested by business faculty; this helps connect her with internship
• Does not know college has transfer assistance center	• Applies to business programs at 2 universities with assistance from department advisors
Still lacks direction Getting discouraged	*Has program goal and completion plan Builds on early momentum*

FIGURE C.3. Progress phase: from program entry to completion of program requirements.

ally skipped semesters. After earning sixty college-level credits—the minimum amount required for the associate degree in business—she finally visits the advising center and discusses possibilities for transfer. The advisor tells her that several of the credits she has earned will not be accepted by local university business programs. However, her transcript does meet the requirements for an associate degree in general studies. The student decides to graduate with a general studies degree, take a break from school, and go back to work full-time. With only a general studies associate degree, however, she finds herself stuck in low-level clerical jobs she gets through a temp agency, and has difficulty finding steady work with good benefits.

In contrast, after two years, the guided pathways student completes an associate of arts degree with a focus in business, and enters the marketing program at the local university as a junior. She also starts a part-time job at the marketing firm where she had interned the previous two summers, and plans to continue working there while she finishes her bachelor's degree.

Cafeteria college student	Guided pathways college student
• Has not completed business program after 5 years of sporadic, part-time enrollment	• Completes business program in 2 years
• Realizes that some of the courses she took will not transfer for credit toward business program at state university; discovers that the university's business program has restricted enrollment; decides to graduate with a general studies associate degree	• Accepted into bachelor's program at state university; transfers all credits for junior standing in major
• Continues working in low-wage jobs	• Works part-time at marketing company where she interned, while starting at the university
• Disengaged by lecture-based courses	• Engaged particularly in social science course, based on topical readings and participation in class projects
Earns a general studies degree Employed in series of low-wage jobs	*Graduates in 2 years On track to complete bachelor's in 5 years Employed part-time in field of interest*

FIGURE C.4. Completion phase: completion of credential of value for further education and labor market advancement.

In many ways, the experiences and behaviors of the hypothetical cafeteria college student, shown on the left-hand side of the figures, reflect typical experiences and behaviors of community college students today. Most students attend part-time, take multiple developmental courses initially, take breaks between semesters or drop out entirely, are confused about which courses to take, and, even if they persist, are surprised to find that they have earned college credits that will not apply to graduation or transfer in a specific major. The purpose of the guided pathways approach is to shift students' experiences and behaviors to more closely resemble those of the hypothetical guided pathways student, shown on the right-hand side of the figures.

Previous chapters have provided a variety of concrete recommendations for how colleges might design and implement guided pathways in order to positively affect students' motivation, persistence, and progression through college. While every member of the college will need to be involved in multiple aspects of guided pathways design and implementation, various personnel may wish to focus their energies on different aspects of the redesign, as we discuss below.

Roles in the Redesign Process

Based on our experience in working with colleges that have initiated the guided pathways design process, below we offer some ideas about how key stakeholders might participate in the redesign process at their own institution.

Faculty Members and Academic Administrators

CREATE MAPS FOR ALL PROGRAMS

The guided pathways approach is built around program maps; thus, creating maps for broad exploratory majors or meta-majors, as well as for the specific major programs embedded within them, is a key first step. The process of creating maps needs to be led by faculty from across disciplines, but it should also involve advisors, career services counselors, and other student services professionals as well.

The primary components of program maps include program learning outcomes, term-by-term course sequences, and milestones (such as critical courses students must pass) that mark students' progress toward completion. For transfer programs, learning outcomes should align with requirements for junior standing in related majors at key transfer destinations.

For career programs, learning outcomes should incorporate industry skill standards.

Program maps should also specify how to support students who enter with varying levels of academic preparation, including the types of students who have traditionally been referred to remedial education, focusing on ways to contextualize basic skill building into challenging and program-relevant learning experiences, with the goal of accelerating students into college-level coursework as quickly as possible.

BUILD PARTNERSHIPS WITH TRANSFER DESTINATION PROGRAM FACULTY AND WITH EMPLOYERS

To guarantee that program maps will articulate seamlessly with key transfer destination programs, community college faculty need to build relationships with their counterparts at each transfer destination. Faculty may give priority to building strong transfer pathways with those destinations that serve transfer students effectively, and that themselves have strong labor market and education outcomes for their students. Similarly, career program faculty should work with employers to ensure that the learning outcomes for their programs are aligned with local labor force needs.

FOCUS ON BUILDING SKILLS, CONCEPTS, AND HABITS OF MIND

Program maps provide a key framework for individual instructors to use in improving their own courses' curriculum and instruction. In particular, maps help each instructor identify which learning outcomes are most important to emphasize in order to support students' development of the key skills, concepts, and habits of mind that will be critical to their success in their chosen field. To support one another in the process of redesigning course materials, activities, and instructional approaches, faculty can create intra-departmental or intra-program instructional inquiry groups. Groups may find it most effective to follow a structured process for their inquiry, such as identifying common challenges in the classroom and tackling each challenge in a systematic way by gathering data, developing hypotheses, experimenting with a new approach, and reporting back to the group.

CREATE AN INFRASTRUCTURE FOR FACULTY SUPPORT

Academic administrators must create an infrastructure to support the work of program mapping groups and instructional inquiry teams. For example, teaching and learning centers can move away from providing general workshops or one-on-one assistance to faculty, and instead focus on helping *groups* of faculty by organizing, facilitating, or providing expert advice to program mapping teams, instructional inquiry teams, or collaborative course design teams. After the initial work of program mapping groups is done, academic leaders should consider continuing these teams as part of a long-term governance body, which would be responsible for assessing student learning outcomes, revising program maps as necessary, and supporting efforts to improve instruction over time.

Student Services Staff and Administrators

WORK WITH FACULTY TO DESIGN A MANDATORY PROCESS FOR PROGRAM EXPLORATION AND SELECTION

All new students should be required to choose a broad program area, or meta-major, or a specific program that would be embedded within a meta-major. By requiring new students to choose a meta-major when they first enroll, colleges can provide undecided students with a structured way to explore specific programs over their first semester. However, some students will need up-front academic and career guidance in order to choose a meta-major in the first place. To provide both immediate help with meta-major selection and ongoing help with program exploration, colleges can use a mixture of online and face-to-face components, including online assessments and exploration tools, in-person advising sessions, and student success courses. While student services professionals will be responsible for much of the design and implementation of these components, it is critical to involve faculty perspectives and input in the process, and to keep faculty informed about how these processes affect the students who are interested in, or have selected, meta-majors in their program area.

IMPLEMENT E-ADVISING TOOLS THAT CAN FACILITATE MONITORING AND SUPPORT FOR STUDENT PROGRESS ALONG PROGRAM PATHWAYS

A variety of e-advising tools are now on the market, but few combine student tracking, case management, and early alerts into one package. Based on an ongoing CCRC project that is studying the implementation and adoption of e-advising tools at several community colleges and four-year institutions, we have observed that most institutions spend insufficient time and energy in up-front planning *before* they select their e-advising tool. As a result, tools may not meet advisors' and students' needs, resulting in an expensive product that few people use in an effective way. Before purchasing a product, we recommend at least a semester-long process of tool exploration—conducted not just by the technology staff but also by professional and faculty advisors—in order to ensure that the selected tool meets the needs of the college's new guided pathways organization and to explore how the work and responsibilities of faculty and staff would have to change to make effective use of the new tool.

Institutional Researchers

TRACK LOSS AND MOMENTUM POINTS ALONG STUDENTS' PATHS THROUGH COLLEGE

Institutional researchers can track cohorts of entering first-time college students longitudinally, in order to locate "loss points," that is, places along the path where students tend to struggle, and "momentum points" (for example, entering a program of study within one year) that, based on the experience of students in the past, are associated with an increased likelihood of completing a credential. Researchers should highlight variations in such loss and momentum points by program area.[4] Not only do student pathways differ by program (because requirements vary), but faculty are most interested in students who are in their programs (or who could potentially be recruited into their programs) and therefore are most likely to be engaged by data on the progress of their own students.

FOLLOW STUDENTS AS THEY CONTINUE THEIR EDUCATION

Community colleges will find it helpful to track the success of transfer students after they depart. Data from the National Student Clearinghouse can be used to identify not only which institutions but also which programs students are likely to major in (based on the majors of program graduates). Special attention should be given to how well transfer students perform at their destination institutions. If students have much worse outcomes at some destinations compared to others, community colleges may wish to steer their students to the higher-performing institutions (and programs within them), and build strong transfer partnerships that further reinforce students' success at those institutions.

FOLLOW STUDENTS INTO THEIR CAREERS

To the extent feasible, institutional researchers should track students' employment outcomes. Surveys of program completers are typically insufficient to understand the real labor market benefits of a community college education. Instead, it is more useful to work with state agencies to match student records to unemployment insurance wage records. Colleges should examine labor market outcomes by program area both for students who complete programs and those who do not. Such data are useful for making a case to local and state stakeholders regarding the value of the college's education programs. In addition to these analyses, however, colleges also need to maintain strong communication with employers in relevant fields to ensure that their programs are up-to-date and continue to meet employer needs.

College CEOs and Other Top Administrators

REFLECT ON COMMITMENT TO STUDENT SUCCESS IN BUDGETARY DECISIONS

College leaders should clearly demonstrate their commitment to student success through a willingness to commit resources to guided pathways efforts that promise to improve outcomes on a substantial scale. For example, leaders may need to reallocate funds to support professional development or release time for cross-functional teams and collaborative inquiry groups, or to rethink the teaching loads and benefit packages of talented adjunct faculty. Leaders should also be willing to adopt practices (such as requiring all students to choose a major or meta-major; requiring orientation, advising, or student success courses for new students; and expecting students to update their program and academic plan each semester) that may risk reduced enrollment income in the short term but will improve student retention and completion in the long term. To fund these budgetary decisions, leaders should seek to identify college practices that do not help students enter and complete high-quality programs of study, and reallocate those resources to redesigned practices, programs, or services that support student progress into and through program pathways.

RETHINK COMMITTEE STRUCTURES TO FOCUS ON STUDENT SUCCESS

Too often, academic and administrative committees devote more attention to bureaucratic issues than to monitoring and improving student success. Colleges need to have some governance body that has strong representation from faculty as well as student services staff, and that is responsible for keeping a sharp focus on student success and for identifying ways to improve outcomes at scale. For such a committee to work, it needs to have clout. Therefore, top administrators should "lead by listening," taking the recommendations of such a body seriously. Responsibilities and leadership of departmental bodies may also need to be rethought to shift their focus from offering courses to recruiting and supporting students through programs of study.

HIRE AND PROMOTE FACULTY AND STAFF WITH A STRONG COMMITMENT TO IMPROVING STUDENT OUTCOMES

Faculty and professional staff should be centrally involved in rewriting their own job descriptions and promotion criteria in ways that focus on assessing and improving student success. However, this process of rewriting hiring and promotion policies is unlikely to happen without strong and unequivocal support from the top of the college. Leaders should also ensure that rewritten policies communicate the importance of shared responsibility for student outcomes and emphasize the importance of collaboration and inquiry in every position across the college.

The Way Ahead for Guided Pathways

Community colleges across the country are already experimenting with elements of the guided pathways approach by implementing program maps, exploratory meta-majors, e-advising and early alert systems, accelerated and contextualized developmental education, and faculty inquiry groups. To achieve substantial improvements in student completion rates, however, more colleges will need to embark on guided pathways, and those that have already begun the process will need to expand from implementing only one or two elements to implementing the full suite of elements in an integrated and systematic way. As we conclude this book, we consider how the dynamics of higher education reform, ongoing research and evidence gathering, and political and economic pressures may influence the adoption and expansion of guided pathways.

A Framework for Higher Education Reform

Higher education has entered a period of intense experimentation and innovation in which a variety of reform-oriented proposals and initiatives jockey for the attention of individual colleges and state systems. Rather than seeing the guided pathways model as yet another competing reform, we believe the model provides a framework around which to structure and focus many of these reforms—particularly those that are intended to improve outcomes for the typical community college student.

Current higher education policy debates and associated reform ideas revolve around college costs, the use of educational technology and online education, developmental education, advising and counseling, faculty development, competency-based education, financial aid regulation, performance funding, and the matriculation of high-performing disadvantaged students into elite colleges (and the associated undermatching problem).[5] Below, we briefly summarize how the guided pathways framework can help shape and focus each of these issues.

We agree that colleges should reduce *costs*, but the discussion of this issue has focused on cost per enrollment or cost per credit hour. The guided pathways model directs our attention to two different concepts of cost: the full pathway cost per student, as opposed to the cost in one year or semester, and the cost per desired outcome (that is, completion of a high-quality credential that propels the student into further education and career advancement). As we have argued, the focus on cutting costs per student has led colleges to adopt practices that hurt outcomes. The guided pathways framework shifts colleges' attention to minimizing the cost per successful outcome, thereby making best use of colleges' limited resources to help students succeed.

Reformers have looked to *educational technology* and *online programs* to increase access to higher education and lower costs. We are skeptical about the potential costs saving, but in designing the use of technology, a focus on guided pathways leads us to ask how and under what circumstances these technologies can be used to address the educational needs of typical community college students. We have argued that it is often difficult to motivate such students in fully online programs. The guided pathways focus suggests that educational technology and online programs will be more effective if they are incorporated into well-structured programs that provide students with clear guidance, small class sizes, intensive student-faculty interaction, and a learning facilitation approach to teaching.

Advocates of *competency-based education* hope that it will both lower costs and allow colleges to do a better job of identifying and assessing the competencies needed for degrees and credentials. The guided pathways model encourages the development and definition of program-level competencies, and it emphasizes the need to incorporate those into well-structured programs. To the extent that reformers hope to use competency-based education for an unbundled approach to learning, they will need to consider how to support the many prospective students who are not already well focused and highly motivated.

There are now widespread efforts to reform and improve *developmental education*. The guided pathways model reconceptualizes remediation as part of the beginning of a college-level program of study. This perspective highlights the problem that for many students developmental education diverts them from college-level programs. In our view, developmental education should be designed to accelerate all students into college-level program-relevant coursework as quickly as possible, while providing the support necessary to ensure their success without lowering standards.

Educators agree that *student services,* including *advising,* are crucial for student success, and a variety of current reforms focus on hiring additional advisors or leveraging new technology to provide information and track students. The guided pathways perspective suggests that reforms to student services will be much more effective if they are implemented in concert with the development of program maps that provide a default course of study that students can follow to achieve clearly specified end goals for further education and employment. The perspective also highlights the need to integrate e-advising services and student success courses into students' everyday experience, in order to free up advisors to focus their one-on-one time on the students who need it most.

Financial aid reform is at the top of the federal education reform agenda. Much of this discussion has focused on simplifying the application process. Simplification is certainly consistent with guided pathways, but the model also directs our attention to two additional issues with financial aid. First, deadlines and dates for the application and reapplication process—for example, for transfer-bound students, application dates for four-year college aid—should be incorporated into student milestones within their program maps. Second, while the current requirement that students be enrolled in a program in order to be eligible for federal financial aid is sensible, our analysis implies that many students meet this requirement by enrolling in a "program" that is poorly organized and delineated. If financial aid policies required students to enroll in a coherent program of study that clearly leads to employment and further education, this would encourage colleges to develop such programs and to create mechanisms that help entering students choose among them, thus making a real difference in students' college experiences.

Every college has a program for *faculty development,* but most are based on a self-service model, and in cases where they are mandatory, they often fail to meet the real challenges that faculty face in the classroom. The guided pathways model implies that faculty development should be organized around collaborative activities designed to strengthen programs, develop program-level learning objectives, and experiment with new pedagogical approaches.

Performance funding policies are designed to help motivate colleges to focus more on improving student outcomes. An analysis based on guided pathways suggest that they are more likely to be effective if they are accompanied by other policies, such as those that encourage the creation of clearer programmatic pathways to baccalaureate transfer or to career advancement in high-demand fields. Funding models might also include incentives for progress on the critical milestones developed in program maps.

The reform of *community to four-year college transfer* in the past has focused on developing common course numbering and guaranteed transfer of credit. The guided pathways approach suggests that transfer policy is more likely to be effective if it is incorporated into a system in which two- and four-year college faculty work together to create coherent programmatic pathways with well-constructed maps that cross the transfer divide— and that lead to career-path employment and further education at the graduate level in fields where it is required.

Finally, the *undermatching* problem has received intense focus from policymakers and researchers in recent years. Researchers have shown that many low-income students with strong high school academic records do not apply to selective colleges and therefore end up at local less-selective, more poorly funded colleges where they are thought to receive a lower-quality education and encounter weaker opportunities for long-term success. Providing useful and timely information to these students increases their chances of applying to and enrolling in a selective college.[6] The guided pathways perspective is certainly consistent with providing more information to high school students, although we emphasize that it should be connected to well-organized college programs and that information should be provided for all students, not only those with strong academic records. Moreover, while the undermatching discussion implies a fixed distribution of quality among colleges, the guided pathways approach is designed to improve the quality of education throughout the less-selective sectors of higher education so as to improve all college outcomes—not just those of disadvantaged students with strong academic records, but also those of the large majority of students whose records would not gain them admission to a selective college.

In general, the guided pathways model provides a useful lens through which to analyze many reform strategies. Central to the guided pathways model—and its implications for a wide variety of reforms—is the development of coherent, relevant, and easily understood programs of study that ideally stretch back into the high school, as well as forward into bachelor's institutions and the labor market. This approach of providing clear educational pathways can help colleges and policymakers focus and leverage their ongoing reform efforts in ways that will have a substantial impact on student success.

Gathering Further Evidence

In this book, we have drawn evidence in support of our recommendations from a variety of sources. In particular, we have strong evidence that the current cafeteria structure of community colleges does not serve students well, and that reforms popular in the 1990s and early 2000s had little impact on either the basic structure or the outcomes of these colleges. We also have strong evidence for key design features of the guided pathways model: for example, behavioral economics research demonstrates that providing a structure for decision making in the face of complex choices can lead to better, more satisfactory decisions, and psychological research demonstrates that motivation is strengthened by creating strong interpersonal connections. The field is also increasingly compiling qualitative, case study, and preliminary quantitative evidence about the effectiveness of specific guided pathway elements. For example, we presented evidence on how underprepared students can be engaged and motivated, and how they can ultimately succeed at a higher level with accelerated developmental education strategies that focus on immediate exposure to challenging and relevant course material coupled with a learning facilitation approach to teaching. Finally, colleges that have implemented major elements of the guided pathways model are enthusiastic about them; they feel they are moving in the correct direction, and point to encouraging preliminary student outcomes to support that view.

We believe that this foundation of knowledge, together with the vital importance of significantly improving college performance and student outcomes, justifies the ambitious and comprehensive model that we have proposed. But we still have many questions. How effective is the overall model? Which of its elements are most important? What are the most significant barriers to its implementation? Without answers to these questions, many colleges may be hesitant to take on the risks and challenges of guided pathways reform.

It is very difficult for researchers to rigorously evaluate whole-institution reforms such as the guided pathways approach. Most random-assignment studies in higher education have created program and control groups within one institution, which is not an option in this case. While K–12 researchers can sometimes randomly assign institutions to a specific reform (particularly in large cities with potentially hundreds of elementary or middle schools), college personnel are unlikely to agree to the random assignment of institutions; and even if they did, the number of colleges within a given system or state tends to be too small to yield the power necessary for a reasonable test of the reform. On the other hand, if a guided pathways college received many more student applications than it could accept, the college could determine admissions by lottery in order to randomly assign students to an intervention group (attending the guided pathways college) versus a control group (attending another local college). This strategy could work in dense urban areas in which students have access to several different colleges, such that being denied admission to the guided pathways college would not automatically translate into delaying college enrollment entirely. To capitalize on this opportunity, college systems in urban areas might consider introducing and evaluating a comprehensive guided pathways model in one or more colleges before scaling it system-wide.

Thus far, however, given that no institutions have yet adopted *all* the integrated elements of the overall model (although CUNY's newest community college, Guttman, might come closest to doing so), we cannot yet evaluate guided pathways as a holistic reform. Yet as more colleges adopt guided pathways elements, researchers can begin to track the trajectory of these colleges' outcomes and compare them to the trajectories of similar colleges that have not implemented guided pathways. Much can be learned from this approach, although it does not yield definitive causal results.

Another useful evidence-gathering approach is to focus on specific features of the model. For example, we have emphasized the importance of helping students to choose meta-majors at enrollment, and to choose specific programs of study within a semester or two. To better understand this element of the model, researchers could focus on questions such as these: What are the best and most effective ways to help support student choice of meta-majors and programs? How does the process work in colleges that have implemented meta-majors or other structures and practices designed to facilitate career and program choices? After students make their initial choice, how many change majors, and how disruptive is that change to their progress? Are students at colleges with structured decision-making processes more satisfied with their program decisions, compared to similar peers at similar colleges?

Of course, focusing on specific elements of the model does have one key drawback: a central tenet of the guided pathways approach is that it seeks to support student progress across entire program pathways, which implies significant coordination among groups of faculty and staff who currently have only limited interaction—for example, among developmental education and college-level faculty in disciplines outside of English and math, and among faculty and student services personnel. It also implies coordinated changes in curricula, pedagogic approaches, professional development, and student records. Implementing and studying only individual elements of the model will have a much more limited impact than implementing the full integrated model. However, studies of individual elements can still yield many insights about design, implementation, feasibility, and potential impacts. The recent study of ASAP at the City University of New York also indicates that it is possible to evaluate a program that contains a cluster, though not all, of the features of the guided pathways approach.

The guided pathways model represents a comprehensive reform, and no one study of it will be definitive. But a varied program of research can build a base of knowledge for the continued development and improvement of elements of the model, and can add to the body of evidence to assess the model's effects.

Economic and Political Pressures to Redesign Colleges

Until recently, the cafeteria structure has been the foundation of a successful business model for community colleges. Low tuition, widespread locations, and a welcoming attitude to full- and part-time students generated a steady flow of enrollments—and if a self-service approach to course enrollment and student support services contributed to many students exiting college after only one or two semesters, that fact did not hurt (and indeed may have helped) a college's financial bottom line.

In reaction to increasing political pressure for higher graduation rates over the past two decades, colleges began to reexamine their student outcomes and to experiment with new approaches to improve those outcomes. These reforms had many benefits: they were often exciting and engaging, appealed to funders, raised the profile of the colleges that implemented them, generated inspiring stories of individual student success, engaged highly dedicated faculty and staff, and generated an overall atmosphere of reform and innovation. Yet while these reforms clearly helped some students, they also tended to be small in scale, avoided disrupting the underlying structure and operations of the college, and did not require the participation of most faculty, student services professionals, and administrators. Not surprisingly, then, student outcome improvements were limited at the institutional level, and political pressures for improved college performance have continued to mount.

At the same time that colleges face pressure to improve outcomes, they also face pressure to cut costs. Accordingly, the guided pathways approach may not be immediately appealing, because it may entail increased costs. Moreover, the approach may raise fears that the college will risk losing students. For example, encouraging students to attend full-time, implementing more time-intensive intake processes, or requiring students to enroll in meta-majors may drive some prospective students away. To the extent that these fears are borne out, by working more closely with local high schools and adult basic education programs and particularly by clarifying the structure and value of their programs for prospective students, colleges should be able to replace lost recruits. And of course, the guided pathways approach should also help retain more students into subsequent semesters. However, given that continuing students tend to take more expensive courses, their retention may not entirely cover the costs of any first-semester enrollment losses. Along those same lines, we have observed examples of colleges that lost revenue when they helped significant numbers of new students avoid inexpensive remedial courses and instead enroll directly into more-expensive college-level courses.[7] And while we argue that guided pathways will reduce colleges' cost per successful outcome, unfortunately that is not the way that colleges are funded. Publicizing a lower cost per outcome is little consolation if the college's financial condition is deteriorating. In general, until policymakers recognize the perverse incentives involved in funding-by-enrollment and more explicitly support colleges in their attempts to cost-effectively improve students' longer-term outcomes, it will take courage for college leaders to embark on guided pathways reform.

On the other hand, there are some indications that the traditional cafeteria model may be less sustainable than it has been in the past. After experiencing dramatic enrollment increases during and after the Great Recession, by 2014, enrollments in many community colleges were falling. This trend may start to shift the relative cost of new recruitment versus retention, making retention-focused models such as guided pathways more attractive relative to recruiting new students. In some geographic areas, enrollment declines have also created excess capacity. Given fixed classroom and faculty salary costs, colleges in these areas will lose substantial amounts of money unless they can fill these classrooms with continuing students. As a result, enrollment declines may help lower the additional incremental costs of moving to a guided pathways model.

Federal financial aid funding, which increased immediately after the Great Recession, has also leveled off, and more students are competing for these funds. This, combined with more stringent federal financial aid regulations—in particular, reducing the number of terms students are eligible for Pell grants from eighteen to twelve, and introducing increasingly strict standards for satisfactory academic progress—have put pressure on colleges not only to make greater efforts to retain students but also to help students get through faster.

Broader political trends may also provide a stronger impetus for reform in the future. There is no question that the scrutiny of student outcomes has strengthened over time, and the growing prevalence of performance funding will add fiscal and political incentives to improve student outcomes. Continued state and federal emphasis on increasing the number of degrees and certificates will raise the political cost of poor performance. If colleges can show that they are substantially improving student outcomes, they will be more attractive to students and will put themselves in a better political position when arguing for increased public funding, or when working to shape other state education policies. In our experience, policymakers are often sympathetic to community colleges; thus, if community colleges can show effective efforts to improve, policymakers may be willing to continue and expand their support for these institutions.

Overall, with all of the controversy and debate surrounding higher education, it is easy to forget that the focused attention on improving college outcomes is a relatively recent phenomenon. In contrast to the decades of activity and reform in elementary and high schools, the intensive activity in higher education stretches back only ten to twenty years. We still have a great deal to learn about how to meet the challenge of increasing postsecondary student success, but the guided pathways model synthesizes our best knowledge thus far, and it offers a framework within which to align promising reform strategies. It will take a combination of economic, political, and evidence-based influences to persuade college leaders and policymakers to make the necessary investments—and take on the risks involved—in implementing guided pathways reforms. We believe that those reforms will enable community colleges to better serve their vital role in educating the millions of Americans who attend them each year.

Notes

Introduction

1. As of the 2011–2012 school year, 43 percent of all undergraduate students, or approximately 10.5 million students, were enrolled in public two-year colleges. Authors' calculations using 12-month unduplicated headcounts from the Integrated Postsecondary Education Data System (IPEDS), http://nces.ed.gov /ipeds/datacenter/.
2. Berkner, Choy, & Hunt-White (2008); National Center for Public Policy and Higher Education (2011).
3. Radford, Berkner, Wheeless, & Shepherd (2010).
4. State Higher Education Executive Officers (2013), figure 3, p. 21.
5. President's Commission on Higher Education (1947), pp. 36–39.
6. Snyder & Dillow (2013), table 221, "Total fall enrollment in degree-granting institutions, by attendance status, sex of student, and control of institution: Selected years, 1947 through 2011."
7. Ibid., table 223, "Total fall enrollment in degree-granting institutions, by control and level of institution: 1970 through 2011."
8. The percentage of recent high school graduates who enrolled in a two- or four-year college increased from 45 percent in 1960 to 68 percent in 2011. See Snyder & Dillow (2013), table 234, "Recent high school completers and their enrollment in two-year and four-year colleges, by sex: 1960 through 2011."
9. Regulations for the SRK graduation rates were finally published in the *Federal Register* in December 1995. Colleges for which a two-year associate degree was the highest degree offered had to make their rates available to prospective students no later than January 2000, and colleges whose highest degree took four years did not have to make their rates available until January 2003.
10. For community colleges, the SRK graduation rate measures the percent of first-time, full-time students who graduate from the initial college of enrollment within three years. This measure does not include part-time students (a majority of community college students) and the many students who

transfer in, and for the most part does not count transfer to a four-year college without completing an associate degree (most transfers do not complete the associate degree) as a positive outcome. In 2010, the Department of Education impaneled a task force to reform the measure.

11. According to a 2012 AASCU study, thirty states have enacted or are considering enacting performance funding (Kelderman, 2013).

12. Snyder & Dillow (2012), table 345, "Graduation rates of first-time postsecondary students who started as full-time degree/certificate-seeking students, by sex, race/ethnicity, time to completion, and level and control of institution where student started: Selected cohort entry years, 1996 through 2007." Here the "more selective peers" are public four-year colleges that accept fewer than 25 percent of applications.

13. For a review of the research see Oreopoulos & Petronijevic (2013); for research on the returns to sub-baccalaureate credentials see Belfield & Bailey (2011).

14. Roughly 90 percent of community college students enroll intending to obtain a formal credential or to transfer to a four-year institution (Hoachlander, Sikora, & Horn, 2003).

15. Horn & Skomsvold (2011).

16. Shapiro et al. (2012), figure 12, p. 33.

17. Schneider & Yin (2011).

18. OECD (2013), Indicator A1, p. 26.

19. In 2010, ATD became an independent not-for-profit that continued to raise money from many sources to further the type of works started under the original grant.

20. Parry, Field, & Supiano (2013).

21. Rutschow et al. (2011).

22. Bailey (2009); Karp (2011); Rutschow & Schneider (2011).

23. Quint, Jaggars, Byndloss, & Magazinnik (2013).

24. These results measure trends for colleges that joined ATD in it first years of implementation. In 2010, ATD became an independent nonprofit organization, and the analysis discussed here does not relate to activities of the nonprofit Achieving the Dream Inc.

25. Rutschow et al. (2011), chapter 8, pp. 121–145.

26. Mayer et al. (2014), chapter 2.

27. Belfield, Crosta, & Jenkins (2014).

28. About 40 percent of students who are deemed college-ready complete a postsecondary credential in eight years, compared to 25 percent of those who take at least one remedial course. See Bailey (2009).

29. Rutschow et al. (2011), chapter 4, pp. 53–70.

30. Achieving the Dream (2009).

31. For a review of the literature see Jenkins (2011), pp. 6–10.

32. Rutschow et al. (2011), chapter 7, pp. 111–120.

33. For a review see Jenkins (2011), pp. 10–12.

34. Western Governors University is the probably the best-known example of this trend. See Connell (2011).

35. The book *Stretching the Higher Education Dollar: How Innovation Can Improve Access, Equity, and Affordability,* edited by Andrew Kelly and Kevin Carey (2013), is a collection of chapters by some of the leading thinkers who are advocating for or predicting major changes as a result of the development of online education and associated innovations.

1. Redesigning College Programs

1. Scott-Clayton (2011).
2. Ibid.
3. Ibid., p. 13.
4. Deil-Amen & Rosenbaum (2003).
5. Rosenbaum, Deil-Amen, & Person (2009).
6. Dadgar (2012); Horn & Nevill (2006).
7. J. Johnson, Rochkind, Ott, & DuPont (2009).
8. Bertrand, Mullainathan, & Shafir (2006), p. 8.
9. Auguste, Cota, Jayaram, & Laboissière (2010); Complete College America (2011).
10. Zeidenberg (2012).
11. Rosenbaum, Deil-Amen, & Person (2009), p. 104.
12. Grubb (2006), p. 197.
13. Nodine, Jaeger, Venezia, & Bracco (2012).
14. Booth et al. (2013).
15. Horn & Skomsvold (2011).
16. Shapiro et al. (2013), figure 1, p. 17.
17. Of students who first entered higher education through a community college in 2003–2004, 37 percent indicated that they were undecided about a major in their first year. Thirteen percent declared a major in liberal arts and sciences, and the remaining half indicated an intent to major in business or another occupational field. Authors' calculations using the 2004/09 Beginning Postsecondary Students Longitudinal Study (BPS:04/09). See http://nces.ed.gov/surveys/bps/about.asp.
18. Gardenhire-Crooks, Collado, & Ray (2006).
19. Grubb (2006).
20. Norton & Wilson (2012).
21. Mullin (2012); Smith (2010).
22. Reed (2013), p. 110.
23. Interviews with administrators, faculty, and staff at Guilford Technical Community College, Jamestown, NC, by Davis Jenkins and Peter Crosta of the Community College Research Center, June 6, 2013. Note that the fifty-eight North Carolina community colleges have a common course numbering system that ensures equivalency of courses in the system. The University of North Carolina system does not have such a policy.
24. Gross & Goldhaber (2009); Roksa & Keith (2008).
25. Monaghan & Attewell (2014).

26. Audits of the transcripts of bachelor's programs graduates who transferred from a community college have also found inefficiencies in the credit transfer process. For example, according to a June 2001 report by the Texas Transfer Issues Advisory Committee (2001) convened by the Texas Higher Education Coordinating Board, a degree audit conducted by five Texas universities—Midwestern State University, Texas A&M International University, University of Texas at Austin, University of Houston, and University of North Texas—of transcripts of transfer students who had earned at least thirty semester credit hours from a Texas community college found that 83 percent of credit hours presented were accepted for transfer, but only 70 percent were applied to a degree. Our reading of the results presented in the report suggests that as many as one in five credits transferred from a Texas community college to a state university was not accepted toward a degree for no clear reason.

27. Venezia, Bracco, & Nodine (2010).

28. R. D. Cox (2009).

29. Ignash (1997).

30. Kadlec & Gupta (2014).

31. Kadlec & Martinez (2013).

32. Jaggars & Fletcher (2014).

33. Public Agenda (2012).

34. Hossler et al. (2012).

35. Shapiro et al. (2013).

36. Ibid.

37. King (1994).

38. This summary was taken from the full set of principles for learning and teaching listed on the website for Carnegie Mellon University's Eberly Center for Teaching Excellence, where these researchers who developed them are employed: http://www.cmu.edu/teaching/eberly/.

39. Kuh, Jankowski, Ikenberry, & Kinzie (2014).

40. Kerrigan & Jenkins (2013).

41. In 2010–2011, community colleges conferred 640,000 associate degrees. Of those, only 22,000 (under 4 percent) were in specific social science, humanities, and physical science fields. In contrast, 290,000 (45 percent) were associate of arts or sciences with no major discipline specified, while the remainder were in occupational fields. Source: Institute of Education Sciences, National Center for Education Statistics, "College and Career Tables Library," table 38, "Degrees conferred at Title IV public institutions, by level of degree and field of study: United States, academic year 2009–2010," http://nces.ed.gov/datalab/tableslibrary/viewtable.aspx?tableid=8491.

42. Rosenbaum, Deil-Amen, & Person (2009), pp. 225–227.

43. Rosenbaum, Deil-Amen, & Person (2009); Stephan, Rosenbaum, & Person (2009).

44. Merisotis & Jones (2010).

45. Using data from the National Longitudinal Study (NELS:88), Stephan, Rosenbaum, & Person (2009) found that students attending private two-year insti-

tutions were more likely to complete an associate degree or higher than similar students who attended public two-year institutions. But the sample of students at the private colleges they used was small (116 students), and the method used for matching similar students may not have taken account of all relevant differences. As the authors concede, the finding may have been due to unobservable differences in student characteristics (see also Scott-Clayton, 2011, p. 22). The Tennessee Tech Centers attract students who have chosen to enroll in a full-time, relatively short-term, narrowly defined occupational program, whereas comprehensive community colleges enroll many students who have little sense of their goals and programs. These differences distort the interpretation of any comparison between the Tech Centers and Tennessee's comprehensive community colleges.

46. Scott-Clayton (2011), p. 2.
47. Deci & Flaste (1996).
48. Utterback (1998).
49. Norton & Wilson (2012).
50. Nickerson & Rogers (2010).
51. Sunstein (2013), p. 38.
52. Thaler & Sunstein (2008).
53. Keller, Harlam, Loewenstein, & Volpp (2011); Madrian & Shea (2001); Thaler & Sunstein (2008).
54. Choi, Laibson, Madrian, & Metrick (2002, 2003, 2004).
55. E. J. Johnson & Goldstein (2003).
56. McKenzie, Liersch, & Finkelstein (2006), as cited in Keller, Harlam, Loewenstein, & Volpp (2011).
57. Booth et al. (2013).
58. Keller, Harlam, Loewenstein, & Volpp (2011), p. 377.
59. Sunstein (2013), pp. 119–120.
60. Ibid., p. 121.
61. Jaggars & Fletcher (2014).
62. Keller, Harlam, Loewenstein, & Volpp (2011).
63. Kadlec, Immerwahr, & Gupta (2013), p. 18.
64. Ibid., p. 20.
65. Grant & Dweck (2003); Marzano (2000); Popham (2000); Tyler (2000).
66. Ericsson, Krampe, & Tesch-Romer (1993).
67. Ambrose, Bridges, DiPietro, Lovett, & Norman (2010).
68. Newmann, Smith, Allensworth, & Bryk (2001); see also Bryk, Sebring, Allensworth, Luppescu, & Easton (2010).
69. Newmann, Smith, Allensworth, & Bryk (2001), p. 299.
70. Collins & Porras (1994).
71. Sources on ASU pathways: presentation by Art Blakemore, senior vice provost and ASU online executive vice provost, at Complete College America meeting in Chicago on "Guided Pathways to Success," August 29, 2012; Philip Regier, executive vice provost and dean, ASU Online and Extended Campus, "Making the University Student-Centric: eAdvisor at ASU," presentation at annual

meeting of Complete College America, in New Orleans, December 14, 2013; telephone interview with Maria Hesse, vice provost for academic partnerships, Arizona State University, and former president, Chandler-Gilbert College, Maricopa Community College District, by Davis Jenkins and Jeffrey Fletcher, May 13, 2013.

72. A map for an exploratory major in social and behavioral sciences is available at https://webapp4.asu.edu/programs/t5/roadmaps/ASU00/UCSBSEXPL/2013. A map for an exploratory major in business is available at https://webapp4.asu.edu/programs/t5/roadmaps/ASU00/BABUSEXP/2013.

73. Telephone interview with Michele Cuomo, by Davis Jenkins and Jeffrey Fletcher, May 6, 2013. Cuomo has since moved to another college but oversaw the initial implementation of the Queensborough academies.

74. Telephone interview with Victor Fichera, principal investigator for Academy Assessment Protocol, Queensborough Community College, by Davis Jenkins and Jeffrey Fletcher, May 9, 2013.

75. Ibid.

76. http://www.aacu.org/value/rubrics/index_p.cfm?CFID=64784705&CFTOKEN=91647612.

77. Rodicio, Mayer, & Jenkins (2014).

78. Among these are generic skills that apply to all programs and students, including (1) communicate effectively using listening, speaking, reading, and writing skills; (2) use quantitative analytical skills to evaluate and process numerical data; (3) solve problems using critical and creative thinking and scientific reasoning; and seven others.

79. Data on "Retention and Graduation Rates for Full-Time FTIC Students," provided by the Florida State University Office of Institutional Research. See also Yeado, Haycock, Johnstone, & Chaplot (2014).

80. Telephone interview with Maria Hesse by Davis Jenkins and Jeffrey Fletcher, May 13, 2013.

81. Telephone interview with Andrea Buehman, associate vice chancellor (in charge of curriculum and transfer partnerships), Maricopa Community College District, by Davis Jenkins and Jeffrey Fletcher, May 13, 2013.

82. This description of the ASU exploratory majors is drawn from a presentation by Maria Hesse, Arizona State University, at a December 6, 2013, Jobs for the Future meeting in Boston on transfer policy.

83. Telephone interview with Maria Hesse by Davis Jenkins and Jeffrey Fletcher, May 13, 2013.

84. Weinbaum, Rodríguez, & Bauer-Maglin (2013), pp. 28–29.

85. Ibid.

86. Information in this paragraph is taken from the CUNY Pathways initiative website: http://www.cuny.edu/academics/initiatives/pathways.html.

87. Faculty charged that the initiative was driven more by concern among administrators to improve graduation rates and reduce "excess credits" than to improve the quality of teaching and student learning. They expressed concern

that Pathways will put pressure on colleges to reduce foreign language instruction, science courses with lab sessions, and other offerings important to
student learning (Clark, 2013).

88. PowerPoint presentation by Philip Regier, executive vice provost and dean,
ASU Online and Extended Campus, "Making the University Student-Cen-
tric: eAdvisor at ASU," at annual meeting of Complete College America, in
New Orleans, December 14, 2013.

89. Telephone interview with Maria Hesse by Davis Jenkins and Jeffrey Fletcher,
May 13, 2013.

90. Queensborough data from PowerPoint presentation shared by Victor Fichera,
principal investigator for Academy Assessment Protocol, Queensborough
Community College.

91. City University of New York, Office of Institutional Research and Assessment (2014).

92. Authors' calculations using the Integrated Postsecondary Education Data
System (IPEDS). See http://nces.ed.gov/ipeds/.

93. Guttman Community College (2014).

2. Guiding Students

1. Author calculations from NELS, using an eight-year time frame from students' initial entry into community college.

2. Venezia, Kirst, & Antonio (2003).

3. L. Gordon (2013).

4. For example, see Jaggars & Fletcher (2014).

5. Community College Survey of Student Engagement (2012).

6. Grubb (2006); Jaggars & Fletcher (2014).

7. Community College Survey of Student Engagement (2012); Venezia, Bracco,
& Nodine (2010).

8. Center for Community College Student Engagement (2012).

9. The Detroit study is discussed in detail in Jaggars & Fletcher (2014).

10. Grubb & Associates (1999), p. 5.

11. Public Agenda (2012), p. 5.

12. See Grubb (2006). This discussion is drawn from Karp (2013); Karp, O'Gara,
& Hughes (2008); and O'Gara, Karp, & Hughes (2009).

13. Karp, O'Gara, & Hughes (2008), p. 17.

14. See, for example, V. N. Gordon (2006); Hartung & Blustein (2002); Holland
(1997); Krumbotlz (1996); Lent (2005); O'Banion (1972); Parsons (1909);
Super (1990).

15. Peterson, Sampson, & Reardon (1991); Reardon, Lenz, Sampson, & Peterson,
2011.

16. Bialik (2010); U.S. Bureau of Labor Statistics (2012, 2014).

17. National Academic Advising Association (NACADA) (2006). See, for example, Campbell & Nutt (2008); Hagen & Jordan (2008).

18. National Academic Advising Association (NACADA) (2006).
19. Campbell & Nutt (2008); Crookston (1972); Hagen & Jordan (2008); Low-enstein (2005); O'Banion (1972).
20. Grubb (2006); Rosenbaum, Deil-Amen, & Person (2009).
21. Karp, O'Gara, & Hughes (2008).
22. Gore & Metz (2008).
23. Karp (2013).
24. Ibid.
25. Community College Survey of Student Engagement (2007); Deil-Amen & Rosenbaum (2003); Goomas (2012); Nodine, Jaeger, Venezia, & Bracco (2012).
26. Karp, O'Gara, & Hughes (2008); Jaggars & Fletcher (2013); Public Agenda (2012).
27. Kadlec, Immerwahr, & Gupta (2013).
28. Ibid.
29. Scrivener & Weiss (2013).
30. Visher, Butcher, & Cerna (2010).
31. See, for example, Steele & McDonald (2008), cited in V. N. Gordon, Habley, & Grites (2008).
32. Van Noy, Weiss, Jenkins, Barnett, & Wachen (2012).
33. Margolin, Miller, & Rosenbaum (2013).
34. Jaggars & Fletcher (2014).
35. Ibid., based on 2012 (pre-intervention) results.
36. Grubb (2006); Karp, O'Gara, & Hughes (2008).
37. Schudde & Scott-Clayton (2014).
38. Center for Community College Student Engagment (2012); Karp et al. (2012).
39. Center for Community College Student Engagment (2012).
40. See Bourdon & Carducci (2002).
41. Karp et al. (2012); O'Gara, Karp, & Hughes (2009).
42. Community College Survey of Student Engagement (2010).
43. Boudreau & Kromrey (1994); Cho & Karp (2012); Schnell & Doetkott (2003); Strumpf & Hunt (1993); Zeidenberg, Jenkins, & Calcagno (2007).
44. Rutschow, Cullinan, & Welbeck (2012); Scrivener, Sommo, & Collado (2009); Weiss, Brock, Sommo, Rudd, & Turner (2011).
45. The remainder of this section is drawn from Karp et al. (2012).
46. Bransford, Brown, & Cocking (2000); Flavell (1979); Perin & Hare (2010).
47. Karp & Fletcher (2014).
48. Keup & Petschauer (2011).
49. Stella and Charles Guttman Community College course catalog, June 5, 2013, p. 30.
50. Sunstein (2013), p. 64.
51. Ross, White, Wright, & Knapp (2013), pp. 29–30.
52. Castleman & Page (2014).
53. Shute (2008).
54. Jenkins (2011), pp. 2–12.

55. Karp & Fletcher (2014).

56. Johns (2006), p. 58.

57. Ibid.

58. Jaggars & Fletcher (2014).

59. Ibid.; Karp & Fletcher (2014).

60. This discussion is based on unpublished observations we made during the course of a larger study of Virginia's student development courses; see Karp et al. (2012).

61. Jaggars & Fletcher (2014).

62. http://www.cuny.edu/academics/programs/notable/asap/about.html.

63. Scrivener & Weiss (2013).

64. Levin & Garcia (2012). In Chapter 6 we discuss the implications of cost-per-student versus cost-per-completion models in more detail.

65. Presentation by Art Blakemore, senior vice provost and ASU online executive vice provost, at Complete College America meeting on "Guided Pathways to Success," Chicago, August 29, 2013. See also Parry (2012).

66. Personal communication with Maria Hesse, vice provost for academic partnerships, Arizona State University.

67. Information on Austin Peay from presentation by Tristan Denley, provost, Complete College America meeting on "Guided Pathways to Success," Chicago, August 29, 2012.

68. Presentation by Karen Laughlin, dean of undergraduate studies, Florida State University, on effective mapping with intrusive advising, at Complete College America meeting on "Guided Pathways to Success," Chicago, August 29, 2012.

69. Telephone interview with Maria Hesse, vice provost for academic partnerships, Arizona State University, and former president, Chandler-Gilbert Colleges, by Davis Jenkins and Jeffrey Fletcher, May 13, 2013.

3. Rethinking Student Instruction

1. However, only a small proportion of that research has been conducted in the context of postsecondary education, and an even smaller proportion has addressed the unique context of instruction in the community college. The major exceptions to this lack of attention are two books by Norton Grubb: Grubb (2013); Grubb & Associates (1999).

2. Twenty-six percent of community college students fall within the 125th percentile of the federally established poverty threshold, compared to 20 percent of four-year college students (Horn & Nevill, 2006).

3. Bailey (2009); also, according to Center for Community College Student Engagement (2012), 66 percent of SENSE entering students and 72 percent of CCSSE "promising practices" survey students said they needed developmental coursework in at least one area. According to Scott-Clayton's calculations using BPS 2009, half of all undergraduates and 68 percent of community

college students take at least one remedial course (Scott-Clayton, Crosta, & Belfield, 2014; and personal communication with Judith Scott-Clayton, September 16, 2014).

4. Horn & Nevill (2006).
5. Center for Community College Student Engagement (2012); J. Johnson & Rochkind (2009).
6. Horn & Nevill (2006).
7. For example, see R. D. Cox (2009); Grubb (2013).
8. Hiebert et al. (2003).
9. Common Core State Standard Initiative (2010).
10. Applebee & Langer (2011); Karp (2006).
11. Cromley, Snyder-Hogan, & Luciw-Dubas (2010); Johns (1985); Karp (2006); Thiede, Griffin, Wiley, & Anderson (2010); D. Wang (2009).
12. Bickerstaff, Barragan, & Rucks-Ahidiana (2012).
13. R. D. Cox (2009); Dickie & Farrell (1991); Karp (2012).
14. Karp (2006).
15. Zimmerman & Pons (1986), p. 623. For a review of how metacognition and other "noncognitive" factors affect academic performance see Farrington et al. (2012).
16. R. D. Cox (2009); Grubb (2013); Karp & Bork (2014).
17. The terms "knowledge transmission" and "learning facilitation" come from Kember & Gow (1994), but they are also known by other names; for example, the knowledge transmission approach has also been termed as a "banking" model. The learning facilitation approach is deeply interconnected with the notion of "active learning" and a philosophy known as "learner-centered" or "learning-centered" teaching—see, for example, Barr & Tagg (1995); O'Banion (1997); Weimer (2002).
18. Kember & Gow (1994).
19. Waskow (2006), p. 51.
20. California Commission on Teacher Credentialing & California Department of Education (1997).
21. Barnes (1983); Grubb (2013); Haas & Keeley (1998); Nunn (1996); Weimer (2002).
22. Hoxby (2014).
23. Chaudhury (2011); Redish, Saul, & Steinberg (1998).
24. Kuh, Cruce, Shoup, Kinzie, & Gonyea (2008); Laird, Chen, & Kuh (2008); Reason, Cox, McIntosh, & Terenzini (2010); Umbach & Wawrzynski (2005).
25. Cabrera et al. (2002); Fullilove & Treisman (1990); Hodara (2011); D. W. Johnson & Johnson (2009); Lasry, Mazur, & Watkins (2008); Saville & Zinn (2011); Tinto (1997); Watkins & Mazur (2013).
26. Schuetz (2002).
27. O'Gara, Karp, & Hughes (2009).
28. As a result, few students receive this type of instruction in any forum. One survey estimated that only 14 percent of undergraduates were ever taught how to study (Gardiner, 1998).

29. Karp & Bork (2014), p. 26.
30. For a practitioner-oriented review of much of this research see Ambrose, Bridges, DiPietro, Lovett, & Norman (2010).
31. Kember & Gow (1994); Waskow (2006).
32. Weimer (2002), p. 31.
33. Cormier & Bickerstaff (2013); Grubb (2013).
34. Michael (2007); Weimer (2002).
35. R. D. Cox (2009); Kearney & Plax (1992); Weimer (2002).
36. Michael (2007); Weimer (2002).
37. See Weimer (2002), chapter 3, for a fuller discussion of how the typical college's focus on "covering" content defeats the goal of leveraging content to support deeper learning.
38. Grubb (2012).
39. Michael (2007); Waskow (2006); Weimer (2002).
40. Haas & Keeley (1998), p. 66.
41. Kezar (2013).
42. Ibid.
43. Grubb (2013); Marincovich (1998); Murray (2002); Waskow (2006).
44. Bickerstaff & Edgecombe (2012).
45. Waskow (2006).
46. For example, see Grubb (2013); Hutchings, Huber, & Ciccone (2011); Marincovich (1998).
47. Marincovich (1998); Murray (2002).
48. Baker & Zey-Ferrell (1984); Bickerstaff & Edgecombe (2012); M. D. Cox (2004); Fugate & Amey (2000); Rice, Sorcinelli, & Austin (2000); Shulman (1993).
49. Haas & Keeley (1998); Hull (2004); Kember & Gow (1994); Michael (2007); Weimer (2002).
50. Murray (2002), p. 91; emphasis added.
51. See, for example, Grubb (2013); Perin (2004).
52. Center for Community College Student Engagement (2012).
53. Pascarella & Terenzini (2005).
54. The available research on tutoring and supplemental instruction is plagued by self-selection issues, making it difficult to estimate the strength of these services' positive impacts, although qualitative and correlational studies consistently show positive results. As with student success courses, the short- and long-term effectiveness of these services may depend in large part on how they are implemented. Research suggests that unless tutors are systematically trained, tutoring may be ineffective. Similarly, supplemental discussion sessions that simply retread the material covered in class appear to be less effective than those that emphasize collaborative and connected learning. See Boylan, Bliss, & Bonham (1997); Pascarella & Terenzini (2005); Rutschow & Schneider (2011).
55. Center for Community College Student Engagement (2012).
56. Ibid.

57. This was an improvement compared to the 43 percent who did not receive encouragement, but still disappointing. After revising the encouragement to a "requirement" (although an unenforced one), still only 69 percent of the students visited the learning center. See Scrivener & Weiss (2009).

58. Karp, O'Gara, & Hughes (2008); Perin (2004), p. 579.

59. The following description of learning communities draws from Grubb (2013); Karp (2011); Minkler (2002); Visher, Weiss, Weissman, Rudd, & Wathington (2012).

60. Minkler (2002); Visher, Weiss, Weissman, Rudd, & Wathington (2012).

61. Karp (2011); Minkler (2002); Moore & Shulock (2009). A more rigorous quasi-experimental study at a university also found strong impacts on students' first-semester GPAs, particularly among black students; a year later, however, these effects had been cut in half (Hotchkiss, Moore, & Pitts, 2006). In a random-assignment study of learning communities, participants also reported a greater sense of integration and belonging on campus (Scrivener et al., 2008).

62. The proportion of learning community faculty reporting that they engaged in each behavior "more than 5 times per term" was 18 percent for collaborating on syllabi or assignments, 35 percent for communicating about shared students, and 34 percent for discussing course content with other instructors (Visher, Weiss, Weissman, Rudd, & Wathington, 2012).

63. Karp, O'Gara, and Hughes (2008).

64. Jaggars (2012); Jaggars & Xu (2010); D. Xu & Jaggars (2011a).

65. Jaggars (2014).

66. Jaggars & Xu (2010); D. Xu & Jaggars (2011a, 2011b, 2013).

67. H. Johnson & Mejia (2014); Streich (2014).

68. See, for example, how the negative effects of online learning increase as the models become increasingly rigorous, in H. Johnson & Mejia (2014) and D. Xu & Jaggars (2013).

69. H. Johnson & Mejia (2014); Kaupp (2012); D. Xu & Jaggars (2014).

70. This section draws from the following CCRC reports: Bork & Rucks-Ahidiana (2013), Jaggars (2014), and Jaggars & Xu (2013).

71. For a review of rigorous research on these three components of motivation see Deci & Flaste (1996). Also see empirical and qualitative studies on how each component relates to learning: for autonomy, Bain & Zimmerman (2009); Kerekes & Huber (1998); Mitchell (1993); S. M. Ross (1983); Weimer (2002); for competence, Bickerstaff, Barragan, & Rucks-Ahidiana (2012); Cohen, Steele, & Ross (1999); Covington (2007); Farrington et al. (2012); Latham & Locke (2007); Schunk & Rice (1991); Shute (2008); van Etten, Pressley, Freebern, & Echevarria (1998); for interpersonal connections, E. A. Barnett (2011); Hausmann, Schofield, & Woods (2007); Karp & Hughes (2008); Mendoza-Denton, Downey, Purdie, Davis, & Pietrzak (2002); Nora, Urick, & Cerecer (2011); Tinto (1993); van Etten, Pressley, Freebern, & Echevarria (1998); Walton, Cohen, Cwir, & Spencer (2012).

72. Bambara, Harbour, Davies, & Athey (2009); Jaggars (2014); Jaggars & Xu (2013).
73. Jaggars (2014); Jaggars & Xu (2013).
74. Jaggars & Xu (2013), p. 21.
75. R. Clark (1989); Kardash (1999); Kardash & Wallace (2001); Kirschner, Sweller, & Clark (2006); Stefanou, Perencevich, DiCintio, & Turner (2004); Weimer (2002).
76. Bork & Rucks-Ahidiana (2013); Jaggars (2014); Jaggars & Xu (2013).
77. Cormier (2014).
78. For more on tactics students use to balance their lives see Karp & Bork (2014).
79. The American Association for Higher Education noted in 1992 that learning "involves not only knowledge and abilities but values, attitudes, and habits of mind that affect both academic success and performance beyond the class-room" (Astin et al., 1992). For a review of research on such habits of mind, how they are important to student success, and how they are taught, see Far-rington et al. (2012).
80. For a digestible review of the research on this topic see Ambrose, Bridges, DiPietro, Lovett, & Norman (2010).
81. For more on the necessity of conceptual representation in learning mathe-matics see Brenner et al. (1997); Chappell (2006); Rittle-Johnson, Siegler, & Alibali (2001).
82. Bain (2004).
83. Chappell (2006), p. 36.
84. Allen, Donham, & Bernhardt (2011); Prince & Felder (2007).
85. Barragan & Cormier (2013).
86. New York Times (2011).
87. Casazza (1998); Norwood (1995); Safford-Ramus (2008).
88. American Association for Higher Education, American College Personnel Association, & National Association of Student Personnel Administrators (1998); American College Personnel Association (1994); Frost, Strom, Downey, Schultz, & Holland (2010); Harvey-Smith (2003); O'Banion (2000); Schuh & Gansemer-Topf (2010).
89. For example, Doucette & Dayton (1989); Harvey-Smith (2003); Newton & Smith (1996).
90. Grubb (2013).
91. Frost, Strom, Downey, Schultz, & Holland (2010).
92. As the Association of College and Research Libraries defines it, for any given task an "information literate" person is able to determine the extent of infor-mation needed; access the needed information effectively and efficiently; evaluate information and its sources critically; incorporate selected informa-tion into one's knowledge base; use information effectively to accomplish a specific purpose; understand the economic, legal, and social issues surrounding the use of information; and access and use information ethically and legally (Association of College and Research Libraries, 2000, pp. 2–3). In recent

years, all six regional accreditation agencies have incorporated these skills into their guidelines or requirements, the American Association of Community Colleges has endorsed their importance, and several states have considered requiring the integration of information literacy into college curricula (American Association for Community Colleges, 2008; Cunningham, 2012; DaCosta & Dubicki, 2012). Employers—even those who employ high school and career-technical education graduates—also endorse the importance of these particular skills and complain that their employees are weak in them (Katz, Haras, & Blaszczynski, 2010; Weiner, 2012).

93. Katz, Haras, & Blaszczynski (2010) report that a commercially available information literacy assessment known as "iSkills" predicted students' grades in an upper-division business writing course with correlations in the 0.30–0.32 range, even after controlling for students' GPA. These are substantially stronger predictive relationships than we see with math and English placement tests; see Scott-Clayton, Crosta, & Belfield (2014).

94. Everett (2010); Haas & Keeley (1998).

95. Cunningham (2012), p. 159; Walter (2008).

96. Cunningham (2012); Warren (2006); Zachery (2010).

97. For example, a community college librarian who created career-specific information literacy activities that could be quickly and easily integrated into career-technical courses (her first such workbook was titled *The Information Literate Chef*). See Cunningham (2012), p. 260.

98. For example, see Dhanesar (2006); Lindstrom & Shonrock (2006).

99. For example, the best-regarded online courses are typically designed with a team-based approach—for example, Alvarez, Blair, Monske, & Wolf (2005); Hawkes & Coldeway (2002); Hixon (2008); Knowles & Kalata (2007); Puzziferro & Shelton (2008); Thille (2008); H. Xu & Morris (2007).

100. Bass (2012); Bernstein & Greenhoot (n.d.).

101. Bernstein & Greenhoot (n.d.), p. 16.

102. Cook-Sather & Shore (2007), p. 7. For another excellent example of team-based course design, including innovative technology integration to promote information literacy, see Millet, Donald, & Wilson (2009).

103. For more details on Guttman's instructional teams see Weinbaum, Rodríguez, & Bauer-Maglin (2013).

104. Weinbaum, Rodríguez, & Bauer-Maglin (2013), p. 20.

105. This notion is very similar to that of faculty "professional learning communities"; see Bryk, Gomez, & Grunow (2010); Bryk et al. (2013).

106. The distinction between technical and adaptive challenges and their solutions is articulated in Heifetz (1998).

107. Heifetz (1998).

108. Ancess (2000), p. 616; Boyer (1990); Darling-Hammond, Wei, Andree, Richardson, & Orphanos (2009); Guskey & Yoon (2009); Hutchings, Huber, & Ciccone (2011); Kennedy (1998); Windschitl, Thompson, & Braaten (2011).

109. Capitalizing on this similarity, some prominent proponents of faculty inquiry have packaged inquiry as an explicitly research-oriented process known as

"scholarship of teaching and learning," in which the fruits of one's research are publicly shared with a larger scholarly community: see Hutchings, Huber, & Ciccone (2011). Of course, faculty inquiry need not be scientifically formal in order to be personally useful, nor need it be polished to the extent required for public sharing. Still, some faculty will still need some logistical and technical support in order to feel confident tackling it, as we discuss later.

110. Huber (2010); Hutchings, Huber, & Ciccone (2011).

111. Phifer (2010).

112. Ibid., p. 105.

113. See Kegan & Lahey (2001, 2009); Wagner et al. (2005).

114. Kegan & Lahey (2001).

115. For example, Brookfield (2002); Feldman & Paulsen (1999); Hutchings, Huber, & Ciccone (2011); Marincovich (1998); Phifer (2010); Sam (2002); Steadman (1998); Waskow (2006); Wildman, Hable, Preston, & Magliaro (2000).

116. Sam (2002), p. 193.

117. Brookfield (2002).

118. Bryk, Sebring, Allensworth, Luppescu, & Easton (2010); Fulton & Britton (2011); Goddard, Goddard, & Tschannen-Moran (2007); Leana (2011); Little (1982); Louis & Marks (1998); Mourshed, Chijioke, & Barber (2010).

119. Lampert, Boerst, & Graziani (2011); Little (1982).

120. Lampert et al. (2011), pp. 1369–1370.

121. M. D. Cox (2004); Wildman et al. (2000).

122. Huber (2008).

123. Ibid.

124. Weinbaum, Rodríguez, & Bauer-Maglin (2013), pp. 13–15.

125. Ibid., p. 16.

126. Ibid., p. 24.

127. Cormier & Bickerstaff (2013).

128. Grubb (2013), pp. 98–99.

129. Mitchell (1993).

130. For example, a U.S. Department of Education, Office of Planning, Evaluation, and Policy Development (2010) meta-analysis discusses mixed findings regarding online quizzes, embedded audio and video, and other technical frills. Mitchell (1993) and Hidi & Renninger (2006) find that two autonomy-supportive methods—showing how the topic relates to students' lives or interests, or encouraging students to build their own learning through hands-on activities, such as working on a project, writing, or learning new concepts within a group work setting—seem to be key to *holding* students' interest in a topic after their interest is initially caught by a fun or novel activity.

131. Sitzmann (2011).

132. R. E. Mayer et al. (2009).

133. Bowen, Chingos, Lack, & Nygren (2012); Lovett, Meyer, & Thille (2008).

134. Bowen, Chingos, Lack, & Nygren (2012), p. 22.

135. Ibid.; see also report supplement, Ithaka S+R (2012), for survey questions and scales. The "interest" scale ranged from 0 ("Not at all") to 4 ("A great deal"). The average response of 1.7 is slightly below 2 ("Some") (personal communication with Matthew Chingos, September 16, 2014).
136. U.S. Department of Education, Office of Planning, Evaluation, and Policy Development (2010).
137. For a review of the impact of learning software on student math performance see Hodara (2011), particularly pp. 61–62.
138. For example, see Grant & Courtoreille (2007); L. Wang (2008).
139. This instructor taught both Chemistry 111 and 112 online, and we descriptively compared her online course outcomes to those of students in the same online courses across the state system. For Chemistry 111, 77 percent of her students stayed in the course until the end of the semester, and of those who remained, they earned an average grade of 3.0; across the state, the comparable numbers were 79 percent and 2.38. For Chemistry 112, 93 percent of her students stayed, with an average grade of 3.93, compared to the statewide average of 89 percent and 2.08. See Jaggars, Edgecombe, & Stacey (2013).
140. Martinez & Martinez (1992, 1999); Slavin (1990).
141. Cormier (2014).
142. Reddy et al. (2013).
143. Reddy et al. (2013) do not provide a specific number; our number of 35 percent is an estimate based on a visual figure and other contextual information.
144. Barragan (2011).
145. Stillson & Alsup (2003), p. 334.

4. Helping Underprepared Students

1. Bailey (2009).
2. In general, pass rates for these courses are often below 80 percent and tend to be far lower in college-level math and science courses; see Zeidenberg, Jenkins, & Scott (2012).
3. Bailey, Jeong, & Cho (2010).
4. Barragan & Cormier (2013); Grubb (2013).
5. Scott-Clayton & Rodríguez (2012).
6. Unpublished analysis based on Achieving the Dream data, including cohorts of students entering community colleges between 2006 and 2008. The analyses include 63,650 students referred to a three-course sequence in remedial math, and 11,210 students referred to a three-course sequence in remedial reading. The updated numbers cited here are similar to those published in Bailey, Jeong, & Cho (2010), which focused on earlier cohorts of Achieving the Dream students.
7. Calcagno & Long (2008); Clotfelter, Ladd, Muschkin, & Vigdor (2013); Dadgar (2012); Martorell & McFarlin (2011); Scott-Clayton & Rodríguez

(2012); D. Xu (2013). While some large-scale studies using regression discontinuity or instrumental variable analysis show some positive results, they tend to be scattered among a much larger number of null and negative results: see Bettinger & Long (2005, 2009) (in the latter study, note that negative coefficients for a negative outcome translate to a positive result, while positive coefficients for a negative outcome translate to a negative result); Boatman & Long (2010). For a more detailed discussion see Bailey, Jaggars, & Scott-Clayton (2013).

8. See Bailey, Jaggars, & Scott-Clayton (2013).

9. This interpretation aligns with work from the K–12 literature demonstrating that academically lagging students benefit from more-challenging courses taken with more-advanced peers. See Burris, Wiley, Welner, & Murphy (2008); Levin (2007).

10. Clotfelter, Ladd, Muschkin, & Vigdor (2013); Scott-Clayton & Rodríguez (2012).

11. Hodara, Jaggars, & Karp (2012).

12. Jaggars & Hodara (2011).

13. For example, see Clotfelter et al. (2013); Collins (2008); Fields & Parsad (2012); Hodara, Jaggars, & Karp (2012); Jaggars & Hodara (2011).

14. Bettinger & Long (2003), p. 18.

15. Jaggars & Hodara (2013).

16. Scott-Clayton (2012), figure 3.

17. Scott-Clayton (2012).

18. Ibid.

19. Venezia, Bracco, & Nodine (2010).

20. Fay, Bickerstaff, & Hodara (2013).

21. Ibid.; Jaggars & Hodara (2011).

22. Grubb (2013), p. 52.

23. Jaggars & Hodara (2011), p. 27.

24. R. D. Cox (2009).

25. See Bailer (2006); Fox (2009); R. E. Mayer & Wittrock (1996); Nash-Ditzel (2010).

26. Zeidenberg, Jenkins, & Scott (2012).

27. Hodara, Jaggars, & Karp (2012).

28. For example, see Virginia Community College System (2010, 2011).

29. Hodara, Jaggars, & Karp (2012).

30. Ibid.

31. Bowen, Chingos, & McPherson (2009), p. 124.

32. Data provided by John Hetts, director of institutional research, Long Beach City College.

33. Bailey, Jeong, & Cho (2010); Hern (2010).

34. Bailey, Jeong, & Cho (2010).

35. Edgecombe (2011).

36. Grubb (2013); Jaggars & Hodara (2011).

37. Results presented in this section draw from Jaggars, Hodara, Cho, & Xu (forthcoming, 2015). Estimates control for a variety of student characteristics (such as gender, ethnicity, placement test scores, and prior academic achievement).

38. Fain (2012, 2013).

39. Jaggars, Hodara, Cho, & Xu (forthcoming, 2015). However, our analyses were able to compare these low-scoring accelerated students only to the low-scoring non-accelerated students who were most similar to them. While there were an ample number of these similar students, the fact remains that we could not effectively compare low-scoring students who chose acceleration with low-scoring students who were quite dissimilar from them and who also opted against the accelerated path. It is possible that these dissimilar students, who are currently very unlikely to opt for an accelerated path, avoid it because they suspect they would not thrive in it.

40. Jaggars, Hodara, Cho, & Xu (forthcoming, 2015).

41. CUNY internal study.

42. Wachen, Jenkins, Belfield, & Van Noy (2012).

43. Zeidenberg, Cho, & Jenkins (2010). Bearing in mind that not all basic-skills occupational students within these colleges participated in I-BEST, these estimates likely underestimate the true impact on program participants.

44. Rodríguez (2014).

45. Van Campen, Sowers, & Strother (2013). Although no rigorous studies have yet been conducted, CCRC is currently partnering with MDRC to evaluate the New Mathways Project.

46. PowerPoint presentation by Peter Adams, "Beyond Anecdotal Evidence," http://alp-deved.org/2011/07/beyond-anecdotal-evidence/.

47. Callahan & Chumney (2009).

48. Dweck (2006).

49. Aronson, Fried, & Good (2002).

50. Paunesku, Yeager, Romero, & Walton (2012), as cited in Yeager & Dweck (2012).

51. Barnett & Fay (2013).

52. Venezia & Voloch (2012).

53. Howell, Kurlaender, & Grodsky (2010).

54. Hodara (2013).

55. Barnett, Fay, Trimble, & Pheatt (2013).

56. For a recent review of the research on dual enrollment, including the results of a new random-assignment study on early-college high schools, see Berger et al. (2013). For further CCRC work on the topic see Hughes, Rodríguez, Edwards, & Belfield (2012); Karp, Calcagno, Hughes, Jeong, & Bailey (2007); Karp, Hughes, & Cormier (2012); Speroni (2011a, 2011b).

57. See Karp (2006).

58. Personal communication with Scott Ralls, director of the North Carolina Community College System.

59. Berger et al. (2013).

5. Engaging Faculty and Staff

1. Bradshaw & Fredette (2009).
2. Waskow (2006), p. 68.
3. See, for example, Bradshaw & Fredette (2009); Gallos (2009).
4. Gallos (2009), p. 137.
5. Bryk & Schneider (2002).
6. Ibid., p. 31.
7. Ibid. See also Feldman & Paulsen (1999).
8. Tschannen-Moran & Hoy (2000), cited in Louis, Mayrowetz, Smiley, & Murphy (2009), pp. 161–162; Uphoff (2000).
9. Bryk, Camburn, & Louis (1999). For an example in the private sector see Tucker, Nembhard, & Edmondson (2007).
10. Bryk & Schneider (2002), p. 26.
11. From an interview conducted as part of the project reported in Jaggars & Fletcher (2014).
12. Kezar & Lester (2009).
13. Taylor (2009); Taylor & Steenpoorte (2007).
14. Quillian (2004).
15. Taylor (2009).
16. Taylor & Steenpoorte (2007), p. 28; emphasis in the original.
17. Taylor (2009); Taylor & Steenpoorte (2007).
18. Bryk & Schneider (2002), p. 23.
19. Telephone interview with Michele Cuomo, associate dean for academic affairs, Queensborough Community College, by Davis Jenkins and Jeffrey Fletcher, May 6, 2013.
20. The quotes from Davidson County Community College personnel are from interviews conducted at the college on June 7, 2013, by Davis Jenkins and Peter Crosta.
21. Kegan & Lahey (2009), p. 73.
22. Gates & Robinson (2009), p. 153.
23. Kegan & Lahey (2009).
24. Ibid., p. 85.
25. Waskow (2006). Such reflection is surprisingly easy to evoke, simply by asking people questions. For example, in interviews with community college instructors who taught under the knowledge transmission model, Waskow's basic open-ended questions (such as, "The words 'to teach' can mean different things to different people. For you, what does it mean to teach?") had powerful effects. As she put it, "Instructors in this study made comments like, 'Well, now that I'm thinking about it' or 'Gosh, I never really thought about it before,' yet followed up with meaningful reflections regarding their own goals and methods. In effect, the interview process appears to have provided an opportunity for some instructors to reflect and articulate their own pedagogies *for the first time*" (p. 99; emphasis in the original).
26. Jaggars & Fletcher (2014).

27. Waskow (2006). For a contrast between espoused beliefs in critical thinking and actual instructional behaviors, see Haas & Keeley (1998).
28. McDonough (2000).
29. Interviews conducted during site visit to Sinclair Community College, June 10, 2013, by Davis Jenkins and Jeffrey Fletcher, Community College Research Center.
30. McDonough (2000).
31. Ibid.
32. Ibid.
33. Grubb (2013); Murray (2002).
34. Jassawalla & Sashittal (1999), p. 50.
35. McDonough (2000).
36. Cormier & Bickerstaff (2013).
37. The college chose its list of high-impact practices from the research literature and, in particular, George Kuh's work on practices that benefit underserved students, for example, Kuh (2008).
38. Cormier & Bickerstaff (2013).
39. Isoda, Stephens, Ohara, & Miyakawa (2007).
40. Kezar & Lester (2009), p. 196.
41. Ibid., p. 204.
42. Carstens & Howell (2012), pp. 54–55.
43. Murray (2002).
44. Corcoran, Fuhrman, & Belcher (2001), p. 81.
45. Carstens & Howell (2012), p. 55.
46. Brookfield (2002); Hutchings, Huber, & Ciccone (2011).
47. Wiseman (2010).
48. Deci (1996).
49. Kegan & Lahey (2009), p. 213.
50. Grubb (2013), p. 192.
51. Ibid.
52. For example, Fowler-Hill (2001).
53. Valencia's process is discussed in detail in Aspen Institute (2013).
54. Ibid., p. 7.
55. Aspen Institute (2013).
56. Fuhrmann (1995).
57. Hutchings, Huber, & Ciccone (2011); Kezar & Lester (2009); National Task Force on Civic Learning and Democratic Engagement (2012).
58. Dweck (2006).
59. Knapp, Kelly-Reid, Ginder, & Miller (2008).
60. Kezar (2013).
61. Blatt (2008).
62. Benjamin (2002, 2003); Bettinger & Long (2006); Eagan & Jaeger (2009); Ehrenberg & Zhang (2005); Harrington & Schibik (2001); Jacoby (2006); Jaeger & Eagan (2009); Schuetz (2002); Umbach (2007).

63. Figlio, Schapiro, & Soter (2013); Sherman (2014).
64. U.S. House of Representatives, Committee on Education and the Workforce (2014).

6. The Economics of College Redesign

1. C. M. Christensen & Eyring (2011); Coy (2014); Kelly & Carey (2013).
2. For example, Sebastian Thrun at Stanford University (Leckart, 2012) and Clay Shirky at New York University (http://www.shirky.com/weblog/2012/11/napster-udacity-and-the-academy/).
3. Baum & Ma (2013).
4. Ibid., figure 10.
5. Community college students who do have debt carry an average of $8,750 in loans (calculations from the 2007–2008 National Postsecondary Student Aid Study [NPSAS:08]; see http://nces.ed.gov/surveys/npsas/). Among first-time community college students tracked for six years, nearly 60 percent never borrow, and 75 percent borrow less than $6,000 (the corresponding figures for students at for-profit two-year institutions are 8 percent and 24 percent, respectively; for public four-year institutions, they are 39 percent and 50 percent (authors' calculations from the 2004/09 Beginning Postsecondary Students Longitudinal Study [BPS: 04/09]; see http://nces.ed.gov/surveys/bps/about.asp).
6. Kirshstein & Hurlburt (2012), figure S2, pp. 7–9.
7. Desrochers & Kirshstein (2012), figure 2, p. 6. As a result, community colleges were the only sector in higher education that did not increase educational expenditures in that period.
8. Baum & Ma (2013), p. 23.
9. Eagan & Jaeger (2009); Ehrenberg & Zhang (2005); Jacoby (2006). However, as we discussed in Chapter 5, this effect may be reversed if adjunct faculty hold full-time positions with opportunities for advancement; see Figlio, Schapiro, & Soter (2013). Adjunct faculty with close ties to the job market may also be more effective in certain occupational fields; see Bettinger & Long (2010).
10. Bound, Lovenheim, & Turner (2010).
11. Belfield & Jenkins (2014).
12. For example, success rates in fully online developmental education courses are so abysmally low that most community colleges now offer few to none of these sections online. See Jaggars & Xu (2010); D. Xu & Jaggars (2011b, 2014).
13. See for example, Desrochers & Hurlburt (2014).
14. Some research has examined the question of postsecondary "efficiency" by calculating cross-section cost per degree—see Belfield (2012a) for a review—but cross-section cost-per-degree calculations do not take account of variation in the costs of different programs, different types of students (for example,

beginning versus more advanced students), or other factors, and are therefore of limited use to colleges in understanding the costs of serving particular groups of students or the economic consequences of specific reforms.

15. See Belfield, Crosta, & Jenkins (2014). Data for this research were collected and compiled from the general ledger accounts of a large community college. These ledgers reported disaggregated spending by department and function (instruction, student support, administration), and in some cases by course. These data were used to calculate instructional spending (including instructional overhead) for each course by credit hour. Noninstructional operating expenditures were also included in the overall cost measures on a prorated FTE basis.

16. Crosta (2014).

17. N. Johnson (2009) presents a variety of approaches to measuring the cost per graduate: catalog cost, transcript method, and full cost attribution. These are much more useful than cross-sectional costs per graduate, and the transcript method and full cost attribution do take account of the actual courses that students take. In contrast to our method, Johnson uses an average cost per course rather than the actual cost of courses. These approaches have not been applied to community colleges, nor do they calculate the pathway cost per student, for all students and for completers and for different types as students, as we will do in this chapter.

18. The figure is based on calculations using data from Belfield, Crosta, & Jenkins (2014).

19. Note that by "costs" in this figure, we mean expenditures, both instructional and noninstructional. Instructional expenditures (which include the direct cost of instruction, instructional equipment, and academic department overhead) were calculated by summing the instructional spending for all courses that each student took based on student transcript data. Noninstructional expenditures (including student support services, college administration, facilities, and all other operating costs; capital costs were not included) were apportioned to each group of students based on the number of students in the group.

20. A student who receives an associate degree is counted as one completion. If a student completes a thirty-five-credit occupational certificate program, and the average associate degree program at the college requires seventy credits, then that student would count as half a completion. Similarly, if a student transfers to a four-year institution with thirty-five credits but without having earned an associate degree, he or she would also count as half a completion (even though most transfer students do not graduate from their destination institutions within five semesters). A potential criticism of this calculation is that it puts no value on credits accumulated by students who do not earn any credential or transfer. An alternative might be to calculate the value of every credit, but this would essentially return us to a cost per enrollment model. For a full discussion of the advantages of the method we use see Belfield (2012a).

21. Table 6.1 uses data from the same college and cohort of students as Figure 6.1. As before, completion rates are measured in terms of associate degree equivalents. Data on revenue—derived from the fee structure of the college and the state funding formula—were attached to individual courses, allowing us to calculate the revenue associated with a student's progression along a pathway. "Net revenue" is defined as total revenue minus expenditures. For details on the calculation of simulated costs and revenues see Belfield, Crosta, & Jenkins (2014).

22. Also, career-technical students may be more likely to take courses requiring expensive equipment as they progress.

23. Decreasing the number of students who have earned thirty or more credits but with no degree or certificate after five years is estimated to have no effect on net revenue.

24. Aspen Institute & Achieving the Dream (2013), p. 9.

25. Grubb (2013), p. 183.

26. Ibid., p. 183.

27. Ibid., pp. 144–145.

28. Ibid., p. 145.

29. Rodicio, Mayer, & Jenkins (2014).

30. See http://www.successnc.org/initiatives/code-green-super-cip-curriculum -improvement-project.

31. Kelderman (2013).

32. Dougherty & Reddy (2013).

33. Ibid.

34. Zumeta (2001).

35. Dougherty & Hong (2005); Sanford & Hunter (2011). In the state of Washington, for example, less than 1 percent of the community and technical college system's operating budget is allocated through the state's performance funding policy (according to authors' February 3, 2014, e-mail correspondence with Washington State Board for Community and Technical Colleges staff, the state appropriations for fiscal years 2014 and 2015 were $617,965,000 and $625,259,000, respectively, of which $5,250,000 was dedicated to the state's performance funding policy, the Student Achievement Initiative, in each year).

36. Dougherty & Reddy (2013).

37. Postsecondary Analytics (2013).

38. Clotfelter, Ladd, Muschkin, & Vigdor (2013). The North Carolina Community College System, like Washington's State Board for Community and Technical Colleges, has since adopted a different set of metrics for measuring college performance. See North Carolina Community College System (2013).

39. Sanford & Hunter (2011).

40. Jenkins & Shulock (2013).

41. To measure students' forward progress or momentum over one year, CCRC researcher Clive Belfield (2012b) classified students in Washington community and technical colleges in a given year according to their main program

type or area—adult basic education, precollege remediation, academic transfer, or workforce—and then counted the number of additional milestones (beyond those that students had already accumulated prior to the given year) that each student had achieved by the following year. This method would allow states to measure student momentum year over year, without having to wait multiple years. But we know of no state that has adopted such an approach.

42. The changes in the Student Achievement Initiative policy are described in documents on the website of the Washington State Board for Community and Technical Colleges, at http://www.sbctc.ctc.edu/college/_e-student-achieve ment-2012.aspx.

43. Dougherty & Reddy (2013).

44. Belfield (2013).

45. Mullin (2012); see figure 1, p. 6.

46. This and the three paragraphs following are based on Sherman & Andreas (2012); Washington Higher Education Coordinating Board (2006, 2009); Washington State Board for Community and Technical Colleges (WSBCTC) (2013); and a telephone interview with Michelle Andreas, vice president for instruction, South Puget Sound Community College, and former staff member, Washington State Board for Community and Technical Colleges, January 15, 2014.

47. Handel & Williams (2012), pp. 29–31.

48. Fain (2014).

49. Gross & Goldhaber (2009); Roksa & Keith (2008). We are not aware of similar research on the efficacy of employment-oriented pathways other than the research on the returns to community college occupational programs mentioned earlier.

50. Roksa & Keith (2008).

51. See Spillane, Reiser, & Reimer (2002) for an overview.

52. Coburn & Stein (2006).

53. Loeb & McEwan (2006).

54. For example, Spillane, Reiser, & Reimer (2002) found that teachers who engaged in discussions with other teachers and with administrators about new district policies and their implications for practice were more likely to understand the policies in ways that were consistent with their original intent.

55. Spillane & Burch (2006); Spillane, Reiser, & Gomez (2006).

56. Crosta (2014).

57. Interviews with faculty and staff at Guilford Technical Community College, Jamestown, NC, by Davis Jenkins and Peter Crosta of CCRC, June 6, 2013.

58. Belfield & Bailey (2011).

59. Belfield (2013); Belfield, Liu, & Trimble (2014); Jaggars & Xu (2014).

60. Dadgar & Trimble (2014); D. Xu & Trimble (2014).

61. Belfield & Bailey (2011); Oreopoulos & Petronijevic (2013).

62. Baum, Ma, & Payea (2013); Belfield & Levin (2007); Cutler & Lleras-Muney (2010).

63. Trostel (2010).
64. Belfield (2012a), table 1.
65. Kelly & Carey (2013).
66. Connell (2011); Fain (2014).
67. Bell & Federman (2013).
68. North Carolina General Assembly, Program Evaluation Division (2010), p. 7.
69. Bichelmeyer et al. (2011), p. 6.
70. Christensen et al. (2013); Ho et al. (2014).
71. Straumsheim (2013).
72. Hoxby (2014).
73. Using data from the Beginning Postsecondary Student transcript study, Hoxby (2014) estimates that 36 percent of courses in nonselective postsecondary institutions cover basic or general material that is contained in standard textbooks.
74. Hoxby (2014) uses data from the 2004 National Survey of Postsecondary Faculty to estimate that 70 percent of courses at nonselective institutions use multiple-choice examinations, which are often supplied with the textbook.
75. Using measures of students' academic integration available in the Beginning Postsecondary Student study, Hoxby (2014) finds that the average freshman at nonselective institutions has an academic integration score of 56, compared to an average of 78 for freshmen at all postsecondary institutions. Only 29 percent of freshmen in nonselective institutions meet informally with faculty, only 57 percent meet with an advisor, and only 39 percent participate in study groups.
76. Griffiths, Chingos, Mulhern, & Spies (2014).
77. Ibid., p. 21.
78. Baum & Ma (2013).
79. See College Navigator at National Center for Education Statistics website: http://nces.ed.gov/collegenavigator/?q=western+governors+university&s=all &id=433387#retgrad.
80. Berrett (2014).

Conclusion

1. These are the four phases of the student "loss-momentum" framework developed as part of Completion by Design (CBD), a community college reform initiative funded by the Bill & Melinda Gates Foundation. CCRC participated in the development of CBD and has worked with other organizations to formulate its guiding principles and provide technical assistance to participating colleges. See Rassen, Chaplot, Jenkins, & Johnstone (2012).
2. Adapted from the "Tale of Two Terrys," a schematic developed as part of Completion by Design. See Couturier (2012).
3. Attewell, Heil, & Reisel (2012); Horn, Cataldi, & Sikora (2005).
4. To support the process of program mapping, researchers can work with program faculty to examine the courses taken by students who completed their

programs in the past. Did these students take the courses faculty would expect based on the "catalog program requirements"? Did they take courses in the expected sequence? Did they take more courses than they needed? What courses are critical to predicting students' success in a program? When in a student's program should those courses be taken? Should students who do not pass the course be allowed to continue in the program? What are some viable alternative program pathways for such students? See the *Completion by Design Student Pathways Analysis Toolkit,* an online guide that CCRC helped to develop: http://completionbydesign.org/our-approach/step-3-diagnose-the-issues/pathway-analyses-toolkit.

5. Bowen, Chingos, & McPherson (2009); Hoxby & Turner (2013).
6. Bowen, Chingos, & McPherson (2009); Hoxby & Turner (2013).
7. For example, in the North Carolina Community College System, President Scott Ralls framed the money saved by the state as a result of the system's developmental education redesign as the "developmental dividend" and argued that the system should be allowed to keep some of the savings generated by its reform; see "Community college system must thrive so NC can thrive" (2014).

References

Achieving the Dream. (2009). *Field guide for improving student success.* http://achievingthedream.org/resource/178/field-guide-for-improving-student-success.

Allen, D. E., Donham, R. S., & Bernhardt, S. A. (2011). Problem-based learning. *New Directions for Teaching and Learning* 2011(128): 21–29.

Alvarez, D. M., Blair, K., Monske, E., & Wolf, A. (2005). Team models in online course development: A unit-specific approach. *Journal of Educational Technology and Society* 8(3): 176–186.

Ambrose, S. A., Bridges, M. W., DiPietro, M., Lovett, M. C., & Norman, M. K. (2010). *How learning works: 7 research-based principles for smart teaching.* San Francisco: Jossey-Bass.

American Association for Community Colleges. (2008). AACC position statement on information literacy. http://www.aacc.nche.edu/About/Positions/Pages/ps05052008.aspx.

American Association for Higher Education, American College Personnel Association, & National Association of Student Personnel Administrators. (1998). *Powerful partnership: A shared responsibility for learning.* Washington, DC.

American College Personnel Association. (1994). *The student learning imperative: Implications for student affairs.* Washington, DC.

Ancess, J. (2000). The reciprocal influence of teacher learning, teaching practice, school restructuring, and student learning outcomes. *Teachers College Record* 102(3): 590–619.

Applebee, A. N., & Langer, J. A. (2011). A snapshot of writing instruction in middle schools and high schools. *English Journal* 100(6): 14–27.

Aronson, J., Fried, C. B., & Good, C. (2002). Reducing the effects of stereotype threat on African American college students by shaping theories of intelligence. *Journal of Experimental Social Psychology* 38(2): 113–125.

Aspen Institute. (2013). *Creating a faculty culture of student success.* Washington, DC.

Aspen Institute & Achieving the Dream. (2013). *Crisis and opportunity: Aligning the community college presidency with student success.* Washington, DC.

Association of College and Research Libraries. (2000). *Information literacy competency standards for higher education.* Chicago.

Astin, A. W., Banta, T. W., Cross, K. P., El-Khawas, E., Ewell, P. T., Hutchings, P., et al. (1992). *Principles of good practice for assessing student learning.* Washington, DC: American Association for Higher Education.

Attewell, P., Heil, S., & Reisel, L. (2012). What is academic momentum? And does it matter? *Educational Evaluation and Policy Analysis* 34(1): 27–44. doi: 10.3102/0162373711421958.

Auguste, B. G., Cota, A., Jayaram, K., & Laboissière, M. C. A. (2010). *Winning by degrees: The strategies of highly productive higher-education institutions.* New York: McKinsey & Company.

Bailer, D. L. (2006). *A multivariate analysis of the relationship between age, self-regulated learning, and academic performance among community college developmental education students.* PhD diss., Touro University International. Ann Arbor, MI: ProQuest Dissertations & Theses Full Text database, UMI No. 3201703.

Bailey, T. (2009). Challenge and opportunity: Rethinking the role and function of developmental education in community college. *New Directions for Community Colleges* 2009(145): 11–30. doi: 10.1002/cc.352.

Bailey, T., Jaggars, S. S., & Scott-Clayton, J. (2013). Characterizing the effectiveness of developmental education: A response to recent criticism. *Journal of Developmental Education* 36(3): 18–25.

Bailey, T., Jeong, D. W., & Cho, S.-W. (2010). Referral, enrollment, and completion in developmental education sequences in community colleges. *Economics of Education Review* 29(2): 255–270.

Bain, K. (2004). *What the best college teachers do.* Cambridge, MA: Harvard University Press.

Bain, K., & Zimmerman, J. (2009). Understanding great teaching. *Peer Review* 11(2): 9–12.

Baker, P. J., & Zey-Ferrell, M. (1984). Local and cosmopolitan orientations of faculty: Implications for teaching. *Teaching Sociology* 12(1): 82–106. doi: 10.2307/1318320.

Bambara, C. S., Harbour, C. P., Davies, T. G., & Athey, S. (2009). Delicate engagement: The lived experience of community college students enrolled in high-risk online courses. *Community College Review* 36(3): 219–238.

Barnes, C. P. (1983). Questioning in college classrooms. In *Studies of college teaching*, edited by C. L. Ellner & C. P. Barnes, 61–81. Lexington, MA: Lexington Books.

Barnett, E. A. (2011). Validation experiences and persistence among community college students. *Review of Higher Education* 34(2): 193–230.

Barnett, E. A., & Fay, M. P. (2013). *The Common Core state standards: Implications for community colleges and student preparedness for college.* New York: National Center for Postsecondary Research.

Barnett, E. A., Fay, M. P., Trimble, M. J., & Pheatt, L. (2013). *Reshaping the college transition: Early college readiness assessments and transition curricula in four states.* New York: Columbia University, Teachers College, Community College Research Center.

Barr, R. B., & Tagg, J. (1995). From teaching to learning: A new paradigm for undergraduate education. *Change* 27(6): 12–25. doi: 10.2307/40165284.

Barragan, M. (2011). *Beyond bells and whistles: Leveraging interactive technologies to enhance online learning.* Paper presented at the 17th Annual Sloan Consortium International Conference on Online Learning, Lake Buena Vista, FL.

Barragan, M., & Cormier, M. S. (2013). *Enhancing rigor in developmental education.* Inside Out series publication. New York: Columbia University, Teachers College, Community College Research Center.

Bass, R. (2012). Disrupting ourselves: The problem of learning in higher education. *EDUCAUSE Review* 47(2): 22–33.

Baum, S., & Ma, J. (2013). *Trends in college pricing.* Washington, DC: The College Board.

Baum, S., Ma, J., & Payea, K. (2013). *Education pays: The benefits of higher education for individuals and society.* Washington, DC: The College Board.

Belfield, C. (2012a). *Measuring efficiency in the community college.* CCRC Working Paper No. 43. New York: Columbia University, Teachers College, Community College Research Center.

———. (2012b). *Washington State Student Achievement Initiative: Achievement points analysis for academic years 2007–2011.* New York: Columbia University, Teachers College, Community College Research Center.

———. (2013). *The economic benefits of attaining an associate degree before transfer: Evidence from North Carolina.* CCRC Working Paper No. 62. New York: Columbia University, Teachers College, Community College Research Center.

Belfield, C., & Bailey, T. (2011). The benefits of attending community college: A review of the evidence. *Community College Review* 39(1): 46–68.

Belfield, C., Crosta, P., & Jenkins, D. (2014). Can community colleges afford to improve completion? Measuring the costs and efficiency effects of college reforms. *Educational Evaluation and Policy Analysis* 36(3): 327–345. doi: 10.3102/0162373713517293.

Belfield, C., & Jenkins, D. (2014). *Community college economics for policymakers: The one big fact and the one big myth.* CCRC Working Paper No. 67. New York: Columbia University, Teachers College, Community College Research Center.

Belfield, C., & Levin, H. M. (2007). *The price we pay: Economic and social consequences of inadequate education.* Washington, D.C.: Brookings Institution Press.

Belfield, C., Liu, Y. T., & Trimble, M. J. (2014). *The medium-term labor market returns to community college awards: Evidence from North Carolina.* CAPSEE Working Paper. New York: Center for Analysis of Postsecondary Education and Employment.

Bell, B. S., & Federman, J. E. (2013). E-learning in postsecondary education. *Future of Children* 23(1): 165–185.

Benjamin, E. (2002). How over-reliance on contingent appointments diminishes faculty involvement in student learning. *Peer Review* 5(1): 4–10.

———. (2003). Reappraisal and implications for policy and research. In *Exploring the role of contingent instructional staff in undergraduate learning,* edited by E. Benjamin, 79–113. San Francisco: Jossey-Bass.

Berger, A., Turk-Bicakci, L., Garet, M., Song, M., Knudson, J., Haxton, C., et al. (2013). *Early college, early success: Early college high school initiative impact study.* Washington, DC: American Institutes for Research.

Berkner, L., Choy, S., & Hunt-White, T. (2008). *Descriptive summary of 2003–04 beginning postsecondary students: Three years later.* NCES 2008-174. Washington, DC: National Center for Education Statistics.

Bernstein, D., & Greenhoot, A. (n.d.). *Final narrative report on Spencer/Teagle Foundations project.* Lawrence: University of Kansas.

Berrett, D. (2014). College, on your own. *Chronicle of Higher Education,* July 14. http://chronicle.com/article/College-On-Your-Own/147659/?cid=at &utm_source=at&utm_medium=en.

Bertrand, M., Mullainathan, S., & Shafir, E. (2006). Behavioral economics and marketing in aid of decision making among the poor. *Journal of Public Policy and Marketing* 25(1): 8–23.

Bettinger, E. P., & Baker, R. (2014). The effects of student coaching: An evaluation of a randomized experiment in student advising. *Educational Evaluation and Policy Analysis* 36(1): 3–19. doi: 10.3102/0162373713500523.

Bettinger, E. P., & Long, B. T. (2003). *The effects of remediation on student outcomes: The plight of underprepared students in higher education.* Cleveland: Case Western University.

———. (2005). Remediation at the community college: Student participation and outcomes. *New Directions for Community Colleges* 2005(129): 17–26.

———. (2006). The increasing use of adjunct instructors at public institutions: Are we hurting students? In *What's happening to public higher education? The shifting financial burden,* edited by R. G. Ehrenberg, 51–69. Baltimore: Johns Hopkins University Press.

———. (2009). Addressing the needs of underprepared students in higher education: Does college remediation work? *Journal of Human Resources* 44(3): 736–771.

———. (2010). Does cheaper mean better? The impact of using adjunct instructors on student outcomes. *Review of Economics and Statistics* 92(3): 598–613.

Bialik, C. (2010). Seven careers in a lifetime? Think twice, researchers say. *Wall Street Journal,* September 4. http://online.wsj.com/articles/SB100014240527 4870420680457546816280587990.

Bichelmeyer, B., Keucher, S., Eddy, M., Sadowski, M., Bott, J., & Hannon, B. (2011). *Costs and pricing of distance/online education programs.* Bloomington, IN, West Lafayette, IN, and Muncie, IN: Indiana University, Purdue University, & Ball State University.

Bickerstaff, S., Barragan, M., & Rucks-Ahidiana, Z. (2012). *"I came in unsure of everything": Community college students' shifts in confidence.* CCRC Working

Paper No. 48. New York: Columbia University, Teachers College, Community College Research Center.

Bickerstaff, S., & Edgecombe, N. (2012). *Pathways to faculty learning and pedagogical improvement.* Inside Out series publication. New York: Columbia University, Teachers College, Community College Research Center.

Blatt, R. (2008). Organizational citizenship behavior of temporary knowledge employees. *Organization Studies* 29(6): 849–866. doi: 10.1177/0170840608088704.

Boatman, A., & Long, B. T. (2010). *Does remediation work for all students? How the effects of postsecondary remedial and developmental courses vary by level of academic preparation.* NCPR Working Paper. New York: National Center for Postsecondary Research.

Booth, K., Cooper, D., Karandjeff, K., Large, M., Pellegrin, N., Purnell, R., et al. (2013). *Using student voices to redefine success: What community college students say institutions, instructors and others can do to help them succeed.* Berkeley: Research and Planning Group for California Community Colleges.

Bork, R. H., & Rucks-Ahidiana, Z. (2013). *Role ambiguity in online courses: An analysis of student and instructor expectations.* CCRC Working Paper No. 64. New York: Columbia University, Teachers College, Community College Research Center.

Boudreau, C. A., & Kromrey, J. D. (1994). A longitudinal study of the retention and academic performance of participants in freshman orientation course. *Journal of College Student Development* 35(6): 444–449.

Bound, J., Lovenheim, M. F., & Turner, S. (2010). Why have college completion rates declined? An analysis of changing student preparation and collegiate resources. *American Economic Journal: Applied Economics* 2(3): 129–157. doi: 10.1257/app.2.3.129.

Bourdon, C. M., & Carducci, R. (2002). *What works in the community colleges: A synthesis of literature on best practices.* Los Angeles: University of California, Los Angeles, Graduate School of Education.

Bowen, W. G., Chingos, M. M., Lack, K. A., & Nygren, T. I. (2012). *Interactive learning online at public universities: Evidence from randomized trials.* New York: Ithaka S+R.

Bowen, W. G., Chingos, M. M., & McPherson, M. S. (2009). *Crossing the finish line: Completing college at America's public universities.* Princeton, NJ: Princeton University Press.

Boyer, E. L. (1990). *Scholarship reconsidered: Priorities of the professoriate.* Princeton, NJ: Carnegie Foundation for the Advancement of Teaching.

Boylan, H. R., Bliss, L. B., & Bonham, B. S. (1997). Program components and their relationship to student performance. *Journal of Developmental Education* 20(3): 2–8.

Bradshaw, P., & Fredette, C. (2009). Academic governance of universities: Reflections of a senate chair on moving from theory to practice and back. *Journal of Management Inquiry* 18(2): 123–133. doi: 10.1177/1056492608326320.

Bransford, J. D., Brown, A. L., & Cocking, R. R. (2000). Technology to support learning. In *How people learn: Brain, mind, experience and school,* expanded edition, edited by J. D. Bransford, A. L. Brown, and R. R. Cocking, 206–230. Washington, DC: National Academies Press.

Brenner, M. E., Mayer, R. E., Moseley, B., Brar, T., Durán, R., Reed, B. S., & Webb, D. (1997). Learning by understanding: The role of multiple representations in learning algebra. *American Educational Research Journal* 34(4): 663–689.

Brookfield, S. D. (2002). Using the lenses of critically reflective teaching in the community college classroom. *New Directions for Community Colleges* 2002(118): 31–38.

Bryk, A. S., Camburn, E., & Louis, K. S. (1999). Professional community in Chicago elementary schools: Facilitating factors and organizational consequences. *Educational Administration Quarterly* 35(5): 751–781. doi: 10.1177/0013 161x99355004.

Bryk, A. S., Gomez, L. M., & Grunow, A. (2010). *Getting ideas into action: Building networked improvement communities in education.* Stanford, CA: Carnegie Foundation for the Advancement of Teaching.

Bryk, A. S., & Schneider, B. (2002). *Trust in schools: A core resource for improvement.* New York: Russell Sage.

Bryk, A. S., Sebring, P. B., Allensworth, E., Luppescu, S., & Easton, J. Q. (2010). *Organizing schools for improvement: Lessons from Chicago.* Chicago: University of Chicago Press.

Bryk, A. S., Yeager, D. S., Hausman, H., Muhich, J., Dolle, J. R., Grunow, A., et al. (2013). *Improvement research carried out through networked communities: Accelerating learning about practices that support more productive student mindsets.* Stanford, CA: Carnegie Foundation for the Advancement of Teaching.

Burris, C. C., Wiley, E., Welner, K. G., & Murphy, J. (2008). Accountability, rigor, and detracking: Achievement effects of embracing a challenging curriculum as a universal good for all students. *Teachers College Record* 110(3): 571–607.

Cabrera, A. F., Crissman, J. L., Bernal, E. M., Nora, A., Terenzini, P. T., & Pascarella, E. T. (2002). Collaborative learning: Its impact on college students' development and diversity. *Journal of College Student Development* 43(1): 20–34.

Calcagno, J. C., & Long, B. T. (2008). *The impact of postsecondary remediation using a regression discontinuity approach: Addressing endogenous sorting and noncompliance.* NBER Working Paper No. 14194. Cambridge, MA: National Bureau of Economic Research.

California Commission on Teacher Credentialing & California Department of Education. (1997). *California standards for the teaching profession.* Sacramento, CA.

Callahan, M. K., & Chumney, D. (2009). "Write like college": How remedial writing courses at a community college and a research university position "at-risk" students in the field of higher education. *Teachers College Record* 111(7): 1619–1664.

Campbell, S., & Nutt, C. L. (2008). Academic advising in the new global century: Supporting student engagement and learning outcomes achievement. *Peer Review* 10(1): 4–7.

Carstens, L., & Howell, J. B. (2012). Questions that matter: Using inquiry-guided faculty development to create an inquiry-guided learning curriculum. *New Directions for Teaching and Learning* 2012(129): 51–59.

Casazza, M. E. (1998). Strengthening practice with theory. *Journal of Developmental Education* 22(2): 14–20.

Castleman, B. L., & Page, L. C. (2014). *Freshman year financial aid nudges: An experiment to increase FAFSA renewal and college persistence.* EdPolicy Works Working Paper No. 28. Charlottsville: University of Virginia, Center for Education Policy and Workforce Competitiveness.

Center for Community College Student Engagement. (2012). *A matter of degrees: Promising practices for community college student success (A first look).* Austin: University of Texas at Austin, Community College Leadership Program.

Chappell, K. K. (2006). Effects of concept-based instruction on calculus students' acquisition of conceptual understanding and procedural skill. In *Research in collegiate mathematics education VI,* edited by F. Hitt, G. Harel, and A. Seldon, 27–60. Providence, RI: American Mathematical Society.

Chaudhury, S. R. (2011). The lecture. *New Directions for Teaching and Learning* 2011(128): 13–20. doi: 10.1002/tl.464.

Cho, S.-W., & Karp, M. M. (2012). *Student success courses and educational outcomes at Virginia community colleges.* CCRC Working Paper No. 40. New York: Columbia University, Teachers College, Community College Research Center.

Choi, J. J., Laibson, D., Madrian, B. C., & Metrick, A. (2002). Defined contribution pensions: Plan rules, participant choices, and the path of least resistance. In *Tax Policy and the Economy,* vol. 16, edited by J. M. Poterba, 67–113. Cambridge, MA: MIT Press.

———. (2003). Optimal defaults. *American Economic Review* 93(2): 108–185.

———. (2004). For better or for worse: Default effects and 401(k) savings behavior. In *Perspectives on the economics of aging,* edited by D. A. Wise, 81–125. Chicago: University of Chicago Press.

Christensen, C. M., & Eyring, H. J. (2011). *The innovative university: Changing the DNA of higher education from the inside out.* San Francisco: Jossey-Bass.

Christensen, G., Steinmetz, A., Alcorn, B., Bennett, A., Woods, D., & Emanuel, E. J. (2013). *The MOOC phenomenon: Who takes massive open online courses and why?* Working Paper. Philadelphia: University of Pennsylvania.

City University of New York, Office of Institutional Research and Assessment. (2014). System retention and graduation rates of full-time first-time freshmen in associate programs by year of entry: Queensborough. http://www.cuny .edu/irdatabook/rpts2_AY_current/RTGS_0001_FT_FTFR_ASSOC_COMM -QB.pdf.

Clark, F. (2013). 92% vote no confidence in Pathways, CUNY's new curriculum. Press release. http://psc-cuny.org/latest-news/92-vote-no-confidence -pathways-cunys-new-curriculum.

Clark, R. (1989). How much and what type of guidance is optimal for learning from instruction? In *constructivist theory applied to instruction: Success of failure?*, edited by S. Tobias and T. M. Duffy, 158–183. New York: Routledge.

Clotfelter, C. T., Ladd, H. F., Muschkin, C. G., & Vigdor, J. L. (2013). *Developmental education in North Carolina community colleges.* Washington, DC: Center for the Analysis of Longitudinal Data in Education Research.

Coburn, C. E., & Stein, M. K. (2006). Communities of practice theory and the role of teacher professional community in policy implementation. In *Confronting complexity: Defining the field of education policy implementation*, edited by M. I. Honig, 25–46. Albany, NY: SUNY Press.

Cohen, G. L., Steele, C. M., & Ross, L. D. (1999). The mentor's dilemma: Providing critical feedback across the racial divide. *Personality and Social Psychology Bulletin* 25(10): 1302–1318. doi: 10.1177/0146167299258011.

Collins, J., & Porras, J. I. (1994). *Built to last: Successful habits of visionary companies.* New York: Harper Business Essentials.

Collins, M. L. (2008). *It's not about the cut score: Redesigning placement assessment policy to improve student success.* Boston: Jobs for the Future.

Common Core State Standard Initiative. (2010). *Common Core state standards for English language arts and literacy in history / social studies, science, and technical subjects.* Washington, DC.

Community College Survey of Student Engagement. (2007). *Committing to student engagement: Reflections on CCSSE's first five years (2007 findings).* Austin: University of Texas at Austin.

———. (2010). *Survey of entering student engagement (SENSE), 2010.* Austin: University of Texas at Austin.

———. (2012). *Survey of entering student engagement (SENSE), 2012.* Austin: University of Texas at Austin.

Community college system must thrive so NC can thrive. (2014). *Asheville Citizen-Times*, May 2. http://www.citizen-times.com/story/opinion/editorials/2014/05/02 /community-college-system-must-thrive-nc-can-thrive/8613801/.

Complete College America. (2011). *Time is the enemy: The surprising truth about why today's college students aren't graduating . . . and what needs to change.* Washington, DC.

Connell, C. (2011). *At no-frills Western Governors University, the path to a college degree is only as long as students make it.* New York: Columbia University, Teachers College, Hechinger Institute on Education and the Media.

Cook-Sather, A., & Shore, E. (2007). Breaking the rule of discipline in interdisciplinarity: Redefining professors, students, and staff as faculty. *Journal of Research Practice* 3(2): article M15.

Corcoran, T., Fuhrman, S. H., & Belcher, C. L. (2001). The district role in instructional improvement. *Phi Delta Kappan* 83(1): 78–84.

Cormier, M. S. (2014). *Examining classroom interactions in computer-mediated developmental mathematics.* Paper presented at the American Educational Research Association (AERA) annual meeting, Philadelphia.

Cormier, M. S., & Bickerstaff, S. (2013). *Faculty learning for instructional improvement: Supporting new ways of teaching in developmental education.* Paper presented at the American Educational Research Association (AERA) annual meeting, San Francisco.

Couturier, L. K. (2012). *Cornerstones of completion: State policy support for accelerated structured pathways to college credentials and transfer, jobs for the future and completion by design.* Boston: Jobs for the Future & Completion by Design.

Covington, M. V. (2007). A motivational analysis of academic life in college. In *The scholarship of teaching and learning in higher education: An evidence-based perspective,* edited by R. P. Perry and J. C. Smart, 661–712. Dordrecht, Netherlands: Springer.

Cox, M. D. (2004). Introduction to faculty learning communities. *New Directions for Teaching and Learning* 2004(97): 5–23. doi: 10.1002/tl.129.

Cox, R. D. (2009). *The college fear factor: How students and professors misunderstand one another.* Cambridge, MA: Harvard University Press.

Coy, P. (2014). The $10,000 bachelor's degree arrives. *Bloomberg Businessweek,* May 5. http://www.businessweek.com/articles/2014-05-05/the-first -online-10-000-bachelors-degree-arrives.

Cromley, J. G., Snyder-Hogan, L. E., & Luciw-Dubas, U. A. (2010). Reading comprehension of scientific text: A domain-specific test of the direct and inferential mediation model of reading comprehension. *Journal of Educational Psychology* 102(3): 687–700. doi: 10.1037/a0019452.

Crookston, B. B. (1972). A developmental view of academic advising as teaching. *Journal of College Student Personnel* 13:12–17.

Crosta, P. M. (2014). Intensity and attachment: How the chaotic enrollment patterns of community college students relate to educational outcomes. *Community College Review* 42(2): 118–142.

Cunningham, A. D. (2012). *Paradoxes and play: An emergent theory of how community college librarians sustain library instruction programs.* EdD diss., California State University, Fullerton. Ann Arbor, MI: ProQuest Dissertations & Theses Full Text database, UMI No. 3529069.

Cutler, D. M., & Lleras-Muney, A. (2010). Understanding differences in health behaviors by education. *Journal of Health Economics* 29(1): 1–28. http://dx .doi.org/10.1016/j.jhealeco.2009.10.003.

DaCosta, J. W., & Dubicki, E. (2012). From lampitt to libraries: Formulating state standards to embed information literacy across colleges. *Library Trends* 60(3): 611–636.

Dadgar, M. (2012). *The academic consequences of employment for students enrolled in community college.* CCRC Working Paper No. 46. New York:

Columbia University, Teachers College, Community College Research Center.

Dadgar, M., & Trimble, M. J. (2014). Labor market returns to sub-baccalaureate credentials: How much does a community college degree or certificate pay? *Educational Evaluation and Policy Analysis*. Advance online publication. doi: 10.3102/0162373714553814.

Darling-Hammond, L., Wei, R. C., Andree, A., Richardson, N., & Orphanos, S. (2009). *Professional learning in the learning profession: A status report on teacher development in the United States and abroad*. Oxford, OH: National Staff Development Council.

Deci, E. L. (1996). Making room for self-regulation: Some thoughts on the link between emotion and behavior. *Psychological Inquiry* 7(3): 220–223.

Deci, E. L., & Flaste, R. (1996). *Why we do what we do: Understanding self-motivation*. New York: Penguin Books.

Deil-Amen, R., & Rosenbaum, J. E. (2003). The social prerequisites of success: Can college structure reduce the need for social know-how? *Annals of the American Academic of Political and Social Science* 586(1): 120–143.

Desrochers, D. M., & Kirshstein, R. J. (2012). *College spending in a turbulent decade: Findings from the delta cost project*. Washington, DC: Delta Cost Project at American Institutes for Research.

Desrochers, D. M., & Hurlburt, S. (2014). *Trends in college spending: 2001–2011*. Washington, DC: Delta Cost Project at American Institutes of Research.

Dhanesar, S. (2006). *The impact of collaboration between faculty and librarians to improve student information literacy skills at an urban community college*. EdD diss., Morgan State University, Baltimore. Ann Arbor, MI: ProQuest Dissertations & Theses Full Text database, UMI No. 3258435.

Dickie, L. O., & Farrell, J. E. (1991). The transition from high school to college: An impedance mismatch? *Physics Teacher* 29(7): 440–445.

Doucette, D. S., & Dayton, L. L. (1989). A framework for student development practices: A statement of the League for Innovation in the Community College. *New Directions for Community Colleges* 1989(67): 61–71.

Dougherty, K., & Hong, E. (2005). *State systems of performance accountability for community colleges: Impacts and lessons for policymakers*. CCRC Policy Brief. New York: Columbia University, Teachers College, Community College Research Center.

Dougherty, K., & Reddy, V. (Eds.). (2013). Performance funding for higher education: What are the mechanisms? What are the impacts? *ASHE Higher Education Report* 39(2).

Dweck, C. (2006). *Mindset: The new psychology of success*. New York: Ballantine Books.

Eagan, M. K., Jr., & Jaeger, A. J. (2009). Effects of exposure to part-time faculty on community college transfer. *Research in Higher Education* 50(2): 168–188. doi: 10.1007/s11162-008-9113-8.

Edgecombe, N. (2011). *Accelerating the academic achievement of students referred to developmental education.* CCRC Working Paper No. 30. New York: Columbia University, Teachers College, Community College Research Center.

Ehrenberg, R. G., & Zhang, L. (2005). Do tenured and tenure-track faculty matter? *Journal of Human Resources* 40(3): 647–659. doi: 10.2307/4129555.

Ericsson, K. A., Krampe, R. T., & Tesch-Römer, C. (1993). The role of deliberate practice in the acquisition of expert performance. *Psychological Review* 100(3): 363–406. doi: 10.1037/0033-295X.100.3.363.

Everett, J. B. (2010). *A study of faculty teaching of information literacy in Alabama's public associate's colleges.* EdD diss. University of Alabama. Ann Arbor, MI: ProQuest Dissertations & Theses Full Text database, UMI No. 3439809.

Fain, P. (2012). How to end remediation. *Inside Higher Ed,* April 4. http://www.insidehighered.com/news/2012/04/04/connecticut-legislature-mulls-elimination-remedial-courses#ixzz38lJgCxOQ.

———. (2013). Remediation if you want it. *Inside Higher Ed,* June 5. http://www.insidehighered.com/news/2013/06/05/florida-law-gives-students-and-colleges-flexibility-remediation#ixzz38lLtw6s3.

———. (2014). Competency and affordability. *Inside Higher Ed,* May 6. https://www.insidehighered.com/news/2014/05/06/college-america-hits-10000-mark-new-competency-based-bachelors-degrees.

Farrington, C. A., Roderick, M., Allensworth, E., Nagaoka, J., Keyes, T. S., Johnson, D. W., & Beechum, N. O. (2012). *Teaching adolescents to become learners: The role of noncognitive factors in shaping school performance.* Chicago: University of Chicago Consortium on Chicago School Research.

Fay, M. P., Bickerstaff, S., & Hodara, M. (2013). *Why students do not prepare for math placement exams: Student perspectives.* CCRC Research Brief No. 57. New York: Columbia University, Teachers College, Community College Research Center.

Feldman, K. A., & Paulsen, M. B. (1999). Faculty motivation: The role of a supportive teaching culture. *New Directions for Teaching and Learning* 1999(78): 71–78. doi: 10.1002/tl.7807.

Fields, R., & Parsad, B. (2012). *Tests and cut scores used for student placement in postsecondary education: Fall 2011.* Washington, DC: National Assessment Governing Board.

Figlio, D. N., Schapiro, M. O., & Soter, K. B. (2013). *Are tenure track professors better teachers?* NBER Working Paper No. 19406. Cambridge, MA: National Bureau of Economic Research.

Flavell, J. H. (1979). Metacognition and cognitive monitoring: A new area of cognitive-developmental inquiry. *American Psychologist* 34(10): 906–911.

Fowler-Hill, S. A. (2001). *Full-time faculty recruitment and selection strategies practiced by learning-centered community colleges.* EdD diss., Oregon State University. Ann Arbor, MI: ProQuest Dissertations & Theses Full Text database, UMI No. 3024373.

Fox, E. (2009). The role of reader characteristics in processing and learning from informational text. *Review of Educational Research* 79(1): 197–261. doi: 10.2307/40071165.

Frost, R. A., Strom, S. L., Downey, J., Schultz, D. D., & Holland, T. A. (2010). Enhancing student learning with academic and student affairs collaboration. *Community College Enterprise* 16(1): 37–51. doi: 10.1002/ SS.234.

Fugate, A. L., & Amey, M. J. (2000). Career stages of community college faculty: A qualitative analysis of their career paths, roles, and development. *Community College Review* 28(1): 1–22. doi: 10.1177/009155210002800101.

Fuhrmann, B. S. (1995). Campus strategies: The "prompts" project prompts academic and student affairs collaboration. *Assessment Update* 7(6): 10. doi: 10.1002/au.3650070607.

Fullilove, R. E., & Treisman, P. U. (1990). Mathematics achievement among African American undergraduates at the University of California, Berkeley: An evaluation of the Mathematics Workshop Program. *Journal of Negro Education* 59(3): 463–478. doi: 10.2307/2295577.

Fulton, K., & Britton, T. (2011). *STEM teachers in professional learning communities: From good teachers to great teaching.* Washington, DC: National Commission on Teaching and America's Future.

Gallos, J. V. (2009). Reframing shared governance: Rediscovering the soul of campus collaboration. *Journal of Management Inquiry* 18(2): 136–138. doi: 10.1177/1056492608326326.

Gardenhire-Crooks, A., Collado, H., & Ray, B. (2006). *A whole'nother world: Students navigating community college.* New York: MDRC.

Gardiner, L. F. (1998). Why we must change: The research evidence. *Thought & Action* 14(1): 71–87.

Gates, G., & Robinson, S. (2009). Delving into teacher collaboration: Untangling problems and solutions for leadership. *NASSP Bulletin* 93(3): 145–165. doi: 10.1177/0192636509354375.

Goddard, Y. L., Goddard, R. D., & Tschannen-Moran, M. (2007). A theoretical and empirical investigation of teacher collaboration for school improvement and student achievement in public elementary schools. *Teachers College Record* 109(4): 877–896.

Goomas, D. T. (2012). Closing the gap: Merging student affairs, advising and registration. *Community College Journal of Research and Practice* 36(1): 59–61. doi: 10.1080/10668926.2012.617652.

Gordon, J., Ludlum, J., & Hoey, J. J. (2008). Validating NSSE against student outcomes: Are they related? *Research in Higher Education* 49(1): 19–39.

Gordon, L. (2013). College recruiters give low-income public campuses fewer visits. *Los Angeles Times,* December 27.

Gordon, V. N. (2006). *Career advising: An academic advisor's guide.* San Francisco: Jossey-Bass.

Gordon, V. N., Habley, W. R., & Grites, T. J. (Eds.). (2008). *Academic advising: A comprehensive handbook,* 2nd ed. San Francisco: Jossey-Bass.

Gore, P. A., & Metz, A. J. (2008). Foundations: Advising for career and life planning. In *Academic advising: A comprehensive handbook*, 2nd ed., edited by V. N. Gordon, W. R. Habley, and T. J. Grites, 103–118. San Francisco: Jossey-Bass.

Grant, H., & Dweck, C. S. (2003). Clarifying achievement goals and their impact. *Journal of Personality and Social Psychology* 85(3): 541–553. doi: 10.1037/0022-3514.85.3.541.

Grant, L. K., & Courtoreille, M. (2007). Comparison of fixed-item and response-sensitive versions of an online tutorial. *Psychological Record* 57(2): 265–272.

Griffiths, R., Chingos, M., Mulhern, C., & Spies, R. (2014). *Interactive online learning on campus: Testing MOOCs and other platforms in hybrid formats in the University System of Maryland*. New York: Ithaka S+R.

Gross, B., & Goldhaber, D. (2009). *Community college transfer and articulation policies: Looking beneath the surface*. CRPE Working Paper No. 2009_1R. Seattle: University of Washington–Bothell, Center on Reinventing Public Education.

Grubb, W. N. (2006). "Like, what do I do now?" The dilemmas of guidance counseling. In *Defending the community college equity agenda*, edited by T. Bailey and V. S. Morset, 195–222. Baltimore: Johns Hopkins University Press.

———. (2012). Rethinking remedial education and the academic-vocational divide: Complementary perspectives. *Mind, Culture and Activity* 19(1): 22–25. doi: 10.1080/10749039.2011.632055.

Grubb, W. N., & Associates. (1999). *Honored but invisible: Teaching in community colleges*. New York: Routledge.

Grubb, W. N. (with Gabriner, R.). (2013). *Basic skills education in community colleges*. New York: Routledge.

Guskey, T. R., & Yoon, K. S. (2009). What works in professional development? *Phi Delta Kappan* 90(7): 495–500.

Guttman Community College. (2014). Guttman Community College to mark its inaugural commencement on Wednesday, August 27, 2014. Press release. http://www1.cuny.edu/mu/ncc/2014/08/15/guttman-community-college-to -mark-its-inaugural-commencement-on-wednesday-august-27-2014/.

Haas, P. F., & Keeley, S. M. (1998). Coping with faculty resistance to teaching critical thinking. *College Teaching* 46(2): 63–67.

Hagen, P. L., & Jordan, P. (2008). Theoretical foundations of academic advising. In *Academic advising: A comprehensive handbook*, 2nd ed., edited by V. Gordon, W. Habley, and T. Grites, 17–35. San Francisco: Jossey-Bass.

Handel, S. J., & Williams, R. A. (2012). *The promise of the transfer pathway: Opportunity and challenge for community college students seeking the baccalaureate degree*. Washington, DC: College Board Advocacy & Policy Center.

Harrington, C., & Schibik, T. (2001). *Caveat emptor: Is there a relationship between part-time faculty utilization and student learning outcomes and retention?* Paper presented at the 21st annual meeting of the Association for Institutional Research, Long Beach, CA.

Hartung, P. J., & Blustein, D. L. (2002). Race, intuiton, and social justice: Elaborating on Parsons' career decision-making model. *Journal of Counseling & Development* 80(1): 41–47.

Harvey-Smith, A. B. (2003). *The adoption of the learning paradigm in student affairs divisions of vanguard community colleges: A case analysis.* PhD diss., University of Maryland, College Park. Ann Arbor, MI: ProQuest Dissertations & Theses Full Text database, UMI No. 3112600.

Hausmann, L. R. M., Schofield, J. W., & Woods, R. L. (2007). Sense of belonging as a predictor of intentions to persist among African American and white first-year college students. *Research in Higher Education* 48(7): 803–839.

Hawkes, M., & Coldeway, D. O. (2002). An analysis of team vs. faculty-based online course development: Implications for instructional design. *Quarterly Review of Distance Education* 3(4): 431–441.

Heifetz, R. A. (1998). *Leadership without easy answers.* Cambridge, MA: Harvard University Press.

Hern, K. (with Snell, M.). (2010). Exponential attrition and the promise of acceleration in developmental English and math. Sacramento, CA: The RP Group.

Hidi, S., & Renninger, K. A. (2006). The four-phase model of interest development. *Educational Psychologist* 41(2): 111–127.

Hiebert, J., Gallimore, R., Garnier, H., Givvin, K. B., Hollingsworth, H., Jacobs, J., et al. (2003). *Teaching mathematics in seven countries: Results from TIMSS 1999 video study.* NCES 2003-013, revised. Washington, DC: U.S. Department of Education, Institute of Education Sciences, National Center for Education Statistics.

Hixon, E. (2008). Team-based online course development: A case study of collaboration models *Online Journal of Distance Learning Administration* 11(4): 1–8.

Ho, A. D., Reich, J., Nesterko, S., Seaton, D. T., Mullaney, T., Waldo, J., & Chuang, I. (2014). *HarvardX and MITx: The first year of open online courses, Fall 2012–Summer 2013.* HarvardX Working Paper No. 1. Cambridge, MA: Harvard University, HarvardX.

Hoachlander, G., Sikora, A. C., & Horn, L. (2003). *Community college students: Goals, academic preparation and outcomes.* NCES 2003-164. Washington, DC: U.S. Department of Education, Institute of Education Sciences, National Center for Education Statistics.

Hodara, M. (2011). *Reforming mathematics classroom pedagogy: Evidence-based findings and recommendations for the developmental math classroom.* CCRC Working Paper No. 27. New York: Columbia University, Teachers College, Community College Research Center.

———. (2013). *Improving students' college math readiness: a review of the evidence on postsecondary interventions and reforms.* CAPSEE Working Paper. New York: Center for Analysis of Postsecondary Education and Employment.

Hodara, M., Jaggars, S. S., & Karp, M. M. (2012). *Improving developmental education assessment and placement: Lessons from community colleges across the country.* CCRC Working Paper No. 51. New York: Columbia University, Teachers College, Community College Research Center.

Holland, J. (1997). *Making vocational choices: A theory of vocational personalities and work environments,* vol. 3. Odessa, FL: Psychological Assessment Resources.

Horn, L., Cataldi, E. F., & Sikora, A. (2005). *Waiting to attend college: Undergraduates who delay their postsecondary enrollment.* NCES 2005-152. Washington, DC: U.S. Department of Education, Institute of Education Sciences, National Center for Education Statistics.

Horn, L., & Nevill, S. (2006). *Profile of undergraduates in U.S. postsecondary education institutions, 2003–04: With a special analysis of community college students.* NCES 2006-184. Washington, DC: U.S. Department of Education, Institute of Education Sciences, National Center for Education Statistics.

Horn, L., & Skomsvold, P. (2011). *Web tables: Community college student outcomes, 1994–2009.* NCES Publication 2012-253. Washington, DC: U.S. Department of Education, Institute of Education Sciences, National Center for Education Statistics.

Hossler, D., Shapiro, D., Dundar, A., Ziskin, M., Chen, J., Zerquera, D., & Torres, V. (2012). *Transfer and mobility: A national view of pre-degree student movement in postsecondary institutions.* Signature Report No. 2. Herndon, VA: National Student Clearinghouse Research Center.

Hotchkiss, J. L., Moore, R. E., & Pitts, M. M. (2006). Freshman learning communities, college performance, and retention. *Education Economics* 14(2): 197–210.

Howell, J. S., Kurlaender, M., & Grodsky, E. (2010). Postsecondary preparation and remediation: Examining the effect of the early assessment program at California State University. *Journal of Policy Analysis & Management* 29(4): 726–748.

Hoxby, C. M. (2014). *The economics of online postsecondary education: MOOCs, nonselective education, and highly selective education.* NBER Working Paper No. 19816. Cambridge, MA: National Bureau of Economic Research.

Hoxby, C. M., & Turner, S. (2013). *Expanding college opportunity for high-achieving, low income students.* SIEPR Discussion Paper No. 12-014. Stanford, CA: Stanford Institute for Economic Policy Research.

Huber, M. T. (2008). *The promise of faculty inquiry for teaching and learning basic skills.* Stanford, CA: Carnegie Foundation for the Advancement of Teaching.

———. (2010). Caring for students: Pedagogy and professionalism in an age of anxiety. *Emotion, Space and Society* 3(2): 71–79. doi: http://dx.doi.org/10.1016/j.emospa.2009.06.002.

Hughes, K. L., Rodríguez, O., Edwards, L., & Belfield, C. (2012). *Broadening the benefits of dual enrollment: Reaching underachieving and underrepresented students with career-focused programs.* San Francisco: James Irvine Foundation.

Hull, E. B. (2004). *Learning from the experiences of faculty: The process of adopting a learning-centered paradigm.* PhD diss., University of New Orleans. Ann

Arbor, MI: ProQuest Dissertations & Theses Full Text database, UMI No. 3127777.

Hutchings, P., Huber, M. T., & Ciccone, A. (2011). *The scholarship of teaching and learning reconsidered: Institutional integration and impact.* San Francisco: Jossey-Bass.

Ignash, J. M. (1997). Who should provide postsecondary remedial/developmental education? *New Directions for Community Colleges* 1997(100): 5–20.

Isoda, M., Stephens, M., Ohara, Y., & Miyakawa, T. (Eds.). (2007). *Japanese lesson study in mathematics: Its impact, diversity and potential for educational improvement.* Hackensack, NJ: World Scientific.

Ithaka S+R. (2012). *Data collection instruments: Interactive learning online at public universities: Evidence from randomized trials.* Report supplement. New York.

Jacoby, D. (2006). Effects of part-time faculty employment on community college graduation rates. *Journal of Higher Education* 77(6): 1081–1103.

Jaeger, A. J., & Eagan, M. K., Jr. (2009). Unintended consequences: Examining the effect of part-time faculty members on associate's degree completion. *Community College Review* 36(3): 167–194.

Jaggars, S. S. (2011). *Online learning: Does it help low-income and underprepared students?* CCRC Working Paper No. 26. New York: Columbia University, Teachers College, Community College Research Center.

———. (2012). Online learning in community colleges. In *Handbook of distance education,* 3rd ed., edited by M. G. Moore, 594–608. New York: Routledge.

———. (2014). Choosing between online and face-to-face courses: Community college student voices. *American Journal of Distance Education* 28(1): 27–38. doi: 10.1080/08923647.2014.867697.

Jaggars, S. S., Edgecombe, N., & Stacey, G. W. (2013). *Creating an effective online instructor presence.* Online Learning Practitioner Packet Part 3. New York: Columbia University, Teachers College, Community College Research Center.

Jaggars, S. S., & Fletcher, J. (2013). *Navigating a sea of choices: The community college student perspective.* Paper presented at the American Educational Research Association (AERA) annual meeting, San Francisco.

———. (2014). *Redesigning the student intake and information provision processes at a large comprehensive community college.* CCRC Working Paper No. 72. New York: Columbia University, Teachers College, Community College Research Center.

Jaggars, S. S., & Hodara, M. (2011). *The opposing forces that shape developmental education: Assessment, placement, and progression at CUNY community colleges.* New York: Columbia University, Teachers College, Community College Research Center.

———. (2013). The opposing forces that shape developmental education. *Community College Journal of Research and Practice* 37(7): 575–579.

Jaggars, S. S., Hodara, M., Cho, S.-W., & Xu, D. (forthcoming, 2015). Three accelerated developmental education programs: Features, student outcomes, and implications. *Community College Review.*

Jaggars, S. S., & Xu, D. (2010). *Online learning in the Virginia community college system*. New York: Columbia University, Teachers College, Community College Research Center.

————. (2013). *Predicting online student outcomes from a measure of course quality*. CCRC Working Paper No. 57. New York: Columbia University, Teachers College, Community College Research Center.

————. (2014). *Examining the wage trajectories of community college students using a growth curve modeling approach*. Manuscript in preparation.

Jassawalla, A. R., & Sashittal, H. C. (1999). Building collaborative cross-functional new product teams. *Academy of Management Executive* 13(3): 50–63. doi: 10.5465/AME.1999.2210314.

Jenkins, D. (2011). *Redesigning community colleges for completion: Lessons from research on high-performance organizations*. CCRC Working Paper No. 24. New York: Columbia University, Teachers College, Community College Research Center.

Jenkins, D., & Shulock, N. (2013). *Metrics, dollars, and systems change: Learning from Washington State's Student Achievement Initiative to design effective postsecondary performance funding policies*. CCRC State Policy Brief. New York: Columbia University, Teachers College, Community College Research Center.

Johns, A. M. (1985). Summary protocols of "underprepared" and "adept" university students: Replications and distortions of the original. *Language Learning* 35(4): 495–517.

Johns, V. (2006). Degree audit systems: Are they worth it? *College and University* 81(2): 57–58.

Johnson, D. W., & Johnson, R. T. (2009). Energizing learning: The instructional power of conflict. *Educational Researcher* 38(1): 37–51. doi: 10.3102/00 13189X08330540.

Johnson, E. J., & Goldstein, D. (2003). Do defaults save lives? *Science* 302(5649): 1338–1339.

Johnson, H., & Mejia, M. C. (2014). *Online learning and student outcomes in California's community colleges*. San Francisco: Public Policy Institute of California.

Johnson, J., & Rochkind, J. (with Ott, A. N., & DuPont, S.). (2009). *With their whole lives ahead of them: Myths and realities about why so many students fail to finish college*. New York: Public Agenda.

Johnson, N. (2009). *What does a college degree cost? Comparing approaches to measuring "cost per degree."* Washington, DC: Delta Cost Project.

Kadlec, A., & Gupta, J. (2014). *Indiana regional transfer study: The student experience of transfer pathways between Ivy Tech Community College and Indiana University*. New York: Public Agenda.

Kadlec, A., Immerwahr, J., & Gupta, J. (2013). *Guided pathways to student success: Perspectives from Indiana college students and advisors*. New York: Public Agenda.

Kadlec, A., & Martinez, M. (2013). *Putting it all together: Strengthening pathways between comprehensives and community colleges*. Paper presented at the American Enterprise Institute private convening, Comprehending Comprehensives, Washington, DC.

Kardash, C. M. (1999). *Students' perceptions of learning outcomes in an inquiry-driven, introductory-level, undergraduate science class*. Unpublished manuscript.

Kardash, C. M., & Wallace, M. L. (2001). The perceptions of science classes survey: What undergraduate science reform efforts really need to address. *Journal of Educational Psychology* 93(1): 199–210. doi: 10.1037/0022-0663.93.1.199.

Karp, M. M. (2006). *Facing the future: Identity development among College Now students*. PhD diss., Columbia University. Ann Arbor, MI: ProQuest Dissertations & Theses Full Text database, UMI No. 3199561.

———. (2011). *Toward a new understanding of non-academic student support: Four mechanisms encouraging positive student outcomes in the community college*. CCRC Working Paper No. 28. New York: Columbia University, Teachers College, Community College Research Center.

———. (2012). "I don't know, I've never been to college!" Dual enrollment as a college readiness strategy. *New Directions for Higher Education* 2012(158): 21–28. doi: 10.1002/he.20011.

———. (2013). *Entering a program: Helping students make academic and career decisions*. CCRC Working Paper No. 59. New York: Columbia University, Teachers College, Community College Research Center.

Karp, M. M., Bickerstaff, S., Rucks-Ahidiana, Z., Bork, R. H., Barragan, M., & Edgecombe, N. (2012). *College 101 courses for applied learning and student success*. CCRC Working Paper No. 49. New York: Columbia University, Teachers College, Community College Research Center.

Karp, M. M., & Bork, R. H. (2014). "They never told me what to expect, so I didn't know what to do": Defining and clarifying the role of a community college student. *Teachers College Record* 116(5): 1–40.

Karp, M. M., Calcagno, J. C., Hughes, K. L., Jeong, D. W., & Bailey, T. R. (2007). *The postsecondary achievement of participants in dual enrollment: An analysis of students outcomes in two states*. St. Paul: University of Minnesota, National Research Center for Career and Technical Education.

Karp, M. M., & Fletcher, J. (2014). *Adopting new technologies for student success: A readiness framework*. New York: Columbia University, Teachers College, Community College Research Center.

Karp, M. M., & Hughes, K. L. (2008). Information networks and integration: Institutional influences on experiences and persistence of beginning students. *New Directions for Community Colleges* 2008(144): 73–82.

Karp, M. M., Hughes, K. L., & Cormier, M. (2012). *Dual enrollment for college completion: Findings from Tennessee and peer states*. Columbia University, Teachers College, Community College Research Center.

Karp, M. M., O'Gara, L., & Hughes, K. L. (2008). *Do support services at community colleges encourage success or reproduce disadvantage? An exploratory study of students in two community colleges.* CCRC Working Paper No. 10. New York: Columbia University, Teachers College, Community College Research Center.

Katz, I. R., Haras, C., & Blaszczynski, C. (2010). Does business writing require information literacy? *Business Communication Quarterly* 73(2): 135–149. doi: 10.1177/1080569910365892.

Kaupp, R. (2012). Online penalty: The impact of online instruction on the Latino-white achievement gap. *Journal of Applied Research in the Community College* 19(2): 8–16.

Kearney, P., & Plax, T. G. (1992). Student resistance to control. In *Power in the classroom: Communication, control, and concern,* edited by V. P. Richmond and J. C. McCroskey, 85–100. Hillsdale, NJ: L. Erlbaum.

Kegan, R., & Lahey, L. L. (2001). *How the way we talk can change the way we work: Seven languages for transformation.* San Francisco: Jossey-Bass.

———. (2009). *Immunity to change: How to overcome it and unlock the potential in yourself and your organization.* Boston: Harvard Business Press.

Kelderman, E. (2013). College education is expected to remain a high priority for states. *Chronicle of Higher Education,* January 3. http://chronicle.com/article/College-Education-Is-Expected/136427/.

Keller, P. A., Harlam, B., Loewenstein, G., & Volpp, K. G. (2011). Enhanced active choice: A new method to motivate behavior change. *Journal of Consumer Psychology* 21(4): 376–383. doi: http://dx.doi.org/10.1016/j.jcps.2011.06.003.

Kelly, A. P., & Carey, K. (Eds.). (2013). *Stretching the higher education dollar: How innovation can improve access, equity and affordability.* Cambridge, MA: Harvard Education Press.

Kember, D., & Gow, L. (1994). Orientations to teaching and their effect on the quality of student learning. *Journal of Higher Education* 65(1): 58–74. doi: 10.2307/2943877.

Kennedy, M. (1998). *Form and substance in inservice teacher education.* Research Monograph No. 13. Madison: University of Wisconsin–Madison, National Institute for Science Education.

Kerekes, J., & Huber, M. T. (1998). *Exceptional teaching in community colleges: An analysis of nominations for the U.S. Professors of the Year program, 1995–1997.* Stanford, CA: Stanford University, National Center for Postsecondary Improvement.

Kerrigan, M. R., & Jenkins, D. (2013). *A growing culture of evidence? Findings from a survey on data use at Achieving the Dream Colleges in Washington State.* New York: Columbia University, Teachers College, Community College Research Center and MDRC.

Keup, J. R., & Petschauer, J. W. (2011). *Designing and administering the course,* vol. 1. Columbia: University of South Carolina, National Resource Center for the First-Year Experience and Students in Transition.

Kezar, A. (2013). Departmental cultures and non-tenure-track faculty: Willingness, capacity, and opportunity to perform at four-year institutions. *Journal of Higher Education* 84(2): 153–188. doi: 10.2307/23486793.

Kezar, A., & Lester, J. (2009). *Organizing higher education for collaboration: A guide for campus leaders.* San Francisco: Jossey-Bass.

King, A. (1994). Guiding knowledge construction in the classroom: Effects of teaching children how to question and how to explain. *American Educational Research Journal* 31(2): 338–368.

Kirschner, P. A., Sweller, J., & Clark, R. E. (2006). Why minimal guidance during instruction does not work: An analysis of the failure of constructivist, discovery, problem-based, experiential, and inquiry-based teaching. *Educational Psychologist* 41(2): 75–86. doi: 10.1207/s15326985ep4102_1.

Kirshstein, R. J., & Hurlburt, S. (2012). *Revenues: Where does the money come from? A Delta Data update, 2000–2010.* Washington, DC: American Institutes for Research.

Knapp, L. G., Kelly-Reid, J. E., & Ginder, S. A. (2012). *Enrollment in postsecondary institutions, fall 2011; Financial statistics, fiscal year 2011; And graduation rates, selected cohorts, 2003–2008: First look (provisional data).* NCES 2012-174rev. Washington, DC: U.S. Department of Education, Institute of Education Sciences, National Center for Education Statistics.

Knapp, L. G., Kelly-Reid, J. E., Ginder, S. A., & Miller, E. (2008). *Employees in postsecondary institutions, fall 2006, and salaries of full-time instructional faculty, 2006–07.* NCES 2008-172. Washington, DC: U.S. Department of Education, Institute of Education Sciences, National Center for Education Statistics.

Knowles, E., & Kalata, K. (2007). A model for enhancing online course development. *Innovate* 4(2). http://www.cs.scranton.edu/~beidler/infoLit/A_Model _for_Enhancing_Online_Course_Development.pdf.

Krumbotlz, J. D. (1996). A learning theory of career counseling. In *Handbook of career counseling theory and practice,* edited by M. L. Savickas and W. B. Walsh, 55–80. Palo Alto, CA: Davies-Black.

Kuh, G. D., Cruce, T. M., Shoup, R., Kinzie, J., & Gonyea, R. M. (2008). Unmasking the effects of student engagement on first-year college grades and persistence. *Journal of Higher Education* 79(5): 540–563.

Kuh, G. D., Jankowski, N., Ikenberry, S. O., & Kinzie, J. (2014). *Knowing what students know and can do: The current state of student learning outcomes assessment in U.S. colleges and universities.* Champaign: University of Illinois at Urbana–Champaign, National Institute for Learning Outcomes Assessment.

Kuh, G. D. (2008). *High-impact educational practices: What they are, who has access to them, and why they matter.* Washington, DC: Association of American Colleges and Universities.

Laird, T. F. N., Chen, D., & Kuh, G. D. (2008). Classroom practices at institutions with higher-than-expected persistence rates: What student engagement data tell us. *New Directions for Teaching and Learning* 2008(115): 85–99. doi: 10.1002/tl.327.

Lampert, M., Boerst, T. A., & Graziani, F. (2011). Organizational resources in the service of school-wide ambitious teaching practice. *Teachers College Record* 113(7): 1361–1400.

Lasry, N., Mazur, E., & Watkins, J. (2008). Peer instruction: From Harvard to the two-year college. *American Journal of Physics* 76(11): 1066–1069. doi: 10.1119/1.2978182.

Latham, G. P., & Locke, E. A. (2007). New developments in and directions for goal-setting research. *European Psychologist* 12(4): 290–300. doi: 10.1027/10 16-9040.12.4.290.

Leana, C. R. (2011). The missing LINK in school reform. *Stanford Social Innovation Review* 9(4): 30–35.

Leckart, S. (2012). The Stanford education experiment could change higher education forever. *Wired*. March 20. http://www.wired.com/2012/03/ff_aiclass /all/.

Lent, R. W. (2005). A social cognitive view of career development and counseling. In *Career development and counseling: Putting theory and research to work*, edited by S. D. Brown and R. W. Lent, 101–129. New York: John Wiley & Sons.

Levin, H. M. (2007). On the relationship between poverty and curriculum. *North Carolina Law Review* 85(5): 1381–1418.

Levin, H. M., & Garcia, E. (with Morgan, J.). (2012). *Cost-effectiveness of accelerated study in associate programs (ASAP) of the City University of New York (CUNY)*. New York: Columbia University, Teachers College, Center for Benefit-Cost Studies in Education.

Lindstrom, J., & Shonrock, D. D. (2006). Faculty-librarian collaboration to achieve integration of information literacy. *Reference & User Services Quarterly* 46(1): 18–23.

Little, J. W. (1982). Norms of collegiality and experimentation: Workplace conditions of school success. *American Educational Research Journal* 19(3): 325–340. doi: 10.3102/00028312019003325.

Loeb, S., & McEwan, P. (2006). An economic approach to education policy implementation. In *New directions in education policy implementation: Confronting complexity*, edited by M. I. Honig, 169–186. Albany, NY: SUNY Press.

Louis, K. S., & Marks, H. M. (1998). Does professional community affect the classroom? Teachers' work and student experiences in restructuring schools. *American Journal of Education* 106(4): 532–575.

Louis, K. S., Mayrowetz, D., Smiley, M., & Murphy, J. (2009). The role of sensemaking and trust in developing distributed leadership. In *Distributed Leadership*, vol. 7, edited by A. Harris, 157–180. Dordrecht, Netherlands: Springer.

Lovett, M., Meyer, O., & Thille, C. (2008). The Open Learning Initiative: Measuring the effectiveness of the OLI statistics course in accelerating student learning. *Journal of Interactive Media in Education* 2008 (May): 1–16.

Lowenstein, M. (2005). If advising is teaching, what do advisors teach? *NACADA Journal* 25(2): 65–73.

Madrian, B. C., & Shea, D. F. (2001). The power of suggestion: Inertia in 401(k) participation and savings behavior. *Quarterly Journal of Economics* 116(4): 1149–1187.

Margolin, J., Miller, S. R., & Rosenbaum, J. E. (2013). The community college website as virtual adviser: A usability study. *Community College Review* 41(1): 44–62.

Marincovich, M. (1998). *Ending the disconnect between the student evaluation of teaching and the improvement of teaching: A faculty developer's plea.* Stanford, CA: Stanford University, National Center for Postsecondary Improvement.

Martinez, J. G. R., & Martinez, N. C. (1992). Re-examining repeated testing and teacher effects in a remedial mathematics course. *British Journal of Educational Psychology* 62(3): 356–363. doi: 10.1111/j.2044-8279.1992.tb01028.x.

———. (1999). Teacher effectiveness and learning for mastery. *Journal of Educational Research* 92(5): 279–285.

Martorell, P., & McFarlin, I., Jr. (2011). Help or hindrance? The effects of college remediation on academic and labor market outcomes. *Review of Economics & Statistics* 93(2): 436–454.

Marzano, R. J. (2000). *Transforming classroom grading.* Aurora, CO: Association for Supervision and Curriculum Development.

Mayer, A. K., Cerna, O., Cullinan, D., Fong, K., Rutschow, E. Z., & Jenkins, D. (with Chan, D., & Richman, P.). (2014). *Moving ahead with institutional change: Lessons from the first round of Achieving the Dream community colleges.* New York: MDRC.

Mayer, R. E., Stull, A., DeLeeuw, K., Almeroth, K., Bimber, B., Chun, D., et al. (2009). Clickers in college classrooms: Fostering learning with questioning methods in large lecture classes. *Contemporary Educational Psychology* 34(1): 51–57. doi: http://dx.doi.org/10.1016/j.cedpsych.2008.04.002.

Mayer, R. E., & Wittrock, M. C. (1996). Problem-solving transfer. In *Handbook of educational psychology,* edited by D. C. Berliner and R. C. Calfee, 47–62. New York: Macmillan Library.

McDonough, E. F., III. (2000). Investigation of factors contributing to the success of cross-functional teams. *Journal of Product Innovation Management* 17(3): 221–235. doi: http://dx.doi.org/10.1016/S0737-6782(00)00041-2.

McKenzie, C. R. M., Liersch, M. J., & Finkelstein, S. R. (2006). Recommendations implicit in policy defaults. *Psychological Science* 17(5): 414–420.

Mendoza-Denton, R., Downey, G., Purdie, V. J., Davis, A., & Pietrzak, J. (2002). Sensitivity to status-based rejection: Implications for African American students' college experience. *Journal of Personality and Social Psychology* 83(4): 896–918.

Merisotis, J. P., & Jones, S. (2010). Degrees of speed. *Washington Monthly* 42 (May/June): 14–17.

Michael, J. (2007). Faculty perceptions about barriers to active learning. *College Teaching* 55(2): 42–47.

Millet, M. S., Donald, J., & Wilson, D. W. (2009). Information literacy across the curriculum: Expanding horizons. *College & Undergraduate Libraries* 16(2–3): 180–193. doi: 10.1080/10691310902976451.

Minkler, J. E. (2002). ERIC Review: Learning communities at the community college. *Community College Review* 30(3): 46–63. doi: 10.1177/009155521020300 0304.

Mitchell, M. (1993). Situational interest: Its multifaceted structure in the secondary school mathematics classroom. *Journal of Educational Psychology* 85(3): 424–436. doi: 10.1037/0022-0663.85.3.424.

Monaghan, D. B., & Attewell, P. (2014). The community college route to the bachelor's degree. *Educational Evaluation and Policy Analysis*. Advance online publication. doi: 10.3102/0162373714521865.

Moore, C., & Shulock, N. (2009). *Student progress toward degree completion: Lessons from the research literature*. Sacramento: Institute for Higher Education Leadership and Policy.

Mourshed, M., Chijioke, C., & Barber, M. (2010). *How the world's most improved school systems keep getting better*. Toronto: University of Toronto.

Mullin, C. M. (2012). *Transfer: An indispensable part of the community college mission*. AACC Policy Brief No. 2012-03PBL. Washington, DC: American Association of Community Colleges.

Murray, J. P. (2002). The current state of faculty development in two-year colleges. *New Directions for Community Colleges* 2002(118): 89–97.

Nash-Ditzel, S. (2010). Metacognitive reading strategies can improve self-regulation. *Journal of College Reading and Learning* 40(2): 45–63.

National Academic Advising Association (NACADA). (2006). *NACADA concept of academic advising*. http://www.nacada.ksu.edu/Resources/Clearinghouse /View-Articles/Concept-of-Academic-Advising-a598.aspx.

National Center for Public Policy and Higher Education. (2011). *Affordability and transfer: Critical to increasing baccalaureate degree completion*. Policy Alert. San Jose, CA.

National Task Force on Civic Learning and Democratic Engagement. (2012). *A crucible moment: College learning and democracy's future*. Washington, DC: Association of American Colleges and Universities.

Newmann, F. M., Smith, B., Allensworth, E., & Bryk, A. S. (2001). Instructional program coherence: What it is and why it should guide school improvement policy. *Educational Evaluation and Policy Analysis* 23(4): 297–321. doi: 10.2307/3594132.

Newton, F. B., & Smith, J. H. (1996). Principles and strategies for enhancing student learning. *New Directions for Student Services* 1996(75): 19–32. doi: 10.1002/ss.37119967504.

New York Times. (2011). *Class matters*. New York: Macmillan.

Nickerson, D. W., & Rogers, T. (2010). Do you have a voting plan? Implementation intentions, voter turnout, and organic plan making. *Psychological Science* 21(2): 194–199. doi: 10.1177/0956797609359326.

Nodine, T., Jaeger, L., Venezia, A., & Bracco, K. R. (2012). *Connection by design: Students' perceptions of their community college experiences.* San Francisco: WestEd.

Nora, A., Urick, A., & Cerecer, P. D. Q. (2011). Validating students: A conceptualization and overview of its impact on student experiences and outcomes. *Enrollment Management Journal* 5(2): 34–52.

Norton, B., & Wilson, K. (2012). *The liberal arts curriculum a decade after merger: A multiple case study of community colleges in Connecticut, Kentucky, and Louisiana.* ASHE Paper 2012-146. Association for the Study of Higher Education.

North Carolina Community College System (2013). *Performance measures for student success.* Raleigh, NC. http://www.successnc.org/sites/default/files/inititiative-docs/2013%20Performance%20Measures%20Report.pdf.

North Carolina General Assembly, Program Evaluation Division. (2010). *University Distance courses cost more to develop but the same to deliver as on-campus courses.* Report No. 2010-03. Raleigh, NC.

Norwood, K. S. (1995). The effects of the use of problem solving and cooperative learning on the mathematics achievement of underprepared college freshmen. *PRIMUS: Problems, Resources, and Issues in Mathematics Undergraduate Studies* 5(3): 229–252.

Nunn, C. E. (1996). Discussion in the college classroom: Triangulating observational and survey results. *Journal of Higher Education* 67(3): 243–266.

O'Banion, T. (1972). An academic advising model. *Junior College Journal* 42: 62–69.

———. (1997). *Creating more learning-centered community colleges.* Mission Viejo, CA: League for Innovation in the Community College and PeopleSoft.

———. (2000). An inventory for learning-centered colleges. *Community College Journal* 71(1): 14–23.

OECD. (2013). *Education at a glance 2013: OECD indicators.* Paris, France.

O'Gara, L., Karp, M. M., & Hughes, K. L. (2009). Student success courses in the community college: An exploratory study of student perspectives. *Community College Review* 36(3): 195–218.

Oreopoulos, P., & Petronijevic, U. (2013). Making college worth it: A review of the returns to higher education. *Future of Children* 23(1): 41–65.

Parry, M. (2012). College degrees, designed by the numbers. *Chronicle of Higher Education*, July 18. http://chronicle.com/article/College-Degrees-Designed-by/132945/.

Parry, M., Field, K., & Supiano, B. (2013). The Gates effect. *Chronicle of Higher Education*, July 14. http://chronicle.com/article/The-Gates-Effect/140323/.

Parsons, F. (1909). *Choosing a vocation.* Boston: Houghton Mifflin.

Pascarella, E. T., & Terenzini, P. T. (2005). *How college affects students: A third decade of research*, vol. 2. San Francisco: Jossey-Bass.

Paunesku, D., Yeager, D., Romero, C., & Walton, G. (2012). *A brief growth mindset intervention improves academic outcomes of community college students en-*

rolled in development mathematics courses. Unpublished manuscript. Stanford, CA: Stanford University.

Perin, D. (2004). Remediation beyond developmental education: The use of learning assistance centers to increase academic preparedness in community colleges. *Community College Journal of Research and Practice* 28(7): 559–582. doi: 10.1080/10668920490467224.

Perin, D., & Hare, R. (2010). *A contextualized reading-writing intervention for community college students.* CCRC Brief No. 44. New York: Columbia University, Teachers College, Community College Research Center.

Peterson, G. W., Sampson, J. P., Jr., & Reardon, R. C. (1991). *Career development and services: A cognitive approach.* Pacific Grove, CA: Brooks/Cole.

Phifer, T. R. (2010). *Paying attention to students' experiences of learning: A study of liberal arts college professors and their learning about teaching.* EdD diss., Teachers College, Columbia University. Ann Arbor, MI: ProQuest Dissertations & Theses Full Text database, UMI No. 3400646.

Popham, W. J. (2000). *Modern educational measurement: Practical guidelines for educational leaders.* Boston: Allyn and Bacon.

Postsecondary Analytics. (2013). *What's working? Outcomes-based funding in Tennessee.* Tallahassee, FL.

President's Commission on Higher Education. (1947). *Higher education for American democracy: A report of the President's Commission on Higher Education,* vol. 1. New York: Harper & Brothers.

Prince, M., & Felder, R. (2007). The many faces of inductive teaching and learning. *Journal of College Science Teaching* 36(5): 14–20.

Public Agenda. (2012). *Student voices on the higher education pathway: Preliminary insights and stakeholder engagement considerations.* San Francisco: WestEd.

Puzziferro, M., & Shelton, K. (2008). A model for developing high-quality online courses: Integrating a systems approach with learning theory. *Journal of Asynchronous Learning Networks* 12(3): 119–136.

Quillian, B. F. (2004). Making the case for strategic budgeting. *The Presidency* 7(3): 36–37.

Quint, J. C., Jaggars, S. S., Byndloss, D. C., & Magazinnik, A. (2013). *Bringing developmental education to scale: Lessons from the developmental education initiative.* New York: MDRC.

Radford, A. W., Berkner, L., Wheeless, S., & Shepherd, B. (2010). *Persistence and attainment of 2003–04 beginning postsecondary students: After six years.* NCES 2011-151. Washington, DC: U.S. Department of Education, Institute of Education Sciences, National Center for Education Statistics.

Rassen, E., Chaplot, P., Jenkins, D., & Johnstone, R. (2012). *Understanding the student experience through the loss/momentum framework: Clearing the path to completion.* Sacramento: Completion by Design.

Reardon, R. C., Lenz, J. G., Sampson, J. P., & Peterson, G. W. (2011). Big questions facing vocational psychology: A cognitive information processing perspective. *Journal of Career Assessment* 19(3): 240–250.

Reason, R. D., Cox, B. E., McIntosh, K., & Terenzini, P. T. (2010). *Deep learning as an individual, conditional, and contextual influence on first-year student outcomes.* Chicago: Association for Institutional Research.

Reddy, D. M., Pfeiffer, H. M., Fleming, R., Ports, K. A., Pedrick, L. E., Barnack-Tavlaris, J. L., et al. (2013). "U-Pace" instruction: Improving student success by integrating content mastery and amplified assistance. *Journal of Asynchronous Learning Networks* 17(1): 147–154.

Redish, E. F., Saul, J. M., & Steinberg, R. N. (1998). Student expectations in introductory physics. *American Journal of Physics* 66(3): 212–224. doi: http://dx.doi.org/10.1119/1.18847.

Reed, M. (2013). *Confessions of a community college administrator.* San Francisco: Jossey-Bass.

Rice, R. E., Sorcinelli, M. D., & Austin, A. E. (2000). *Heeding new voices: Academic careers for a new generation.* Washington, DC: American Association for Higher Education.

Rittle-Johnson, B., Siegler, R. S., & Alibali, M. W. (2001). Developing conceptual understanding and procedural skill in mathematics: An iterative process. *Journal of Educational Psychology* 93(2): 346–362. doi: 10.1037/0022-0663.93.2.346.

Rodicio, L., Mayer, S., & Jenkins, D. (2014). Strengthening program pathways through transformative change. *New Directions for Community Colleges* 2014(167): 63–72. doi: 10.1002/cc.20111.

Rodríguez, O. (2014). *Increasing access to college-level math: Early outcomes using the Virginia Placement Test.* CCRC Brief No. 58. New York: Columbia University, Teachers College, Community College Research Center.

Roksa, J., & Keith, B. (2008). Credits, time, and attainment: Articulation policies and success after transfer. *Educational Evaluation and Policy Analysis* 30(3): 236–254. doi: 10.2307/25478669.

Rosenbaum, J. E., Deil-Amen, R., & Person, A. E. (2009). *After admission: From college access to college success.* New York: Russell Sage Foundation.

Ross, R., White, S., Wright, J., & Knapp, L. (2013). *Using behavioral economics for postsecondary success.* New York: ideas42.

Ross, S. M. (1983). Increasing the meaningfulness of quantitative material by adapting context to student background. *Journal of Educational Psychology* 75(4): 519–529. doi: 10.1037/0022-0663.75.4.519.

Rutschow, E. Z., Cullinan, D., & Welbeck, R. (2012). *Keeping students on course: An impact study of a student success course at Guilford Technical Community College.* New York: MDRC.

Rutschow, E. Z., Richburg-Hayes, L., Brock, T., Orr, G., Cerna, O., Cullinan, D., et al. (2011). *Turning the tide: Five years of Achieving the Dream in community colleges.* New York: MDRC.

Rutschow, E. Z., & Schneider, E. (2011). *Unlocking the gate: What we know about improving developmental education.* New York: MDRC.

Safford-Ramus, K. (2008). *Unlatching the gate: Helping adult students learn mathematics.* Lexington, KY: Xlibris.

Sam, D. A. (2002). *The journey into community: The professional learning community in one community college.* PhD diss., Michigan State University. Ann Arbor, MI: ProQuest Dissertations & Theses Full Text database, UMI No. 3064303.

Sanford, T., & Hunter, J. M. (2011). Impact of performance-funding on retention and graduation rates. *Educational Policy Analysis Archives* 19(33).

Saville, B. K., & Zinn, T. E. (2011). Interteaching. *New Directions for Teaching and Learning* 2011(128): 53–61. doi: 10.1002/tl.468.

Schneider, M., & Yin, L. (2011). *The hidden costs of community colleges.* Washington, DC: American Institutes for Research.

Schnell, C. A., & Doetkott, C. D. (2003). First year seminars produce long-term impact. *Journal of College Student Retention* 4(4): 377–391.

Schudde, L., & Scott-Clayton, J. (2014). *Satisfactory academic progress requirements: Pell Grant loss prevalence and impact of student outcomes.* Paper presented at the Association for Education Finance and Policy annual conference, San Antonio, TX.

Schuetz, P. (2002). Instructional practices of part-time and full-time faculty. *New Directions for Community Colleges* 2002(118): 39–46.

Schuh, J. H., & Gansemer-Topf, A. M. (2010). *The role of student affairs in student learning assessment.* Occasional Paper No. 7. Champaign, IL: National Institute for Learning Outcomes Assessment.

Schunk, D. H., & Rice, J. M. (1991). Learning goals and progress feedback during reading comprehension instruction. *Journal of Reading Behavior* 23(3):351–364.

Scott-Clayton, J. (2011). *The shapeless river: Does a lack of structure inhibit students' progress at community colleges?* CCRC Working Paper No. 25. New York: Columbia University, Teachers College, Community College Research Center.

———. (2012). *Do high-stakes placement exams predict college success?* CCRC Working Paper No. 41. New York: Columbia University, Teachers College, Community College Research Center.

Scott-Clayton, J., Crosta, P. M., & Belfield, C. R. (2014). Improving the targeting of treatment: Evidence from college remediation. *Educational Evaluation and Policy Analysis* 36(3): 371–393. doi: 10.3102/0162373713517935.

Scott-Clayton, J., & Rodríguez, O. (2012). *Development, discouragement, or diversion? New evidence on the effects of college remediation.* NBER Working Paper No. 18328. Cambridge, MA: National Bureau of Economic Research.

Scrivener, S., Bloom, D., LeBlanc, A., Paxson, C., Rouse, C. E., & Sommo, C. (2008). *A good start: Two-year effects of a freshman learning community program at Kingsborough Community College.* New York: MDRC.

Scrivener, S., Sommo, C., & Collado, H. (2009). *Getting back on track: Effects of a community college program for probationary students.* New York: MDRC.

Scrivener, S., & Weiss, M. J. (2013). *More graduates: Two-year results from a evaluation of accelerated study in associate programs (ASAP) for developmental education students.* Policy Brief. New York: MDRC.

Scrivener, S., & Weiss, M. J. (with Teres, J.). (2009). *More guidance, better results? Three-year effects of an enhanced student services program at two community colleges.* New York: MDRC.

Shapiro, D., Dundar, A., Chen, J., Ziskin, M., Park, E., Torres, V., & Chiang, Y.-C. (2012). *Completing college: A national view of student attainment rates.* Signature Report No. 4. Herndon, VA: National Student Clearinghouse Research Center.

Shapiro, D., Dundar, A., Ziskin, M., Chiang, Y.-C., Chen, J., Harrell, A., & Torres, V. (2013). *Baccalaureate attainment: Outcomes of students who transfer from two-year to four-year institutions.* Signature Report No. 5. Herndon, VA: National Student Clearinghouse Research Center.

Sherman, J., & Andreas, M. (2012). The successful transfer structure in Washington State. *New Directions for Community Colleges* 2012(160): 17–29. doi: 10.1002/cc.20035.

Sherman, M. (2014). David Figlio's research finds infant health has long-term impact on education. Press release. Northwestern University, School of Education and Social Policy.

Shulman, L. S. (1993). Teaching as community property. *Change* 25(6): 6–7.

Shute, V. J. (2008). Focus on formative feedback. *Review of Educational Research* 78(1): 153–189.

Sitzmann, T. (2011). A meta-analytic examination of the instructional effectiveness of computer-based simulation games. *Personnel Psychology* 64(2): 489–528. doi: 10.1111/j.1744-6570.2011.01190.x.

Slavin, R. E. (1990). Achievement effects of ability grouping in secondary schools: A best-evidence synthesis. *Review of Educational Research* 60(3): 471–499.

Smith, M. (2010). *Transfer and articulation policies.* StateNotes. Denver: Education Commission of the States.

Snyder, T. D., & Dillow, S. A. (2011). *Digest of education statistics 2010.* NCES 2011-015. Washington, DC: U.S. Department of Education, Institute of Education Sciences, National Center for Education Statistics.

———. (2012). *Digest of education statistics 2011.* NCES 2012-001. Washington, DC: U.S. Department of Education, Institute of Education Sciences, National Center for Education Statistics.

———. (2013). *Digest of education statistics 2012.* NCES 2014-015. Washington, DC: U.S. Department of Education, Institute of Education Sciences, National Center for Education Statistics.

Speroni, C. (2011a). *Determinants of students' success: The role of advanced placement and dual enrollment programs.* NCPR Working Paper. New York: National Center for Postsecondary Research.

————. (2011b). *High school dual enrollment programs: Are we fast-tracking students too fast?* NCPR Working Paper. New York: National Center for Postsecondary Research.

Spillane, J. P., & Burch, P. (2006). The institutional environment and instructional practice: Changing patterns of guidance and control in public education. In *The new institutionalism in education,* edited by H.-D. Meyer & B. Rowan, 87–102. Albany, NY: SUNY Press.

Spillane, J. P., Reiser, B. J., & Gomez, L. M. (2006). Policy implementation and cognition: The role of human, social, and distributed cognition in framing policy implementation. In *New directions in education policy implementation: Confronting complexity,* edited by M. I. Honig, 47–64. Albany, NY: SUNY Press.

Spillane, J. P., Reiser, B. J., & Reimer, T. (2002). Policy implementation and cognition: Reframing and refocusing implementation research. *Review of Educational Research* 72(3): 387–431. doi: 10.2307/3515992.

State Higher Education Executive Officers (SHEEO). (2013). *State higher education finance FY 2012: Retrends in state appropriation.* Boulder, CO.

Steadman, M. (1998). Using classroom assessment to change both teaching and learning. *New Directions for Teaching and Learning* 1998(75): 23–35. doi: 10.1002/tl.7503.

Steele, G. E., & McDonald, M. L. (2008). Moving through college. In *Academic advising: A comprehensive handbook,* edited by V. N. Gordon, W. R. Habley, and T. J. Grites, 157–177. Hoboken, NJ: Jossey-Bass.

Stefanou, C. R., Perencevich, K. C., DiCintio, M., & Turner, J. C. (2004). Supporting autonomy in the classroom: Ways teachers encourage student decision making and ownership. *Educational Psychologist* 39(2): 97–110.

Stephan, J. L., Rosenbaum, J. E., & Person, A. E. (2009). Stratification in college entry and completion. *Social Science Research,* 38(3): 572–593.

Stillson, H., & Alsup, J. (2003). Smart ALEKS . . . or not? Teaching basic algebra using an Online Interactive Learning System. *Mathematics & Computer Education* 37(3): 329–340.

Straumsheim, C. (2013). Scaling back in San Jose. *Inside Higher Ed,* December 18. https://www.insidehighered.com/news/2013/12/18/san-jose-state-u-res urrects-scaled-back-online-course-experiment-mooc-provider.

Streich, F. E. (2014). *Online education in community colleges: Access, success, and labor-market outcomes.* PhD diss., University of Michigan.

Strumpf, G., & Hunt, P. (1993). The effects of an orientation course on the retention and academic standing of entering freshmen, controlling for the volunteer effect. *Journal of the Freshman Year Experience* 5(1): 7–14.

Sunstein, C. R. (2013). *Simpler: The future of government.* New York: Simon & Schuster.

Super, D. E. (1990). A life-span, life space approach to career development. In *Career choice and development: Applying contemporary theories to practice,* 2nd ed., edited by D. Brown, L. Brooks, and Associates, 197–261. San Francisco: Jossey-Bass.

Taylor, A. (2009). How strategic budgeting can control cost while improving performance. *Journal of Corporate Accounting and Finance* 20(3): 53–58. doi: 10.1002/jcaf.20484.

Taylor, A., & Steenpoorte, H. (2007). The problem with budgeting and how one municipality addressed it. *Management Accounting Quarterly* 8(4): 20–36.

Texas Transfer Issues Advisory Committee. (2001). *Identifying and closing the gaps.* Austin: Texas Higher Education Coordinating Board.

Thaler, R. H., & Sunstein, C. R. (2008). *Nudge: Improving decisions about health, wealth, and happiness.* New Haven, CT: Yale University Press.

Thiede, K. W., Griffin, T. D., Wiley, J., & Anderson, M. C. M. (2010). Poor meta-comprehension accuracy as a result of inappropriate cue use. *Discourse Processes: A Multidisciplinary Journal* 47(4): 331–362.

Thille, C. (2008). Building open learning as a community-based research activity. In *Opening up education: The collective advancement of education through open technology, open content, and open knowledge,* edited by T. Iiyoshi and M. S. V. Kumar, 165–180. Cambridge, MA: MIT Press.

Tinto, V. (1993). *Leaving college: Rethinking the causes and cures of student attrition,* 2nd ed. Chicago: University of Chicago Press.

———. (1997). Classrooms as communities: Exploring the educational character of student persistence. *Journal of Higher Education* 68(6): 599–623.

Trostel, P. A. (2010). The fiscal impacts of college attainment. *Research in Higher Education* 51(3): 220–247. doi: 10.1007/s11162-009-9156-5.

Tschannen-Moran, M., & Hoy, W. K. (2000). A multidisciplinary analysis of the nature, meaning, and measurement of trust. *Review of Educational Research* 70(4): 547–593. doi: 10.2307/1170781.

Tucker, A. L., Nembhard, I. M., & Edmondson, A. C. (2007). Implementing new practices: An empirical study of organizational learning in hospital intensive care units. *Management Science* 53(6): 894–907. doi: 10.2307/20122252.

Tyler, R. W. (2000). A rationale for program evaluation. In *Evaluation models: Viewpoints on educational and human services evaluation,* 2nd ed., edited by D. L. Stufflebeam, G. F. Madaus, and T. Kellaghan, 87–96. Boston: Kluwer Academic Publishers.

U.S. Bureau of Labor Statistics. (2012). Number of jobs held, labor market activity, and earnings growth among the youngest baby boomers: Results from a longitudinal survey. News release. http://www.bls.gov/news.release/pdf/nlsoy.pdf.

———. (2014). Employee tenure in 2014. News release. http://www.bls.gov/news.release/pdf/tenure.pdf.

U.S. Department of Education, Office of Planning, Evaluation, and Policy Development. (2010). *Evaluation of evidence-based practices in online learning: A meta-analysis and review of online learning students.* Washington, DC.

U.S. House of Representatives, Committe on Education and the Workforce. (2014). *The just-in-time professor.* Washington, DC.

Umbach, P. D. (2007). How effective are they? Exploring the impact of contingent faculty on undergraduate education. *Review of Higher Education* 30(2): 91–123.

Umbach, P. D., & Wawrzynski, M. R. (2005). Faculty do matter: The role of college faculty in student learning and engagement. *Research in Higher Education* 46(2): 153–184. doi: 10.1007/s11162-004-1598-1.

Uphoff, N. (2000). Understanding social capital: Learning from the analysis and experience of participation. In *Social capital: A multifaceted perspective,* edited by P. Dasgupta and I. Serageldin, 215–249. Washington, DC: World Bank.

Utterback, J. (1998). Closing the door: A critical review of forced academic placement. *Journal of College Reading and Learning* 29(1): 48–56.

Van Campen, J., Sowers, N., & Strother, S. (2013). *Community college pathways: 2012–2013 descriptive report.* Stanford, CA: Carnegie Foundation for the Advancement of Teaching.

van Etten, S., Pressley, M., Freebern, G., & Echevarria, M. (1998). An interview study of college freshmen's beliefs about their academic motivation. *European Journal of Psychology of Education* 13(1): 105–130.

Van Noy, M., Weiss, M. J., Jenkins, D., Barnett, E. A., & Wachen, J. (2012). *Structure in community college career-technical programs: A qualitative analysis.* CCRC Working Paper No. 50. New York: Columbia University, Teachers College, Community College Research Center.

Venezia, A., Bracco, K. R., & Nodine, T. (2010). *One-shot deal? Students' perceptions of assessment and course placement in California's community colleges.* San Francisco: WestEd.

Venezia, A., Kirst, M., & Antonio, A. L. (2003). *Betraying the college dream: How disconnected K-12 and postsecondary education systems undermine student aspirations.* Stanford, CA: Stanford Institute for Higher Education Research.

Venezia, A., & Voloch, D. (2012). Using college placement exams as early signals of college readiness: An examination of California's Early Assessment Program and New York's At Home in College program. *New Directions for Higher Education* 2012(158): 71–79. doi: 10.1002/he.20016.

Virginia Community College System. (2010). *The critical point: Redesigning developmental mathematics education in Virginia's community colleges.* Richmond, VA.

———. (2011). *The focal point: Redesigning developmental English education in Virginia's community colleges.* Richmond, VA.

Visher, M. G., Butcher, K. F., & Cerna, O. S. (with Cullinan, D., & Schneider, E.). (2010). *Guiding developmental math students to campus services: An impact evaluation of the Beacon program at South Texas College.* New York: MDRC.

Visher, M. G., Weiss, M. J., Weissman, E., Rudd, T., & Wathington, H. D. (with Teres, J., & Fong, K.). (2012). *The effects of learning communities for students in developmental education: A synthesis of findings from six community colleges.* New York: National Center for Postsecondary Research.

Wachen, J., Jenkins, D., Belfield, C., & Van Noy, M. (2012). *Contextualized college transition strategies for adult basic skills students: Learning from Washington State's I-BEST program model.* New York: Columbia University, Teachers College, Community College Research Center.

Wagner, T., Kegan, R., Lahey, L., Lemons, R. W., Garnier, J., Helsing, D., et al. (2005). *Change leadership: A practical guide to transforming our schools.* Hoboken, NJ: Jossey-Bass.

Walter, S. (2008). Librarians as teachers: A qualitative inquiry into professional identity. *College and Research Libraries* 69(1): 51–71.

Walton, G. M., Cohen, G. L., Cwir, D., & Spencer, S. J. (2012). Mere belonging: The power of social connections. *Journal of Personality and Social Psychology* 102(3): 513–532.

Wang, D. (2009). Factors affecting the comprehension of global and local main idea. *Journal of College Reading and Learning* 39(2): 34–52.

Wang, L. (2008). Developing and evaluating an interactive multimedia instructional tool: Learning outcomes and user experiences of optometry students. *Journal of Educational Multimedia and Hypermedia* 17(1): 43–57.

Warren, L. A. (2006). Information literacy in community colleges: Focused on learning. *Reference & User Services Quarterly* 45(4): 297–303.

Washington Higher Education Coordinating Board. (2006). *Consolidated transfer report: Transfer policy and upper-division baccalaureate capacity.* Olympia, WA.

———. (2009). *Transfer and articulation in higher education.* Olympia, WA.

Washington State Board for Community and Technical Colleges (WSBCTC). (2013). *The role of transfer in the attainment of baccalaureate degrees at Washington public bachelor's degree institutions class of 2011.* Olympia, WA.

Waskow, J. A. (2006). *Understanding and application of learner-centeredness among community college faculty.* PhD diss., Walden University. Ann Arbor, MI: ProQuest Dissertations & Theses Full Text database, UMI No. 3218897.

Watkins, J., & Mazur, E. (2013). Retaining students in science, technology, engineering, and mathematics (STEM) major. *Journal of College Science Teaching* 42(5): 36–41.

Weimer, M. (2002). *Learner-centered teaching: Five key changes to practice.* San Francisco: Jossey-Bass.

Weinbaum, A., Rodríguez, C., & Bauer-Maglin, N. (2013). *Rethinking community college for the 21st century.* New York: New Community College at CUNY.

Weiner, S. A. (2012). Institutionalizing information literacy. *Journal of Academic Librarianship* 38(5): 287–293.

Weiss, M. J., Brock, T., Sommo, C., Rudd, T., & Turner, M. C. (2011). *Serving community college students on probation: Four-year findings from Chaffey College's Opening Doors program.* New York: MDRC.

Wildman, T. M., Hable, M. P., Preston, M. M., & Magliaro, S. G. (2000). Faculty study groups: Solving "good problems" through study, reflection, and collaboration. *Innovative Higher Education* 24(4): 247–263. doi: 10.1023/B:IHIE .0000047413.00693.8c.

Windschitl, M., Thompson, J., & Braaten, M. (2011). Ambitious pedagogy by novice teachers: Who benefits from tool-supported collaborative inquiry into practice and why? *Teachers College Record* 113(7): 1311–1360.

Wiseman, L. (with McKeown, G.). (2010). *Multipliers: How the best leaders make everyone smarter.* New York: HarperCollins.

Xu, D. (2013). *Three essays on the impact of cost-saving strategies on student outcomes.* PhD diss., Columbia University. Ann Arbor, MI: ProQuest Dissertations & Theses Full Text database, UMI No. 3561734.

Xu, D., & Jaggars, S. S. (2011a). The effectiveness of distance education across Virginia's community colleges: Evidence from introductory college-level math and English courses. *Educational Evaluation and Policy Analysis* 33(3): 360–377.

———. (2011b). *Online and hybrid course enrollment and performance in Washington State community and technical colleges.* CCRC Working Paper No. 31. New York: Columbia University, Teachers College, Community College Research Center.

———. (2013). The impact of online learning on students' course outcomes: Evidence from a large community and technical college system. *Economics of Education Review* 37: 46–57. doi: http://dx.doi.org/10.1016/j.econedurev .2013.08.001.

———. (2014). Performance gaps between online and face-to-face courses: Differences across types of students and academic subject areas. *Journal of Higher Education* 85(5): 633–659. doi: 10.1353/jhe.2014.0028.

Xu, D., & Trimble, M. J. (2014). *What about certificates? Evidence on the labor market returns to non-degree community college awards in two states.* Manuscript in preparation.

Xu, H., & Morris, L. (2007). Collaborative course development for online courses. *Innovative Higher Education* 32(1): 35–47. doi: 10.1007/s10755-006 -9033-5.

Yeado, J., Haycock, K., Johnstone, R., & Chaplot, P. (2014). *Learning from high-performing and fast-gaining institutions.* Higher Education Practice Guide. Washington, DC: Education Trust.

Yeager, D. S., & Dweck, C. S. (2012). Mindsets that promote resilience: When students believe that personal characteristics can be developed. *Educational Psychologist* 47(4): 302–314. doi: 10.1080/00461520.2012.722805.

Zachery, I. (2010). *The effect of information literacy competency on student learning and success in three California community colleges.* Doctor of arts diss., George Mason University. Ann Arbor, MI: ProQuest Dissertations & Theses Full Text database, UMI No. 3421710.

Zeidenberg, M. (2012). *Valuable learning or "spinning their wheels"? Understanding excess credits earned by community college associate degree completers.* CCRC Working Paper No. 44. New York: Columbia University, Teachers College, Community College Research Center.

Zeidenberg, M., Cho, S.-W., & Jenkins, D. (2010). *Washington State's Integrated Basic Education and Skills Training Program (I-BEST): New evidence of effectiveness.* CCRC Working Paper No. 20. New York: Columbia University, Teachers College, Community College Research Center.

Zeidenberg, M., Jenkins, D., & Calcagno, J. C. (2007). *Do student success courses actually help community college students succeed?* CCRC Brief No. 36. New York: Columbia University, Teachers College, Community College Research Center.

Zeidenberg, M., Jenkins, D., & Scott, M. A. (2012). *Not just math and English: Courses that pose obstacles to community college completion.* CCRC Working Paper No. 52. New York: Columbia University, Teachers College, Community College Research Center.

Zimmerman, B. J., & Pons, M. M. (1986). Development of a structured interview for assessing student use of self-regulated learning strategies. *American Educational Research Association* 23(4): 614–628.

Zumeta, W. (2001). Public policy and accountability in higher education: Lessons from the past for the new millennium. In *The states and public higher education policy: Affordability, Access, and Accountability,* edited by D. E. Heller, 155–197. Baltimore: Johns Hopkins University Press.

Index